Creative Writing Exercises

FOR DUMMIES®

A Wiley Brand

by Maggie Hamand

FOR DUMMIES®
A Wiley Brand

Creative Writing Exercises For Dummies®

Published by: **John Wiley & Sons, Ltd.,** The Atrium, Southern Gate, Chichester, www.wiley.com

This edition first published 2014

© 2014 Maggie Hamand

Registered office

John Wiley & Sons Ltd, The Atrium, Southern Gate, Chichester, West Sussex, PO19 8SQ, United Kingdom

For details of our global editorial offices, for customer services and for information about how to apply for permission to reuse the copyright material in this book please see our website at www.wiley.com.

The right of the author to be identified as the author of this work has been asserted in accordance with the Copyright, Designs and Patents Act 1988

Wiley publishes in a variety of print and electronic formats and by print-on-demand. Some material included with standard print versions of this book may not be included in e-books or in print-on-demand. If this book refers to media such as a CD or DVD that is not included in the version you purchased, you may download this material at http://booksupport.wiley.com. For more information about Wiley products, visit www.wiley.com.

Designations used by companies to distinguish their products are often claimed as trademarks. All brand names and product names used in this book are trade names, service marks, trademarks or registered trademarks of their respective owners. The publisher is not associated with any product or vendor mentioned in this book.

For general information on our other products and services, please contact our Customer Care Department within the U.S. at 877-762-2974, outside the U.S. at (001) 317-572-3993, or fax 317-572-4002. For technical support, please visit www.wiley.com/techsupport.

For technical support, please visit www.wiley.com/techsupport.

A catalogue record for this book is available from the British Library.

ISBN 978-1-118-92105-0 (pbk); ISBN 978-1-118-92106-7 (ebk); ISBN 978-1-118-92107-4 (ebk)

10 9 8 7 6 5 4 3 2 1

Contents at a Glance

Table of Contents

Introduction

Creative writers come in all shapes and sizes. Put the stereotyped bespectacled introvert, hunched over a desk in a dusty attic, out of your mind: no 'typical' writer exists. Whatever your background, age or current situation, if you have the enthusiasm and discipline, you can become a writer.

I designed this book to help you write a novel, a collection of short stories or a piece of narrative fiction or non-fiction. I made it as practical as possible, filling it with exercises and examples from the greats so that you can progress from your first vague ideas through to a completed manuscript.

Without doubt, writing is difficult. One of the main obstacles is that it's a lonely business and often no one's around to help or support you along the way. Plus, creative writing techniques are poorly taught at school, and most education seems designed to drum the creativity out of you, with its focus on grades, results and ticking the right boxes. This regimented approach makes being creative later in life difficult.

All children are naturally creative, and I believe that adults are at their happiest when being creative too. However, taking up an art or a craft after you've finished your education is often hard, because you haven't had the initial training or practice you need. For physical pursuits, you may no longer have the manual strength or dexterity you had as a child (for example, it's hard to be a musician or dancer without physical strength and if you haven't put in the early training). Also some arts or crafts are expensive to practise – paint and canvas can be pricey, sculptors need costly materials to carve into. But writing is something that everyone can do, at any age.

You've picked up this book and are reading this passage, and so you're clearly interested in creative writing. I encourage you to use this book to turn that interest into a concrete reality.

About This Book

I've been leading creative writing classes for 15 years, and I love teaching almost as much as I love writing. One of its pleasures is coming up with relevant texts to illustrate particular topics and devising interesting exercises that help people to develop new techniques and their craft.

Over these years I've collected a large bank of texts and exercises that have worked well in class, and I've been able to ditch quietly the ones I tried that didn't turn out to be so helpful. I know that the exercises in this book help writers to take their projects forward, because I've seen the great results. Many of the students who've taken my courses started off with a vague idea and, by progressing through the different levels from beginner courses to advanced workshops, ended up with complete drafts of novels. If you work your way through all the exercises in the book, in whatever order you choose, you can achieve the same.

Often I read through a final draft and see the exercises I set during the classes blended skilfully into a complete narrative. By completing all the exercises, these writers have been able to start with the opening pages, develop their characters and storyline, and tackle all the different aspects of creating good fiction. Some of these novels have finally been published. One or two have even won prizes.

Seeing these writers take their first tentative steps into fiction is a pleasure and a privilege, as is watching them progress as they gain confidence and develop their voice and their skills. All the writers who finish their projects realise that writing takes a huge amount of commitment and hard work. They also learn to trust their instincts about what they want to write and the way they want to write it. They were willing to learn and remained open to feedback and new ways of working. You too can be like them!

Foolish Assumptions

In writing this book, I make some assumptions about you:

- ✔ **You enjoy books and reading.** All kinds of reading are good, but this book is mainly concerned with narrative fiction and non-fiction – in other words, books that tell a story. Books are about characters, and so I also assume that you're fundamentally interested in human nature – what people do and why they do it. I refer to a lot of books that I've read, and you'll notice that the same books come up again and again. This is because they're well constructed, contain characters you can believe in and illustrate many points so beautifully. I suggest you read these books if you haven't already.

- ✔ **You want to write a full-length book.** This can be a novel, a memoir, a travelogue, a biography or a collection of stories – anything that has a narrative element. Many of the exercises in this book are equally useful for someone writing a play, a screenplay or any other kind of extended narrative.

✔ **You want your book to be as good as you can possibly make it.** Lots of poorly written or unoriginal books are published and have even sold in good quantities, but I assume that you want to aim for the best rather than imitate the mediocre. Even 'bad' books must have appealing aspects to them if they find an audience, but you still don't want to settle for less than the best you can achieve.

✔ **You want to work hard and improve at your writing.** Writing at any length doesn't come easily to many people, and creative writing is different from the kind of factual writing that people tend to do in their everyday lives. With this book, you have the opportunity to develop new techniques and ways of writing and to try out new skills. If you come to this book already thinking that you know everything about writing and have already decided exactly how you're going to proceed, you aren't going to get much out of this book.

Icons Used in This Book

To make finding your way around this book as easy as possible, I use little drawings in the margins, called icons, to highlight important information.

I highlight important advice and tricks of the trade with this icon.

This icon draws your attention to information that you may want to come back to and bear in mind while you're writing.

I like to illustrate points I make with concrete examples to make them more memorable. I suggest that you look at the relevant passages in the books yourself.

This book is packed with helpful exercises designed to take your writing forward. Don't just read about them – do them!

Beyond the Book

As you work your way through the book, don't forget to look at the bonus material available at www.dummies.com/extras/creativewritingexercises.

You can find the book's cheat sheet at www.dummies.com/cheatsheet/creativewritingexercises.

Where to Go from Here

You can use this book in a number of ways:

- You can go through the contents and find an area that especially interests you or where you feel you need particular help.
- You can work through the early chapters in each part, which give more basic information, and then read the later chapters.
- You can turn the page and start reading at the beginning, progressing through to the end.

Whichever way you use the book, I recommend that you do all the exercises as you go. If you complete every exercise in this book, you'll soon be a long way along the road to completing your writing project.

Best of luck with all your creative writing!

Part I
Getting Started with Creative Writing Exercises

In this part . . .

- ✔ Set yourself some simple targets that you can use to help you make progress.

- ✔ Look at ways to define the theme of your writing project and to keep yourself motivated.

- ✔ Find useful tools and techniques to get your imagination going and inspire you on your way.

- ✔ Understand the creative process, with plenty of tips to get you started and support you on your writing journey.

Chapter 1

Preparing to Create Your Written Masterpiece

In This Chapter

▷ Starting your creative writing

▷ Thinking about the process

▷ Embracing confusion

*T*he saying goes that all people have a book inside them. Certainly, all people have their own life stories and many want to write theirs down; everybody has dreams, ideas, hopes and fears, as well as a certain amount of imagination. All that most people lack is the courage and know-how to turn their chosen idea into a story that others want to read.

Many people think that if you want to be a writer, you have to leave your job (or never start one!) and sit all day in a freezing garret. In fact, most writers have other jobs as well – because they have to! Writers write in bed in the mornings before anyone else is awake, they stay up late writing when every-one else has gone to bed, they write on their commute to work, they write in their lunch hours, they write in any small bit of time they have. They write because they want to and because they have something unique to say – while still paying the bills in other ways.

Being passionate about what you write is important, because otherwise you're highly unlikely to find the energy and commitment to finish. A story needs to be burning inside you, wanting to escape. You should love your characters, be fascinated by your themes and want to find out how your story ends.

But good writing is more than just a passion – it's also a craft. You need to discover the techniques and tips of the trade and then practise them to help you make the project you have in mind as good as it can possibly be – which is where this book and this introductory chapter come in! I lead you through some things to consider before you start writing and discuss the basics of creative writing and creative thinking.

Planning for the Writing Journey

Before you physically start writing, a little preparation is a good idea to get the best out of the valuable time you devote to your writing. In this section I discuss helpful ideas such as setting targets and staying confident, as well as how much you do or don't need to think about genre, scope and the title of your work before you start writing.

Setting your writing goals

One of the most helpful things you can do when starting any writing project is to set yourself some simple, realistic and achievable goals and targets. Here are a few examples:

- ✔ **Task targets:** Such as developing a character, finishing a chapter or planning a scene.
- ✔ **Time targets:** A certain number of writing sessions of fixed length, such as three half-hour sessions a week.
- ✔ **Word targets:** A certain number of words or pages, such as 500 words or three pages per week.

None of these targets sounds like much, but you may be surprised how much you achieve if you keep going with them week after week.

If you set writing goals that are too optimistic, you're likely to fail, which undermines your writing instead of supporting it. The good thing about modest targets, especially at the beginning of a project, is that when you exceed them and replace them with slightly more ambitious ones, you can see that you're making real progress. If you do find that you're struggling with the targets you've set, revise them downwards until you have something that you feel is appropriate for you.

Write down an overall long-term goal as well, such as 'I'll have a first draft by this date next year'; it really helps to keep you on track.

Update your goals at regular intervals to keep them relevant and so that you always have something to aim for. Your goals inevitably change as the work develops.

People differ in their strengths and weaknesses: some are planners and others prefer to plunge in and get started. If you're a planner, plunging in probably makes you feel completely overwhelmed and all at sea, and your story's likely to peter out quite quickly. Therefore, you'll find that working out a rough plan or timeline for your story is beneficial, and perhaps even mapping out key scenes before you begin (see Chapters 3 and 19). If you're a more instinctive writer, and planning is a barrier rather than an aid to progress, just jump in and write every day, and watch your story gradually take shape.

Locating the appropriate genre

Books are defined principally by their genre. Go into any bookshop or library and you'll find books listed under headings such as action/adventure, children's, crime, fantasy, historical, horror, mystery, romance, science fiction, thriller, women's and young adult.

Literary fiction is usually listed under general fiction but is sometimes considered a genre on its own. *Literary fiction* is hard to define, but the term is often used to describe books that are original or innovative in form, show deep psychological insight and act metaphorically as well as literally – meaning that you can dip beneath the surface of the story and characters to examine themes or issues or to extract multiple meanings. I cover these sorts of issues and techniques in Chapters 15 and 16.

Before you start writing, a good idea is to consider what genre your story will fall into. Also, read some of the most successful examples of this genre to see how they work. Ask yourself the following types of question:

- ✔ **What's the rough length of books in your chosen genre?**

- ✔ **Do they tend to be written from a first-person or a third-person viewpoint and do they contain one or several points of view?** (Check out Chapter 8 for more details on point of view.)

- ✔ **Are they primarily *plot driven* (that is, the story is the most important element, and the characters mainly exist to fulfil a role within it) with lots of action (see Chapter 12), or *character driven* (the characters' choices and actions drive the story) with lots of internal reflection?**

- ✔ **Is the language simple and direct with relatively short sentences and paragraphs, or are the sentences more complex with more detailed description, including similes and metaphors?** (Chapter 15 has loads of info on these figures of speech and Chapter 11 covers using all the senses for intense descriptions.)

Literary fiction tends to be character driven and commercial fiction plot driven, although this isn't always the case. Many popular and successful novels have well-drawn characters who seem real and that readers can identify with, as well as a well-structured and compelling plot. Thrillers, detective stories and adventure novels tend to fall into the plot-driven category. (The chapters in Part IV have lots of useful information on plot and structure.)

Sometimes people say to me that they don't want to read other novels in their genre, because they don't want to be influenced by them. Unfortunately, this often means that they inadvertently write something that's already been done or that completely fails to match the expectations that readers have when they buy a book in this genre. My mantra is read, read, read! (See the nearby sidebar 'Taking lessons from other writers'.)

Taking lessons from other writers

You can discover an enormous amount about writing from reading books, novels and stories of all kinds. When you read, think consciously about the way the book is written. Look to see whether it's divided into sections, parts and chapters. If so, are the chapters short or long, or varied in length? Are the different parts of equal size? How many points of view and locations exist in the story? (Check out Chapter 20 for loads more on structuring your work.)

Look at the techniques the writer uses to convey the way that people speak in dialogue, to describe a scene or build suspense. See how the plot unfolds, how secrets are hidden and how clues are revealed. Examine how events are foreshadowed and surprises created. (Chapters 4 and 6 discuss dialogue, and Chapters 14 and Chapter 21 creating and maintaining suspense.)

Picking passages you really like from a book and imitating them as closely as possible using your own settings, characters and story can be helpful. It helps you to see how really good fiction works. Consider these to be exercises, like a musician playing scales or an artist making a sketch from a famous painting. You don't even need to put them in your work in progress, although you can use them, often altered, if they fit.

I was once working on a novel based on my experience of working in a women's prison. The beginning just wouldn't come right, so in exasperation I picked up a copy of one of my favourite novels, John le Carré's *The Spy Who Came in from the Cold* (1963). It starts with a terse dialogue at Checkpoint Charlie, where the main character is waiting for someone to cross over. I immediately started my novel with a tense dialogue just before the main character meets the disturbed woman who is the focus of the narrative, ditching the first 20 pages I'd written!

However much you're influenced by other books and other writers – and all writers are – beware of writing something that's too close to a book that exists already. This can constitute *plagiarism* – legally defined as the 'wrongful appropriation, stealing and publication' of another author's 'language, thoughts, ideas or expressions' and passing them off as your own.

Beware of mixing different genres, and in particular of switching genre mid-novel. A romantic story that suddenly changes into a political satire, or a crime novel where the corpse turns out to have been abducted by aliens, defies publishing conventions and gives readers an unpleasant jolt.

Creating the right title

The right title is vital, because it tells readers something important about the story. You don't need to have a title before you start writing your story. Many writers haven't found a title until very late in their project or even after it has finished. Occasionally, literary agents or publishers suggest the title or change the one you already have, and sometimes books have different titles in different countries, especially when they're translated.

You can take your title from different aspects of your story:

- **Name of the main character or one around which the plot pivots:** For example, *David Copperfield, Jane Eyre, Ethan Frome, Mrs Dalloway, Emma, Rebecca.* You can also use a character's profession *(The Piano Teacher, The Honorary Consul, The Secret Agent, The Professor, The Reluctant Fundamentalist, A Man of the People)* or some kind of description of them *(The Woman in White, The Boy in the Striped Pyjamas, A Good Man in Africa, The Woman Who Went to Bed for a Year).*

- **Relationship between two characters:** For example, *The Magician's Nephew, The Time Traveller's Wife, The French Lieutenant's Woman, Sons and Lovers, The Spy Who Loved Me.*

- **Significant place:** For example, *Wuthering Heights, Mansfield Park, Revolutionary Road, Middlemarch, Solaris, Gorky Park.*

    Theme of the book: For example, *War and Peace, Crime and Punishment, Pride and Prejudice, The End of the Affair, The Sense of an Ending.*

- **Biblical or literary quotation:** For example, *East of Eden, Gone with the Wind, For Whom the Bell Tolls, Present Laughter, The Darling Buds of May.* Or you can adapt one, for example, *By Grand Central Station I Sat Down and Wept.*

- **Significant object:** For example, *Brighton Rock, The Golden Bowl, The Subtle Knife, The Moonstone, The Scarlet Letter.*

- **Central element of the plot:** For example, *The Hunt for Red October, The Voyage of the Dawn Treader, Around the World in Eighty Days, Looking for Mr. Goodbar, The War Between the Tates, On Her Majesty's Secret Service.*

- **Word or phrase buried deep in the story:** For example, in Raymond Chandler's *The Big Sleep,* the phrase comes on the last page.

Titles arrive in all sorts of ways

The now famous titles of many books weren't the author's first choices: George Orwell's *1984* was going to be called *The Last Man in Europe*, *To Kill a Mockingbird* was going to be *Atticus* before Harper Lee decided the title was too narrowly focused on one character, and Jane Austen's original title for *Pride and Prejudice* was *First Impressions*.

Books often have different titles in different countries, even when they share the same language. For example, Laurie Lee's *Cider with Rosie* was published in the US as *Edge of Day*, and *Harry Potter and the Philosopher's Stone* was *Harry Potter and the Sorcerer's Stone*. The *Bridges of Madison County* was originally published with the title *Love in Black and White*, and only became a bestseller after the title was changed.

The title can be the first thing that comes to an author, though. Jonas Jonasson, author of *The Hundred-year-old Man Who Climbed Out of the Window and Disappeared*, so loved the title after he thought it up that he felt compelled to write the book itself!

The title you choose highlights in readers' minds a certain element in the story. For example, *The Hobbit*'s alternative title was *There and Back Again*, which emphasised the journey the main character takes.

Don't let not having a good title stop you from getting started or indeed finishing your book!

You may not find the final title of your story or novel for some time, but try this to help you get at least a working one:

1. **Make a list of different possible titles for your story from each of the preceding categories.** Think about which one you like best and why.

2. **Pick a working title for your story.** Having one to hand often helps even if you decide to change it later.

Discovering the scope of your book

Don't worry too much about fixing the scope of your book before you start writing or even while you're drafting it. Many writers find that their story changes and grows as they write it. A novel you begin as a light-hearted romance may take a dark turn when the handsome love interest turns out to be concealing a terrible secret; a crime story can transform into an exposé of the poverty and suffering of a marginalised community; a straightforward thriller may turn out to have a supernatural element.

Sometimes only at the end of a draft do you really know who your characters are and have a good idea of where the story is going. So just keep drafting and leave editing and rewriting until much later. You can always go back and transform the first part of your story so that it fits in with your later discoveries, or expand your original idea to accommodate a new idea or additional characters (see Chapter 22).

If your story takes an unexpected turn, don't stop yourself from writing. If you block yourself because you want to stick to your original idea or are surprised by some of the material coming through, you'll almost certainly find that all the life goes out of your writing.

The foreword to the second edition of JRR Tolkien's *The Lord of the Rings* (1955, George Allen & Unwin) begins with the words: 'This tale grew in the telling'. Tolkien started writing a sequel to *The Hobbit*, but the story took over and turned into a massive three-volume epic aimed more at adults than children.

Silencing the inner critic

I believe that drafting out your entire story before you start to edit anything is best (I discuss editing in Chapters 24 to 26). I read about novelists who write a thousand words in the morning, edit their text and then move on the next day. This may work for experienced writers (though not all), but it's seldom useful when you're starting out. As soon as you look at your work, that voice starts up in your head saying, 'This is rubbish; it's never going to work. You'll never make it as a writer. Go back and change everything.' Somehow, you have to find out how to banish that voice!

The best way I know to get rid of that voice is not to edit at all while you're at an early stage. Just keep writing. Resist the temptation to go back and look at what you've written previously, unless you really have to check a fact such as what name you gave a character or on what day of the week a certain event happened. But don't get out that red pen or turn on the word processor's track changes function and start going over your work, because you may soon find that you have no writing left! You have plenty of time to go over what you've written when you get to the end of your draft.

Reviewing the Creative Writing Process

In this section I have a look at the various stages involved when you want to write a novel, a piece of narrative non-fiction or a series of short stories.

No single right way to set about any creative process can apply to everyone: different people find that different methods of working are best for them. At the beginning, just try out a few different ways of working until you find what clicks with you.

Taking your first steps

When you start writing, the important thing to do is just to gain confidence.

Get a notebook, pen and paper or the kind of computer that suits you – laptop, tablet, desktop – and jot down ideas, anecdotes, sketches, key phrases, character outlines and memories. Write down anything you like, as long as you're writing. If you have a particular project in mind or a story that you want to tell, just write down anything connected with it. At this stage, you simply want to get your pen moving or some words on the screen, so that you have some material to work with. I talk more about recording and using ideas in Chapter 2.

Sometimes when you start a project you have an idea of a key scene: maybe two characters meeting, having an argument or confrontation, or a character discovering something, someone having an important realisation, or a dramatic event taking place. Sometimes ideas come from a family story or something that happened to you or someone you know. If this type of situation applies, begin writing from these starting points.

At this point, don't worry about the quality of what you write: just begin somewhere. The more you get down on paper or on screen, the more confident and skilful your writing becomes. Developing your writing voice takes time, and so don't hurry it or expect too much too soon.

If you find that you're constantly struggling to get started at the beginning of each writing session, try leaving a sentence unfinished so that you can complete it when you next sit down. Alternatively, try making a list of ideas. Usually, getting started takes a while, but then your mind is buzzing by the end of a session and ideas arise more freely – so take advantage of this to help you get started next time.

Here's an exercise to ensure that you always have a repository of ideas to turn to whenever you're stuck. Write down three of the following:

> ✔ **Significant memories from your character's past:** These can be adapted from your own memories. Check out Chapter 3 and Chapter 19 for how to use memories.

- ✔ **Facts about your main characters:** Check out Chapter 3 for how to give them convincing backgrounds and Chapter 5 for detail on creating them physically. Chapters 4 and 6 guide you through teaching them to speak.

- ✔ **Objects your main character possesses:** Chapter 13 has several tips on this aspect.

- ✔ **Incidents your main character can experience:** Read Chapter 18 for all about plotting events for your characters.

- ✔ **Desires or fears of your main character:** Chapters 7 and 9 discuss providing characters with complex inner lives.

Gearing up for the long haul

Writing a whole book is going to take you a long time, and so don't put undue pressure on yourself by trying to get it all done too quickly. Slow and steady is the best way forwards. If you're always rushing ahead to get onto the next scene, you don't allow yourself the challenge and the pleasure of going deeply into the scene that you're writing now.

The fashionable Buddhist concept of mindfulness is really useful for creative writing, because you want to create a space in which you and your characters deeply experience the 'now' of your story. If you're constantly thinking back to previous scenes and worrying that they aren't good enough, or stressing about what on earth you're going to write next, you can't slow down and concentrate on what's happening to your writing or your characters in the present moment.

Every paragraph or page that you write is an important step towards your goal.

Writing in a spiral path

Writing a book isn't a linear process: you don't start at the beginning and go in a straight line towards the end. On the contrary, sometimes you seem to be going backwards rather than forwards, round and round in circles or not going anywhere at all!

I prefer to see my writing as being like walking on a spiral path, sometimes facing backwards, sometimes forwards, but always moving slowly towards my goal. You get a whole lot of writing done only to discover yourself back with the same scene or dilemma or conflict that you were wrestling with earlier.

However, you're never exactly back in the same place, because you've learned a whole lot more about your characters and your story in the meantime, and so you can write the scene again better than you did the first time around.

Using creative writing exercises

The single most helpful tool for developing your creative writing skills is to do creative writing exercises: quick, focused pieces of work that you can complete in 5 to 20 minutes. This book is chock-full of such useful exercises designed to illustrate different aspects of the writing process.

When doing these exercises, I suggest you get started right away and just jot down the first thing that comes into your head without thinking too much about it. These spontaneous and unedited thoughts are often the most useful. As you get used to doing the exercises, jumping in and writing straight away without much prior thought or effort gets easier and easier.

Sometimes you don't see the point of an exercise or feel that what you've written is never going to fit into your story. This doesn't matter. You almost certainly learned something useful and are mastering techniques to put into use at another time or in another place. Don't worry if the results of the exercise don't always seem that great – they're quick writing exercises and no one is expecting prefect prose!

Some of the exercises involve random prompts or elements you can introduce into your story. One problem with writing is the feeling that you have to supply all the ingredients out of your own head, which isn't the way real life works – after all, you don't choose the weather, who sits next to you on the bus or what strange object a friend will leave behind in your house! Read Chapter 13 for more on creative use of objects in your stories.

Using random elements from your environment enables you to create a more complex and lifelike story, as well as giving you new ideas that you can often connect in a fresh and original way.

Living with Creative Confusion

In a non-creative project, having lots of notebooks and computer files with slightly different versions of the same thing is a bad sign. But creative projects, particularly in their early stages, benefit from this level of uncertainty. Having five separate start plans and three endings is fine (I discuss writing openings and endings in Chapters 17 and 23), as is having no clear idea of on what day of the week different events in your story happen.

Resist the urge to 'tidy' your work as you go. A far better idea is to keep writing and then return when you have a first draft to make your final selections and examine the finer details. Don't expect your writing to come out perfectly first time. You have to adjust to a certain amount of chaos. Many people resist the messiness involved in producing creative work, but it's inevitable if you want to produce something worthwhile.

Writing in chaos doesn't mean, however, that your writing space has to be a complete tip (although mine often is when I'm in the middle of a project). Some people just can't work in a messy environment. However, others can't work if everything is too neat and tidy. Find out what kind of person you are, and don't fight against it.

Consider these tips to help you create some order in the chaos:

- ✔ **Get different coloured notebooks or one with different coloured pages.** Write plot ideas in the blue notebook (or on the blue pages), character things in the red, random observations in yellow and so on. This approach makes finding something you've written far easier later on.

- ✔ **Give chapters working titles.** Do so even if you aren't going to keep them in the end.

- ✔ **Write a brief summary of what happens at the top of each chapter.** This helps you to find key scenes easily.

- ✔ **Number and title computer files for easy reference.** Group them in folders and subfolders.

- ✔ **Keep everything.** Buy box files and folders to store your material.

One area in which you may need to be systematic is in sorting files on your computer. Because you can't access things on a computer at a glance as you can with a notebook or typescript, you can easily lose track of what you've written. Create folders with headings such as 'notes', 'sketches', 'characters' (use the names of your main characters) and clearly number each draft. Give chapters a working title in the file name so that you can identify what each chapter is about with no hassle.

Allowing yourself to make mistakes

People learn by making mistakes. Many creative breakthroughs occur when you make a mistake. If you keep going along a safe track, you never discover the exciting avenues you may have gone down if you'd allowed yourself a little more latitude. It's a bit like tourists who stick to the main areas instead of exploring the interesting backstreets where they may discover a charming café or hidden gem.

You often need to start a story or try out a scene in a particular way in order to discover that it isn't working. You're working without knowing enough about the world of your story, and so you're bound to make false starts and go down dead ends. Sometimes you may go down a side turning and realise that lovely as the scene you've written is, it doesn't belong in the narrative you're currently writing. You can always file these scenes for later in the story or for another project. Sometimes, however, you discover something absolutely vital to your story that you hadn't realised before. Unless you write the scene, you'll never know which way it'll go or whether it'll introduce something new and exciting into your story.

The more you write, the more you develop a kind of instinct that helps you discard certain options in advance. But when you begin, you really don't know what's going to be best, and you never will know – unless you try out different approaches.

Almost all writers create far more material than they ever use in their final version, but this doesn't matter. What you see in the finished book is a bit like the one-tenth of an iceberg that appears above the surface of the water. The rest of the material may be hidden or discarded, but it's still a vital part of creating your story.

If you like to plan, you often find that your story refuses to stick to the structure you work out in advance. Maybe you planned that halfway through your novel, character A would divorce character B, but when you get there you realise that your character would never have the courage to confront his wife. You then have to restructure the second part of the book, and the result is usually far stronger than if you'd stuck to your original plan.

Think about making a film: it usually needs a large number of 'takes' to get a scene absolutely as the director wants it. And some of the items that ended up in Picasso's wastepaper basket have been sold for huge sums of money!

Writers who've made 'mistakes' and had to correct them include Sir Arthur Conan Doyle and Ian Fleming, who both killed off their heroes, Sherlock Holmes and James Bond, only to have to backtrack later. The inventor of Sherlock Holmes needed some ingenuity to explain how his character survived what seemed a certain death. When JRR Tolkien wrote the original version of *The Hobbit,* he hadn't yet decided that Bilbo's ring was the One Ring, and so Gollum wasn't overly upset when he lost it. After publishing *The Lord of the Rings,* Tolkien had to go back and correct this incident for all future editions of *The Hobbit.*

Writing what you want to write

One of the most important things I want to stress is that when you start out as a writer you must write *what you want to write* and not allow yourself to be persuaded by anyone to write anything else. Even if you're not sure precisely what you want to write, and your thoughts seem a bit confused at first, don't change what you're writing in order to comply with other people's ideas; after all, you've not written your novel before, and so some uncertainty is inevitable.

You write best when you write the kind of fiction you like to read. Many novelists say that they write the books they want to read – the books didn't exist before, and so they had to create them!

Use this exercise to help you clarify what you love about other people's books:

1. **Make a list of your top ten favourite books of all time.**

2. **Mull over what you love about them: characters, plot (see Chapter 18), setting (see Chapter 10) or perhaps a mixture of all three.**

3. **See whether you can spot any similarities in theme, structure or writing style.**

Nobody's forcing you to write; you do so because you want to, for its own sake, and not because you feel that you ought to write or you think it's going make you rich and famous. So if you're going to take the time and trouble, you may as well write the book you really want to write and not the book you think will appeal to others.

Books and writing are personal. Some writers I can't stand and others I love, and the books I love sometimes leave other people cold. Some books were bestsellers in their time but have long been out of print and forgotten, while other books that were rejected or reviled at the time are now highly respected. Some people will like what you write and others will hate it.

Don't try to please everybody, because you won't. As the saying goes, in trying to please everyone you almost inevitably end up pleasing nobody.

Never worry about what anyone else may think of your work. As soon as you do, you start restricting your writing to fit in with what you think others would like or consider appropriate, or to conceal aspects of yourself you think people may disapprove of.

In particular, don't worry about what literary agents or publishers may think in the early stages of a project. When you begin, you're so far away from being published that thinking about it in any way except as a distant and ultimate goal is pointless. It often just causes you to freeze and give up.

Many people think they have to write in a special way when they're writing fiction, to develop a distinctive 'voice' or 'style' that impresses people. Many published writers do have an individual and recognisable style, but usually they took many years to develop it. I think that all writers have their own voice, just as you can usually recognise everyone you know by the sound of their unique, individual voice. The best way to develop your writing voice is simply to write as clearly, directly and unaffectedly as you can.

Never show your work to friends, family, lovers or indeed anybody too soon. They simply pick up on aspects that you know aren't perfect, which just makes you feel negative about your writing. Also, such people often don't have the knowledge or skills to make any constructive criticism. They may just tell you it's wonderful because they don't want to hurt your feelings or spoil your relationship! Or they may make vague comments such as 'I found this scene boring' or 'I didn't like that chapter', but you won't know what on earth to do about it because they haven't been specific enough.

Writing a book is such hard work that you really have to be obsessed by it. There's no point spending all that time and energy to write something that doesn't totally grip you. You'll find that writing about a topic that really inspires you and that you already know something about, or which you're dying to learn about, is much easier. Let your pen follow your heart and lead you where it wants to go.

Write a list of the things that fascinate you: perhaps a culture, a language, a sport, an art form, an aspect of human psychology, a historical period, a country or district, a profession, a hobby. Are any of these included in your story idea, and if not, why not?

Bad, teacher; good teacher

My eldest son learnt the cello. His first teacher was very enthusiastic, but at a certain point my son stopped making progress. She made comments like 'That note was flat' or 'Your bow is making a scratchy sound', but didn't explain what he should do about it.

His next teacher watched him play and then said 'If you lift up your left elbow, you'll find it much easier to stretch out your arm and reach that top note' and 'I noticed that your bow was a little too close to the bridge in that passage'. Almost immediately, his playing started to develop in leaps and bounds.

Chapter 2

Sketching Out Ideas

*I*f you're starting a writing project and think that it's a question of sitting down in front of a blank piece of paper or a blank screen and waiting for inspiration to strike, you're probably in for a surprise. You may well sit there waiting . . . and waiting . . . and waiting.

This method may work for you, but for most people it simply doesn't. So instead of wasting your valuable time, use the effective, painless ways to kick-start your creativity that I suggest in this chapter. I give you plenty of exercises, ideas and tips to wake up your sleeping creative giant, show you how to use images and objects effectively in your writing, and lead you towards deciding on the appropriate level of research.

Getting Your Creative Juices Flowing

Nine times out of ten, just sitting down to write the story in a linear fashion doesn't work. You tend to freeze at the sight of the blank page and immediately a million questions leap out at you: Where to begin? Who are the main characters? What point of view shall I use? Do I write in the first or third person? Should I do all my research before I start writing? You can see how the result is thought-overload pretty quickly!

In addition, even if you do manage to write a few sentences or paragraphs, you almost always start having doubts: 'This isn't any good. Maybe I'm setting about this the wrong way.' Quite often the whole writing session ends with very little done. After two or three such attempts, you're likely to despair and give up.

Central to getting started is to think of your project as something that's going to take some time to take shape, and find ways to build it gradually. Instead of diving straight in to write what you think will be the book itself, a more productive approach is to start by writing *about* it: thinking about your characters, your setting, some of the events that will take place, the main themes and so on.

Collect materials to help inspire you and start building up the world you want to create before writing. Sketch out ideas and explore the subject matter of your story, and begin building up the main characters so that they can take on a life of their own.

In this section, I suggest three effective ways to become inspired: getting down your first thoughts, making use of mind maps and having a go at brainstorming.

Starting with your first thoughts

A piece of writing can begin in a number of different ways; for example:

- ✔ **From a personal experience:** Some events are so powerful and emotional that you feel compelled to write them down.

- ✔ **From more gradual inspiration:** An idea condenses slowly in your mind over days, weeks, months or even years.

- ✔ **From an incident in the news:** You may have no idea why, but a particular story grabs you while watching TV or reading a newspaper.

- ✔ **From an anecdote that someone tells you:** Even finding yourself thinking 'Is that really true?' or 'I wonder how that panned out?' can be enough to get you started.

What starts you off doesn't matter, as long as something does! But then you have the problem of how to develop the idea to take it from that first seed to something more substantial.

Creating a mind map of ideas

Mind maps (also known as *spider diagrams* or *sunbursts*) are wonderful tools for sparking creativity. They're diagrams used to outline information in a visual and often colourful way. All you do is place a single word or phrase in the centre of a sheet of paper and add associated ideas, words and concepts radiating out from this centre, often with connecting links.

Mind mapping is useful in creative work, because it's a form of non-linear thinking and organisation. One of the main problems with writing an extended piece of work is that you often feel that you have to start at the beginning and write through, step by step, to the end. But most creative people, including most writers, don't work that way. It can take you a long time to work out where your story begins and ends, and you're far more likely to find yourself writing scenes early on that belong towards the end of your story.

In this section, you get the chance to create mind maps for your main character and main theme. You can produce these mind maps simply in one colour, but many people find that using different colours for different parts of the diagram is useful. Do whatever helps generate those ideas.

Mapping your characters

Try building a mind map of a set of characters for a piece of writing. (Check out the example in Figure 2-1.) To do this, use these following steps:

1. **Write the full name of your main character in the middle of the page.**

   Add in any other names your character has: childhood names, pet names, nicknames.

2. **Insert all the people in the main character's life around the name in the centre, and connect them to the protagonist with bold lines.**

   Include names and any details for family, friends, work colleagues, neighbours, lovers and so on.

3. **Add people who the main character doesn't know but who may play a part in the story.**

   Don't draw lines connecting them to the main character yet.

4. **Draw in any connections between other characters in the diagram.**

   I suggest drawing connections your main character knows about in blue, and those he doesn't know about in red.

6. **Identify potential enemies among the characters in these groups.**

   Underline these in a different colour – say, green.

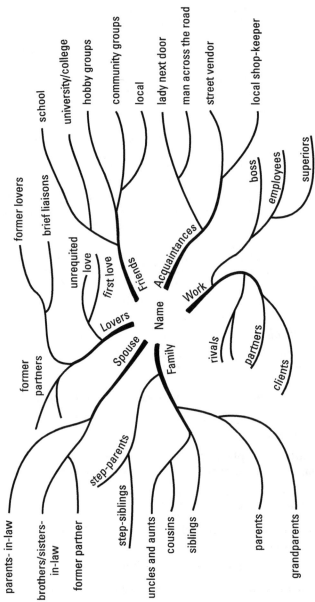

Figure 2-1: A mind map of characters.

As you develop your map, you begin to get a much more complete and complex picture of your main character. The whole plot of your novel starts to reveal itself through the links, and you see possibilities for connections between other characters that you hadn't imagined, or possibilities for their further development.

If you're writing a biography or other non-fictional work, this character mind map can be useful for keeping track of the significant relationships in the real person's life. It may also help you to think of your story in a more dramatic way.

Mapping your main theme

Mind maps are useful in developing your main theme. Follow these steps:

1. **Place the main theme in the middle of the page.**

   Restrict this to just a few key words.

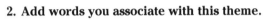

2. **Add words you associate with this theme.**

   Use a thesaurus after you've completed your list, and see whether you can add even more words or phrases.

3. **Jot down possible events that can dramatise your theme.**

   Detail items such as arguments, reconciliations, confrontations, accidents, journeys, meetings, separations, proposals, losses and discoveries.

4. **Note down information about the characters.**

   Think about who the characters are: their ages, jobs, hobbies, families and friends.

5. **Produce a list of the emotions for all parties.**

   These emotions can vary at different times, and so make sure to include the whole range.

6. **Move on to actions and consequences for the characters.**

   Again, write down all the things your characters may do in response to the situations they're in, and the emotions these actions provoke.

To see how the outline of a story can start to emerge from loads of possibilities, many of which you may not have thought about if you hadn't drawn your mind map, I now examine an example story idea about a man's betrayal through a secret love affair. Here's the list I came up with for this story:

- **What two big themes arise as possibilities as a result of a betrayal?** Revenge and forgiveness. Which approach does the main character choose?

- **How was the main character betrayed?** An affair, a lie, a lack of trust or love?

- **With whom?** Work colleague, friend/best friend, former lover/former spouse, relative (cousin, brother/sister), stranger.

- **How long?** Weeks, months, years.

- **Where did they meet?** His place, her place, office, hotel, park, abroad.

- **Is his relationship out of bounds?** Perhaps she's too young, a student or work colleague, or his doctor/therapist.

- **Main character's feelings?** Numb, in denial, sick, anxious, angry, vengeful, frightened, lost.

- **Betrayer's feelings?** Guilt, shame, remorse, anger, self-righteousness, denial, keen to shift the blame.

- **Feelings of third person in the triangle?** Uncertainty, guilt, anxiety, stress.

- **Actions?** Putting pressure on, backing out, confronting the betrayer or the betrayed.

- **Betrayed person's actions?** Screaming, crying, frozen, unable to eat, shaking, fainting, lashing out, walking away, attempting suicide, seeking help, telling others, drowning sorrows in drink.

- **What's the person upset about?** Lies, omissions, being made a fool of, what other people will think, who else knew.

- **Past betrayals?** Former lovers, friends, father/mother.

- **Other betrayals?** Financial, work-related, other previous affairs.

- **Similar events in the news?** Political betrayal, celebrity divorce.

Brainstorming: Creative idea sessions

Although the term sounds negative (as in 'Argh! I'm having a real brainstorm!'), in fact *brainstorming* is a classic way of getting down ideas, clarifying your thoughts and coming up with creative solutions. Brainstorming works so well because it makes you suspend criticism of your project while it's at an early stage, and so allows you to keep all your options open. The problem with a linear way of working is that you keep eliminating possibilities as you go along, whereas brainstorming involves exploring all possibilities and then choosing the options that are most suitable for your story and offer the greatest dramatic potential.

Start by writing down on a piece of paper as many ideas as you can connected to your project, such as specific scenes or characters within it. Don't worry about how stupid they appear to be; if the thought comes to you, write it down! The idea is to get beyond the rational part of your brain and to enable yourself to think outside the box you often create for yourself.

You can brainstorm on your own, but the process often works best in a group. If you know other writers, start regular brainstorming sessions during which you work on one another's projects. Don't be afraid to talk to other people about specific aspects of your idea; often they think of great ideas, show you potential weaknesses and offer interesting angles on situations that you hadn't thought of before.

Although talking to others is useful, beware of giving away too much of your story. Focus on specific scenes or issues instead of trying to explain the whole project in detail. For one thing, taking in a whole story at once is usually too much for people, and for another, talking too much about your idea can sometimes dull it in your imagination and take the edge off the impulse to write.

Here's a great exercise to help you overcome the dreaded 'blank page syndrome'. It generates lots of ideas, giving you plenty of material to develop. Here's how:

1. **Take a large blank sheet of paper.**
2. **Start filling it with as many thoughts and ideas as possible: names of characters, settings, feelings, situations and anything that occurs to you in connection with your writing project.**
3. **Keep on going, pushing yourself until you've filled the whole page.**

Brainstorming needs to be a continuous process: whenever you feel blocked or aren't sure how to carry on, such sessions can be incredibly useful. Often they help you think of more complications, background and consequences than you would've come up with had you just started writing.

Moving Beyond Words with Objects and Images

The secret of good writing is to make readers forget that they're looking at words on a page, and to tell your story in a way that enables them to 'see' the scene, the characters, the setting and everything that happens in their mind's eye – as if they're watching a film or, even better, experiencing the scene themselves. One way to help yourself do this is to use objects and images to create a more concrete reality.

Keeping a scrapbook of ideas and materials

Students of art create notebooks or scrapbooks of ideas and materials as a source of inspiration and ultimately a demonstration of the way in which the final product developed – the influences, the processes and so on. Using these tools is so important that tutors often give as many marks for this stage of the project as for the final piece of work itself.

As a writer, keeping a notebook or scrapbook is just as useful (even if no marks are forthcoming!). You can carry a notebook with you at all times and jot down anything you see or hear that may be useful for your project. You can also write down any thoughts as they occur to you, so that you don't forget those brilliant ideas that come to you in the middle of a boring meeting at work or when you're sitting on the bus or train. You can also make sketches of things or people you see, and maps and diagrams of places.

If you have more than one project on the go, or you're constantly coming up with new ideas for stories or books, keep several notebooks on the go, one for each project. Buy sets in different colours to help organise them.

Get started by building one or more creative-writing scrapbooks that include the following types of material:

- **Ideas and points of inspiration:** If you find a painting, a photograph or an image that inspires you, the scrapbook is the ideal place to store it so that you can use or refer to it later.

- **News clips:** Cut out from magazines or newspapers interesting news stories or articles that are related to your story. You may want to put in real-life events as the background to your story, or perhaps something happens to you personally that you want to include in some way.

- **Postcards, pictures, photos and images:** Collect these from museums, bookshops, market stalls, old drawers in your desk, family albums and attics.

If you store photos and images electronically, printing them out as small thumbnails and storing them in a scrapbook is helpful so that you can look at them whenever you want.

Make notes and observations about your images – jotting down ideas and thoughts as they come to you. Don't worry about how messy or disorganised your scrapbook is – in fact, the messier the better! Good artistic work is seldom neat and tidy while it's being created.

- **Research materials and notes:** Your scrapbook is a good place to keep the results of research you carry out and to make or paste in notes from interviews you conduct. This way you have everything to hand when you need it for instant reference. For more on research, check out the later section 'Considering the Level of Research Required'.

- **Sketches:** If you've created an imaginary town or country for your story, draw a plan of key locations. If you're writing science fiction or fantasy, sketch some of the aliens or creatures involved. The more precise you are about the imaginary details, the more convincing the story is for readers.

You never know how big your scrapbook is going to get, and so buy three or four of the same kind so that you can add new ones as your project develops. Some people get very attached to a certain kind of notebook, and if you find what's right for you, it does make a difference!

Finding images related to your project

Images can help you to clarify what characters look like, pinpoint and describe exact locations, and dramatise your story. They can also act as symbols. Collecting photographs and pictures of certain objects that appear in your story can help you to focus your imagination and develop ideas before you begin writing.

With mobile phones and tablets, you can snap images at a moment's notice, wherever you are, of meals, buildings, views, rooms, houses, streets and situations. Store or print these photos, because they can prove invaluable when you need to describe something later on.

I have a huge collection of images, which I use for writing and teaching. I'm an inveterate collector of postcards – of people, places, objects and scenes of all kinds, all filed by subject. They're just so useful for sparking the imagination and getting going whenever I feel stuck.

Museums and art galleries are fantastic places for finding images and adding to your postcard collections. I prefer paintings of people and landscapes to photographs, because they're less specific and tend to trigger my imagination. For more ideas on creating the appearance of your characters, flip to Chapter 5.

Using a MacGuffin

Alfred Hitchcock referred to 'the thing that the spies are after' in spy films as a 'MacGuffin'. The MacGuffin is, in Hitchcock's own words: 'The thing that the characters on the screen worry about but the audience don't care.' The thing can be unspecified government secrets, papers or information – it really doesn't matter what it is as long as the characters want it and are prepared to kill other characters or risk their own lives to obtain it!

In Hitchcock's classic 1959 film *North by Northwest,* the main character, played by Cary Grant, is the victim of mistaken identity. He's pursued across the USA by agents of a mysterious organisation, who try to stop him interfering in their plans. It finally turns out that the spies are attempting to smuggle microfilm containing government secrets out of the country. But the precise object everyone wants doesn't really matter.

Using objects to enhance your writing

Creating objects for your characters can help you bring them to life and allow you to start creating stories around them.

Look at all the objects in your home. Unless you're a minimalist or unusually good at throwing things away, you may well find a treasure trove of objects. Useful discoveries include the following:

- Family heirlooms passed down from grandparents or great-grandparents
- Family photos of weddings, Christmases or other festivals, and summer holidays
- Pictures and prints hanging on your walls
- Clothes stuffed into the back of cupboards, worn only for special occasions
- Books and ornaments
- Objects you use every day, such as crockery and mugs

All such items not only have a whole history behind them, but also reveal something about you and your unique life. Wherever you can use a concrete object in a piece of writing, you make it stronger.

Here are some examples of how you can use objects in fiction and non-fiction in lots of different ways (I include relevant chapters where I describe using objects elsewhere in this book):

- **As a plot device:** Often the whole plot revolves around an object that everyone wants to have (or to get rid of). (See the nearby sidebar 'Using a MacGuffin' and Chapter 13 for more information on using objects.)

   Think of novels such as *The Maltese Falcon* (1929) by Dashiell Hammett, the Moonstone in the novel of the same name by Wilkie Collins (1868) and *The Lord of the Rings* (1954) by JRR Tolkien, in which the plot revolves around an object that everyone desires.

- **To represent a character:** Think of Piggy's glasses in *Lord of the Flies* (1954) by William Golding – they represent culture and learning and Piggy himself, and what happens to them is also symbolic. You can tell a lot about a person from the kind of objects he possesses, treasures or collects. In Chapter 5, I describe how to create character and personality with carefully selected items.

Edmund de Waal's best-selling memoir *The Hare with Amber Eyes* (2010) is based around a collection of Japanese miniature carvings, or *netsuke*. He uses the collection to explore the history of his family and their travels.

✔ **As a symbol representing something larger than itself:** For example, the Holy Grail of Arthurian legend representing spiritual enlightenment, or the green light in F Scott Fitzgerald's *The Great Gatsby* (1925) representing Gatsby's hopes and dreams – and his attachment to Daisy. (See Chapter 15.)

✔ **As a clue:** Especially in mystery or detective fiction, or to reveal something significant to a character. Sir Arthur Conan Doyle's Sherlock Holmes stories are full of clues – for example, Holmes deduces a huge amount about various characters through a pocket watch, a pipe, a hat and a walking stick! (See Chapter 13 for more information on using clues.)

✔ **To foreshadow something that will happen later in the story:** As Anton Chekhov famously said, a gun hanging on the wall at the beginning of Act 1 must be fired by the end of Act 3. (Chapter 14 has more information on foreshadowing.)

✔ **To trigger a memory or flashback:** Echoing the way people's minds work – such as the *petite madeleine* in Marcel Proust's *Remembrance of Things Past* (1913–1927), which triggers the childhood memories that form the substance of the book. (Check out Chapters 3 and 13 for more on flashbacks.)

✔ **As a device connecting characters' separate stories:** For example, the violin in *The Red Violin* (1998) directed by François Girard, or the 20-dollar bill in *Twenty Bucks,* a 1993 film directed by Keva Rosenfeld (and based on a screenplay originally written by Endre Bohem in 1935). (See Chapter 22 for more information.)

Objects are also useful triggers for a story. Characters can find them, lose them, be given them, give them away, have them stolen, search for them, treasure them, neglect them, lock them up, destroy them and throw them away.

Pick an object in your home that has some meaning for you and construct a scene or short story around it – perhaps the object was lost and then found, or given as a gift from someone, or was inherited from a relative. Make sure that the object triggers a significant event in the life of your character, helping him to make a decision, understand something that happened in the past or turn his life in a different direction.

Objects as inspiration

One day, I found a statue of the Buddhist deity Green Tara in a market. I carried this heavy little object around with me in a plastic bag all day, and several extremely strange coincidences happened:

✔ I had lunch in an Austrian café with a friend, and we chatted to the couple at the next table. The man worked at the United Nations in Vienna, and his father knew a great friend of mine who lived there and who'd died the previous year.

✔ I was thinking of attending a meditation class, but couldn't find one in my area.

I went to my gym and saw that a meditation class was starting at the best possible time in the week for me.

✔ I left to go home and found it was blowing a gale and pouring with rain and I had no umbrella. As I stood wondering what to do, my neighbour came past on her way home and offered to share her umbrella with me all the way to my door.

I used these coincidences as the basis for a story about someone who found a similar statue in a market and then strange things began to happen in her life.

Considering the Level of Research Required

While you're working out the basics of your story, you inevitably have to decide how much research you need to do and at what stage. The answer depends on the nature of your writing project.

For non-fiction such as biography, history or travel writing, a lot of the research comes first. You need to find out the fundamental events or travel somewhere to get the material you need *before* you can put pen to paper. However, getting *all* the information you need to know before you begin writing is usually impossible – often the writing itself makes you aware of what you need and what you don't. Most journalists and travel writers make extensive notes and write pieces as they go; most historical writers or biographers constantly need to find out new facts when they realise they're short of material, and of course remember to use only the parts that will interest the reader!

One of the problems with doing too much research before you begin is that you then feel the need to use it all, whether it fits in the story or not, and regardless of whether it's interesting to readers. Don't allow yourself to fall for this temptation!

When writing a piece of fiction, the best approach is usually to draft out scenes first – you can then set about discovering the necessary facts and find the specific things that will add to your story. There are more tips on using research in Chapter 22.

You often need to research aspects of your characters' lives to make them complex and believable. If a character is a lawyer, for instance, you need to talk to lawyers to see how they operate and to get specific required information. If a character is a doctor, a school teacher, a craftsperson or a musician, you need to find out how these people work and the kinds of issues that would be on their minds.

Don't feel that you have to do all the research before you begin – this is one of the surest routes to endless procrastination and ensures that you never start the actual writing!

Part II
Realising That Character Is Everything

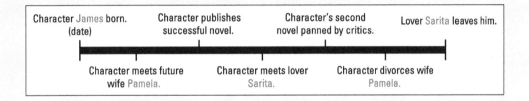

Character James born.
(date)

Character publishes
successful novel.

Character's second
novel panned by critics.

Lover Sarita leaves him.

Character meets future
wife Pamela.

Character meets lover
Sarita.

Character divorces wife
Pamela.

In this part . . .

✔ Develop your characters to convey them convincingly and so readers want to know what will happen to them.

✔ Find out how to write convincing and effective dialogue.

✔ Look at the different aspects of your characters' lives – their inner thoughts and feelings and their physical attributes and backgrounds – including ways to make them act and speak convincingly.

Chapter 3

Developing Your Characters' Backgrounds

▷ Inventing detailed pasts for characters

▷ Deciding to use diaries

*A*ll successful writing starts with character. Readers engage with your story through your characters, whether they're essentially you, based on people you know or completely fictional. The most important thing to remember when you create characters is to make sure they have depth. By that I mean that your characters have a history, come from somewhere and have had experiences that moulded and shaped them.

You can't know too much about your characters' pasts. Even if you don't use all the material you create, it still affects how you depict your characters, because you know what happened to your characters and that influences the way you write about them.

In this chapter, I help you build up your characters' backgrounds so that you can get inside their heads (not literally, of course – for that you'd need *Brain Surgery For Dummies!*) and see what makes them tick. I guide you through creating their families, careers and childhood back stories. I also describe how you can make use of the classic story-telling structure of a diary.

Creating Seriously Deep Characters

Real people don't spring from nowhere, simply materialising in air like the crew in *Star Trek* beaming onto a planet's surface. No, they have pasts and experiences that contribute to who they are – and so your characters need to as well. The aspects of character that can drive a story – such as weaknesses and strengths, sadness and positivity, desire for revenge and so on – often lie in your characters' backgrounds.

In this section I provide four great ways to help provide real depth to your characters: creating family backgrounds, childhood memories, education and work histories, and timelines of the major events in their lives. Using these techniques helps you to produce and have to hand a convincing past for your characters before you start writing your story's text. Although all the information you come up with doesn't necessarily appear directly in your final piece of writing, it acts as a useful background and solid foundation for you to draw on.

Use these exercises for all your main characters. You may also want to think about using some of them for certain minor characters as well.

Detailing your character's family tree

All characters have a family. In some stories, you may want the main character to have a large and complicated family, so that the other family members have important roles to play. In other stories, your protagonist may have fled the family home, or left her relatives far behind. Whichever course you choose, developing a family tree is extremely helpful in creating people who feel real. After all, people are the product of their families, whether your characters like or recognise that fact or not.

Here's how to go about producing a family tree for a main character:

1. **Take a blank sheet of paper, as large as you can find.** A big piece of art paper or flipchart paper is ideal, or you can use sticky tape to join two or four A4 sheets together. You don't want to run out of space just as your tree's getting interesting.

2. **Using your main character and working backwards, write in the brothers and sisters, parents, any previous marriages and step- or half-siblings, and then grandparents, aunts and uncles, and cousins.**

   You don't have to go back much farther than the great-grandparents (unless you're writing a sci-fi time-travel epic!) – most people don't recall their great-grandparents, and none any earlier relatives. If you want to include any colourful or important family members farther back, by all means put them into the tree. You can do this with a dotted line.

3. **Give the characters names.** Even if you never use them, it's fun to do. Remember that names can give a reader a lot of information about a character – popular names change from generation to generation, and being given an ordinary name makes a person feel a little differently to someone who has a very unusual name. Think too about the meaning and origin of a name – and remember that in a family people are often referred to by pet names and nicknames.

   For example, in my father's huge Welsh family, there was an uncle called Christmas Day Jones because his birthday fell on Christmas. He was known by my father and much of the family as 'Uncle C.D.'. My father was christened James but known to everyone by his middle name Eric, except among ex-army friends, and my mother, who call him Jonah.

4. **Add the characters' dates of birth.** This is important; if you work it out accurately, you may find that some characters were born in a year containing an important historical event that you can work into your story.

5. **Write in where the characters lived and any significant things about them.** Remember that every family has black sheep, and so consider picking one of the characters and writing what that person did wrong.

That reminds me! Exploring characters' memories

Providing your characters with memories is a great way to give them depth and create a past for them. Memories are so useful because they occur to characters in the present while they're in the act of remembering, and so memories bring the past into the present of your story extremely effectively.

Keep your characters' memories short, vivid and relevant to what's happening in your story now.

Sparking a memory

Memories work best when you use something happening in the present to trigger them, such as a smell (like freshly mown grass), a sound (like a piece of music), an action that seems familiar (like the way someone runs her hand through her hair), a taste (like the *petite madeleine* dipped in lime-flower tea in Proust's famous *Remembrance of Things Past*, published in volumes between 1913 and 1927), or a visual prompt (like a photograph). Objects are incredibly useful for triggering flashbacks. A childhood toy, a piece of family jewellery and some food with a particular taste can all jolt the character back into the past, almost as if that past is happening again to her now. For more on this, see Chapter 13.

I hate to turn to Marcel Proust again, but he is the master of memory! Look at the way the sound of water running through a pipe seamlessly takes the narrator back to the past:

> The shrill noise of water running through a pipe, a noise exactly like those long-drawn-out whistles which sometimes on summer evenings we heard pleasure-steamers make as they approached Balbec from the sea.
>
> —*Marcel Proust (Remembrance of Things Past/À la recherche du temps perdu, Trans C K Scott Moncrieff, Chatto &, Windus, 1973, first published 1922)*

1. **Make a list of six key childhood memories for your character.**

2. **Now come up with a series of prompts to trigger the memories.**

3. **Make one a sight, one a smell, one a sound, one a taste, one an action and one an object.**

Childhood memories are particularly vivid and can be a great way of explaining things that happened long ago that shaped your character's life, and that may reveal why the person behaves as she does now.

Showing these events through a flashback is far more effective than simply telling readers what happened. For example, you can state directly that when she was a child your character was terrified of her father's rages, but if you dramatise this moment skilfully, readers identify with the character, hear the father's voice and empathise with her fear of him. For example, you can describe the character tying her shoelaces when she was young, which triggers a vivid memory of her father standing over her and shouting at her for going about it the wrong way.

Long slabs of memories of a character's back story – all the things that happened before your story begins – can be fatal to the forward momentum of your narrative. Keep flashbacks short, specific and focused! For much more on flashbacks, check out Chapter 19.

Write about your character doing a simple action now – perhaps eating ice cream, putting on her hat or playing the piano. Have her remember doing the same action as a child. Write for five minutes; don't let the memory go on too long, and come back into the present moment at the end.

Another useful exercise is to dig out some old photographs from your childhood and write about a memory they create. Then write about your character at the same age, experiencing a similar kind of memory. Think about how the experience is the same and in what ways it's different.

Remembering wrongly

Of course, childhood memories aren't always reliable. Many memories are elaborated over time and embroidered with repetition. Sometimes people are actually remembering a *story* of the event they think they remember, rather than the event itself.

Much fiction is built around the failure of memory, or mistakes in memories. The best-selling novel *Before I Go to Sleep* by SJ Watson deals with a woman who can't remember anything that happened before she fell asleep and has to build new memories each day. She tries to overcome this problem by keeping a journal.

Ian McEwan is another novelist who explores, in his novel *Atonement,* the ease with which people can recall things falsely. The main character, Briony, thinks that she recognises a man accused of rape, with devastating consequences for the man and for the woman he loves.

1. **Think about a time when you forgot something important, or remembered something wrongly.**

2. **Write about your character forgetting an important event (perhaps she repressed the memory, was distracted at the time or has a condition that causes poor memory) and see how you can exploit this to create tension in a story.**

3. **Write about the character recalling what happened later on.**

4. **Think about flaws in her recollection and important details she has wrong, and how you can reveal in a story the truth about what really happened.**

Seeing into a character's CV

A character's education is a vital aspect to think about when building up her background. For example, consider:

- ✔ Subjects she liked or was proficient in at school
- ✔ The kind of schooling she had
- ✔ Whether she had higher education and, if so, what she studied

Don't forget the world of work: what has your character done in life so far, and what has she achieved?

Write a detailed CV as if your character's applying for a job:

1. **Place the full name of your main character in the top middle of the CV.**

2. **Add in educational and professional qualifications and where the person studied.**

3. **Add all the jobs she's ever done, including holiday and temporary employment, and state the skills gained from these jobs.**

4. **Write a profile selling the character's personal qualities.**

5. **Provide details of any hobbies or interests.**

If you're writing a biography or other non-fictional work, this CV may be easy to fill in, or you may discover certain gaps where you can't find out the information. This exercise is still useful to do and keep on file. Sometimes you find surprising information while drawing up a CV.

Setting out a character's timeline

Most fiction and non-fiction deals with a certain limited period in your main protagonist's life, such as during childhood, the transition to adulthood in a coming-of-age story, when she's in her 20s or 30s and choosing a partner, when she's in her physical prime and at the height of her abilities, or in old age, when she's looking back over her life.

But even though your story may not begin with the character's birth and end with her death, knowing the whole story is still invaluable: where your character's life begins, where and when it ends, and all the stages in between – in other words a *timeline* of the person's life.

See Figure 3-1 for a simple timeline for a character, highlighting the important events in her career and personal life which will come into a novel. The novel may of course not start with the birth of the main character, but it's useful to include. It can help to add in the dates when each major event happened.

Figure 3-1:
Sample character timeline.

Usually, a short story focuses on a critical moment of a character's life, while a longer piece builds up to this moment. Whatever happens in your story usually determines everything that happens afterwards.

In this exercise, you take a look at the whole span of a character's life from birth to death:

1. **Write a scene in which your character is born.** If you don't know anything about childbirth, talk to someone who does! The birth may impact on the relationship between mother and child – a difficult birth may lead to a difficult relationship later on.

2. **Write a scene about your character as a young child, under ten years of age.** The scene can be set at home or at school. Try not to think too hard about it; just write what comes to you.

3. **Compose a scene about your character as a teenager.** Is the person full of teenage angst, interested in books or music, or drugs or sex? Does she confront her parents and challenge their values, or conform and face problems with her peer group? Does she leave home?

4. **Write a scene about your character as a young adult aged mid-20s to mid-30s.** Is she working and in a relationship or on her own? What are her goals and desires, and is she on her way to achieving them?

5. **Move on to a scene set when the character is aged mid-30s to mid-40s.** Is she having a mid-life crisis? Does something happen that turns her life around? Or does she have what she wanted and finds that it no longer satisfies her?

6. **Progress to a scene when the character's in her mid-40s to 60.** Has a significant change taken place in her life? Does she need to make a big decision to change things? What are her goals and aspirations now?

7. **Portray the character as an old person, looking back on her life.** How does she face the prospect of old age and death? What does she think of her life – is she satisfied or regretful? Does she need to make amends for wrongdoings – or to achieve what she failed to do?

Don't be too rigid about this step – just write what you think is most useful for you. And don't worry if the character dies at the end of the story you have in mind, maybe halfway through her life – just write what would have happened if she hadn't died. In itself, this step can provide useful information about your creation, who by now is a rounded person you're really getting to know.

8. **Write a scene in which the person dies.** For the purposes of this exercise, it's usually best if the person's death occurs in old age and follows on from the scene in step 7. But if you kill the character off early, just write her death scene now!

The question of where, when and how to end a story is a tricky one, to which I devote the whole of Chapter 23. Usually, a story ends at a high point in the narrative, after a dramatic climax. But this isn't always satisfying for readers, who may want the narrative to continue to find out what happens to the characters at the end of the story. The problem with this latter approach is that after the climax, when the main question of the story has been resolved, some readers may not want to go on reading.

One solution to this problem is to write an epilogue, a short piece that reveals what happens at some stage in the future. An example is the end of the seven-volume *Harry Potter* series by JK Rowling, published in the decade from 1997 to 2007, where she jumps ahead to show Harry taking his own son to King's Cross to go to Hogwarts. It brings the story nicely full circle.

Add the events of an epilogue to your timeline, so that you know what happens to your character(s), even if you decide not to use these details. Knowing what happens allows you to hint about the contents of the epilogue before the end of the story itself. Make sure that your epilogue works seamlessly and doesn't just feel tacked on.

Using Diaries, Letters and Reminiscences in Your Writing

The techniques that I provide in the preceding section are invaluable for giving depth to your characters. In this section, I discuss a time-honoured literary format that you can use to help to structure your story and bring the events from your characters' pasts into your narrative: the diary.

You can of course tell a whole story as an exchange of letters or in diary format, but letters and diaries are also incredibly useful as parts of a narrative to fill in information from the past. Information is presented vividly and becomes part of your present narrative as your characters read the old diaries or letters in the present of your story.

Stories are more effective if your character discovers something new about her past through a letter or diary instead of reciting facts that she has known all along. When writing a diary or letter in a larger piece of work, you need to:

✔ Create an individual voice that is different from that of the main narrative.

✔ Ensure that the voice of the diaries or letters is appropriate for the period in which they would have been written.

✔ Make sure that the diaries or letters tell a story in themselves, or the reader will start to skip!

If you are using letters or extracts from diaries, think carefully about how and when to include them. You can use them once to reveal a particular secret, or you can interweave a story that happened in the past with one in the present by alternating a chapter of diary with a chapter of the present story.

The best way to get the hang of using a diary for your story is to read great works that use one. Loads of famous novels are written in journal form, and many more use journals to make up part of the narrative. Bram Stoker's *Dracula* (1897) is one of the best-known and most successful novels to be written in this format; others include Stephen King's *Carrie* (1974), Alice Walker's *The Colour Purple* (1982) and Helen Fielding's *Bridget Jones's Diary* (1996). Some stories divide into two, with one chapter telling the story in the past and another in the present, with the two intersecting. In Barbara Vine's *Asta's Book* (1993) one character's narrative takes place in the 1990s and her grandmother's journals start in 1905, with the story jumping back and forth between the two.

Many books have been based on people's real diaries or letters that relatives discover, perhaps hidden away in desks or attics and found after someone dies (check out the nearby sidebar 'Finding hidden treasure').

Finding hidden treasure

Irène Némirovsky (1903–1942) was a French novelist who died at the age of 39 in Auschwitz concentration camp after being arrested by the Nazis as a Jew. Her older daughter, Denise, kept a notebook containing the manuscript for *Suite Française* for 50 years without reading it, thinking it was her mother's journal or diary, which she imagined would be too painful to read.

In the late 1990s, however, Denise decided to donate her mother's papers to a French archive, and looked at the notebook, only to discover that it contained two novellas portraying life in France between 4 June 1940 and 1 July 1941, when the Nazis occupied Paris. In 2004 she arranged to have the book published in France, where it became a bestseller and was translated into many languages. In 2007 another novel by Némirovsky, *Fire in the Blood,* was published after two French biographers found a complete manuscript in her archives.

Writers often also use material deposited in museums and libraries. Very seldom are these letters, diaries or journals well written and interesting enough to stand on their own; often they require heavy editing, or a writer uses the information in them but rewrites them entirely.

Such sources can be invaluable for providing factual information and for revealing how people thought, felt and wrote during a period.

1. **Find an old diary or letter, either from your family or one printed in a book.**

2. **Write a few paragraphs imitating the style.**

3. **Think about how you can adapt this source material to make it more interesting for a modern reader: what needs to stay, what needs to be added, what taken away?**

4. **Write a story about what's in the letter or journal; add to and elaborate it as much as you like.**

5. **Write about a character finding a copy of that story and reacting to what's in it.**

Chapter 4

Creating Drama through Dialogue

Great dialogue is intrinsically dramatic. Whether you're writing a novel, a play, a film script or a memoir, you need to master the art of dialogue to reveal aspects about your characters and to express conflicts between them.

Dialogue is a wonderful tool because it enables characters to speak directly, giving readers explicit access to their thoughts and personality (see Chapter 6). In addition, lively, snappy dialogue is quick to read and breaks up long slabs of text, making your story more readable and enjoyable.

In this chapter I introduce you to the vitally important skill of writing convincing dialogue, including specific issues relating to choosing a situation, conveying conflict and implying subtext.

Recognising Great Dialogue

Writing effective, successful dialogue takes a lot of practice. You need to take time to really listen to what people say and the way that they say it. As you go about your day-to-day business, make a point of actively listening to how people speak – the words they use, the inflections in their voices, and any mannerisms or quirks of speech (see Chapter 6). Pay attention to accents and to people of different ages and backgrounds, and then jot down phrases that you overhear.

Also, read lots of dialogue. Look at plays and screenplays to see how the dialogue works, and how, in film scripts especially, a little dialogue goes a very long way. Remember that convincing dialogue is all about (re)producing the sound and the rhythm of speech; writing good dialogue is more like writing poetry or music than ordinary prose, in that it needs to be concise, sound good when read aloud, and provoke an emotional response in the reader.

The best way to get your dialogue right is to write lots of it. One great approach to creating lively, realistic dialogue is to practise writing dialogue with another person. If you have a friend who's also a writer or just willing to help and have some fun, arrange to sit down and write dialogues together in which you each control one person in a conversation. Not only is this great fun, but it also helps show you how real dialogue works – one person can't control what the other character says!

While you're writing with a partner, you can develop this exercise a little further with the three following ideas:

- ✔ Write a dialogue in which one of the characters is trying to draw out the other one, asking questions.
- ✔ Write a dialogue in which one of the characters isn't listening to the other.
- ✔ Write a dialogue in which the second character keeps changing the topic of conversation to his own agenda.

Drafting and Developing Dialogue

Most dialogue takes a while to write well, which is why many writers write far more dialogue than they finally use, discarding much when revising their work. Writing the dialogue without worrying about it too much in the first draft is still important, though, because the more dialogue you have to play with, the more chance you have of coming up with that telling phrase that really conveys what you want to say.

In this section I describe some fundamentals and cover the particular skills of creating face-to-face dialogue and phone dialogue, when your characters can't see each other.

Talking about dialogue basics

Here are some basics to be aware of when creating your masterpieces of conversation:

✔ **Keep dialogue short and to the point.** All too often, writers make dialogue too long and have people talk in long, complete, fully thought-out sentences. Most real-life speech doesn't happen in this way. People usually talk in fragments, frequently don't finish sentences and often interrupt one another.

Remember that characters often don't have the time to think out carefully what they want to say in advance, unlike you, the writer. In fact, many characters don't know what to say at all. So don't be afraid to use interruptions, let sentences trail away or employ silences.

Write a dialogue in which the two characters end up saying nothing of any significance at all.

Long dialogue often gets uninteresting, so cut to the chase. You don't need all the build-up: 'Hello, Dan. Nice to see you. How are you doing? How's the family?' and so on. You don't need to know every word that's spoken – the characters may say all this in real life, but the readers don't need it, especially if they know the information already. Similarly, a line of a dialogue is a great way to end a scene; don't spoil it by making the conversation tail off into a series of phrases like 'Nice talking to you', 'Goodbye' and 'See you soon'.

✔ **Never use dialogue to tell readers something they know already.** This is a good time to use reported speech (which I describe in Chapter 6), or simply to skip over this part of the conversation.

✔ **Use speech tags sparingly.** 'He said' and 'she said' are preferable to more complicated words, which draw too much attention. Also, it's best not to use a lot of adverbs to explain the dialogue. Let the dialogue itself make the tone clear. Instead of: 'Go away,' she said angrily, write: 'Get out, you bastard!' Instead of: 'You're very clever,' she said witheringly, write: 'Very clever, ha ha.'

✔ **Lay out your dialogue in the conventional way for the medium in which you're writing.** In scripts for film and plays, you use the character's name followed by a colon. In prose, you use quotation marks to enclose the speech (that is, ' and '). Many modern novelists have experimented with different ways of writing dialogue, such as introducing dialogue with a dash or leaving out speech marks entirely, but using the conventional system to begin with is the way to go.

The acclaimed novelist John le Carré has a great ear for dialogue. Here's a short exchange from one of his novels. Notice how the author keeps phrases really short and has the characters hold back more than they reveal:

'How's Osnard?' she asked.

'How should he be?'

'Why does he think he owns you?'

'He knows things,' Pendel replied.

'Things about you?'

'Yes.'

'Do I know them?'

'I don't think so.'

'Are they bad things?'

'Yes.'

—*John le Carré (The Tailor of Panama, Sceptre, 1999, first published 1996)*

Write a dialogue of your own as terse as this one. Don't write more than ten words per line. Don't let your characters answer the questions they're asked with more than minimal information.

One of the main problems when writing dialogue is deciding how much to let the dialogue stand on its own and how much readers need explained about the characters' thoughts and feelings and what's going on around them when they talk. The only suggestion I can give is for you to practise writing a lot of dialogue and gradually develop an instinct for when it works and when it doesn't.

The following exercise helps you develop your dialogue-writing skills:

1. **Take your notebook or open a new file on your computer and write a dialogue between two people, leaving plenty of space between each line. Write only the lines of dialogue, with nothing else.**

2. **Think about the point of view from which the dialogue is viewed, from just one of the two characters. (Check out Chapter 8 for much more on point of view.)**

3. **Write down in the spaces between the dialogue what the viewpoint character is thinking and feeling.**

4. **Write in any body language that the viewpoint character notices. (See the following section for details on this aspect.)**

5. **Add any external observations that the character makes – perhaps noticing the clock ticking on the wall, the sunshine coming through the window or the traffic passing in the street outside.**

6. **Write any 'he saids' or 'she saids' you need in order to make it clear who's speaking.**

7. **Go through the piece and edit it, taking out anything you feel isn't needed or is over-explained.**

How do you know when the scene is finished? That's hard to say. In the end, you develop an instinct, but ultimately the only way to be sure the scene is finished is when the goals the writer sets for it are achieved and the necessary information, character, conflict or subtext have been conveyed or the tension established.

Getting up close and personal: Face-to-face dialogue

When characters are physically present, they can see one another and pick up a lot of clues about what the other character is thinking, through body language. These behaviours can include posture, gestures, facial expressions and eye movements.

When writing face-to-face dialogue, you need to help readers visualise the scene through use of body language. Think about the following:

- ✔ **How close to one another the characters are standing or sitting:** The closer they are, the more intimate the relationship and perhaps the conversation itself.

  You can show imbalances in power or influence by having one character advance and the other retreat.

- ✔ **Degree of eye contact:** Usually, making eye contact means the characters are comfortable with one another, but it can also show a degree of distrust, with one person unable to look away for fear of missing clues about the other's intentions. Avoidance of eye contact can also indicate disbelief or boredom.

- ✔ **Mirroring gestures:** When one person in a conversation makes a gesture, the other often does the same. Some of this *mirroring* is positive – for example, when characters copy each other's posture and make lots of eye contact they're getting on well – but remember that you can depict negative feedback too, such as people crossing their arms, which can indicate defensiveness.

I can't see what you're saying!

Research shows that a surprisingly high proportion of meaning in a conversation is revealed through intonation and body language, with some experts claiming that as much as 65 per cent of meaning is conveyed non-verbally.

Some professions are trained in reading body language; for example, the police look for clues that a suspect is lying, and poker players watch for signs that give away clues to opponents' hands.

To practise your face-to-face dialogue, try the following exercises, remembering to use body language clues in all three cases:

- ✔ Write a dialogue in which two characters want to get to know one another better.
- ✔ Write a dialogue in which one character wants to get close to the other, but the other doesn't reciprocate this approach.
- ✔ Write a dialogue where two people are really uncomfortable with one another.

Ringing the changes: Phone conversations

In telephone dialogue, the characters can't see one another and therefore don't pick up clues from the gestures or body language of the person they're talking to. For this reason, people are much more likely to misunderstand one another over the phone – which presents a great opportunity for you as a writer.

You can exploit the fact that the other person can't see, by having a character do strange or inappropriate things while on the phone – something that's common in the age of mobiles and cordless phones, and that you can use for dramatic effect. Perhaps your character is having an important conversation while feeding the cat, getting dried after getting out of the bath, cooking a meal, or tidying or shuffling papers at a desk.

Nowadays we have an in-between kind of dialogue with technologies such as Skype, where you can see the person, but only imperfectly, and don't have the possibility of touching them. This offers new dramatic possibilities as in David Foster Wallace's *Infinite Jest* (1996).

Here's a useful exercise for working on your phone dialogue:

1. **Write down a list of activities that a character does in the course of the day.**

2. **Think of a difficult conversation that this person is going to have with someone over the phone.**

3. **Pick an activity at random from your list in step 1 and write the dialogue where the character is doing this activity while on the phone.**

4. **Choose a second activity, write the dialogue and see how this activity makes a difference to the way the conversation unfolds.**

Making the Best Use of Dialogue

When writing dialogue, you have to decide where the interaction takes place and how long it lasts. Get these two aspects right from the start, and you're well on the way to creating a winning conversation. Plus, to use dialogue most effectively, you have to use its great strengths, two of which are depicting conflict and hinting at the underlying and the unsaid.

Deciding where and when conversations happen

One of the most important and often neglected aspects of dialogue in fiction is choosing the location where a conversation takes place. The same conversation often turns out differently depending on where it takes place: for example, in the privacy of someone's home or in a public place where it can be overheard, such as a bar or restaurant.

The setting can have an impact in so many ways: for example, a noisy location causes difficulty for the characters to hear one another, or a public place results in many interruptions. Sometimes people talk more freely when concentrating on another task, such as mending a car or preparing a meal.

Choosing a setting

Think about how in real life you seldom get an opportunity for free and open uninterrupted conversation, with no time limit or outside constraint. You're often trying to tell somebody something over a hurried lunch, just getting going when someone else walks into the room or the person you're trying to talk to is interrupted by a phone call. Similarly, the weather can spoil an outing or a transport delay can make someone late, changing the dynamic between the characters.

Don't be lazy about where you set a conversation and forget that you have many options that can make a conversation more interesting.

In the this exercise, let the dialogue change as it wants to, and think about how the setting completely changes what goes on between the characters:

1. **Think up a dialogue you want to write between two characters.**

2. **Set out the dialogue like a play script. (See the earlier section 'Talking about dialogue basics'.)**

3. **Write the dialogue in one character's home, remembering to include external observations of the scene.**

4. **Write it in the other character's home.**

5. **Write it in a different location in which the characters may meet: a corridor in the office, a third person's house, a neutral space such as a sport's hall or a shop (allow other characters to walk past or speak to the characters).**

6. **Write it in an outside space such as on a street corner, in a park or garden, or in a car park.**

7. **Write the conversation in a crowded bar.**

8. **Write the conversation when the two characters are in a car, driving somewhere.**

Also think about what may be going on around the characters and how that can act as a metaphor (see Chapter 15 for more on metaphors) reflecting something about the conversation. Here are some ideas for a couple talking in a café:

- ✔ A police car streaks past, perhaps hinting at trouble to come.
- ✔ The café is emptying gradually all around them, and they're left alone, which may reveal that the two characters are alone in their dilemma.
- ✔ Something gets spilt on the floor, indicating a potential upset.

Write down some random events that you noticed recently: a child dropping an ice-cream and bursting into tears, a man giving a woman a bunch of tulips, an argument outside a pub. Create about six of these events. Now shuffle them and pick one at random to write in as background to a conversation you've already written – and see what happens!

Using time constraints

The timing of a conversation can be crucial. Think of the difference between a couple having an hour or two in which to talk about their plans for buying a house or having ten minutes outside a solicitor's office.

Restricting a dialogue to a short period of time is one of the best ways to avoid a conversation dragging on and to up the stakes for the characters.

Set up a time limit to a conversation you want to write: perhaps a couple have five minutes before someone arrives, two minutes before the train leaves and one minute before the alarm goes off!

A character's state of mind can have a big impact too. Think about the difference between characters feeling fresh and hopeful first thing in the morning, and at the end of the day when everything has gone wrong and they're exhausted; then try to:

- ✔ Write a conversation taking place over breakfast in the morning.
- ✔ Write the same conversation between the same characters late at night.

Creating and handling conflict

Creative writing is one area in life where creating conflict deliberately is a good thing! After all, dialogue works best when you have conflict. So how do you create conflict in your dialogue?

Often, something has to be wrong and characters have to have different opinions for a dialogue to be worth reading. Any dialogue without conflict is going to be very short or very boring. Make sure that you don't write conversations with long passages but without any conflict, misunderstanding or tension. Otherwise you risk creating the effect of your characters simply batting a verbal ping-pong ball back and forth for no reason other than to keep the conversation going and fill up a few more pages!

To see how dialogue works with and without conflict, try this exercise. Write three little dialogues that begin as follows:

- ✔ 'What are you doing?'
- ✔ 'Something wonderful has happened.'
- ✔ 'Let's do it this way.'

What happens next is up to you. Most people find that each of these conversations inevitably turns into an argument. After all, if everything is wonderful there really isn't much to say about it!

When writing dialogue, think about what each character wants from the exchange. One may want to find something out, the other to conceal it; one may want to share information that the other doesn't want to hear.

Write a short dialogue that begins: 'There's something I need to tell you.' Produce a whole page before you allow your character to say what he wants to say. Or maybe, by the end of the conversation, it becomes clear that the person refuses to say – not this time, at least, and possibly never.

Things that aren't said are always more powerful in a story than those that are openly stated, because, like keeping the lid on a saucepan of boiling water, the pressure builds. Readers feel the increasing tension and know that sooner or later whatever's hidden has to come out, often with real force and drama.

Hinting at what's hidden: Subtext

Dialogue is often more about what your characters don't say than what they do. The best dialogues are those where something's going on under the surface that's not always immediately visible to readers. (I discuss the wider subject of the ineffable in Chapter 16.)

People often talk about mundane things when they're really talking about something more important – something they can't bring themselves to raise or even acknowledge. For an example from my own life, see the nearby sidebar 'Mum: He's got more than me!'.

Write a dialogue in which the characters are arguing about something that symbolises something else.

In Hemingway's short story 'Hills Like White Elephants', a couple talk while waiting for a train. The couple mention an operation that the woman may have, but not what it is. To readers, however, it's perfectly clear because of Hemingway's brilliant use of omission and coded dialogue. Check out this masterpiece in only three pages.

Take two characters and give them something they mustn't mention. The situation can be as extreme as two prisoners waiting to be hanged or as trivial as two characters not wanting to mention that one of them is overweight. They talk of anything but the subject at issue. Now bring in a third person. See if you can get the subtext to emerge.

Mum: He's got more than me!

One day, my three sons were driving me to distraction by arguing among themselves after I'd divided a pizza into three slices for them. Although I took the greatest care to cut it equally, one was convinced his piece was a millimetre smaller than his brother's, and the third one thought he'd been short-changed by having one tiny piece of pepperoni less than the others.

As they squabbled and fought, I remember shouting at them, 'What's the problem? It's only a pizza!' But of course they weren't really arguing about a pizza. They were arguing because they were looking for clues as to whether I loved one of them a tiny bit more than the others – the pizza was simply a symbol of my maternal love and care for them.

Chapter 5

Embodying Your Characters

*A*s a writer, your aim is to create convincing characters to whom readers can relate, and so you need to portray people who inhabit real bodies and live in a believably physical world. After all, the alternative is to write about characters who exist in a vacuum – people readers just can't care about or engage with. Surprisingly often, writers forget that their characters are human and limited by physical constraints. They give a few superficial details – hair colour, eye colour, height – and then for the rest of the story more or less forget them.

In this chapter you get intimate with your characters as I give you loads of great tips for fleshing them out physically. I show you how to surround them with real objects and engage them in real activities. Doing so makes your creations believable – emotionally as well as physically – whether the character is your main character or just has a small walk-on part.

Building a Body for Your Characters to Inhabit

Don't let the heading worry you. I'm talking about making your characters much more real by thinking seriously about their physical qualities and how they react to the world around them.

For example, consider how being very tall affects people – they always stood out at school, they can see over the heads of a crowd, they constantly bang their heads on door frames and light fittings, they may have trouble buying long enough trousers and overall feel self-conscious about their appearance. Knowing the problems and advantages that tall people encounter provides an insight into a character's personality.

In addition, describing your characters' appearances gives readers a great deal of information about them without you needing to tell them too directly. Instead of saying 'Mira was a careless kind of person', you can show them by describing how carelessly she's dressed and her cluttered and messy home.

If you can draw, sketch a picture of some of your characters to keep handy while you're writing. Or perhaps visit an art gallery, look at some portraits and see whether you can use one as a model for a character. Another idea is to flick through some art books at your library or look up images of portraits on the Internet. By all means look at photographs or postcards of faces to get ideas as well – but beware of looking at glossy women's magazines, because the models have been airbrushed and digitally manipulated into 'perfection'!

Look around you as you go about your daily business, and observe the people you meet. Get used to thinking about the way they look and the words you can use to describe them. Carry a notebook and jot down any physical mannerisms or the clothes that people wear.

Write about four ways in which a physical aspect of a character has affected her life. For example, a woman with a large nose may 1) have been teased at school, 2) feel unattractive to men, 3) be constantly trying to save money for cosmetic surgery and 4) go out with the first man who says he likes her nose, even though he's completely unsuitable.

Inventing and describing major characters

When musing on your cast of characters, starting with the main ones and working out in detail what they look like is really helpful. Although you may have a rough idea – say, blonde, tall, slim, with blue eyes – this is too bland and stereotyped to engage the reader. Instead, think about your character in greater detail to help you get an idea of the real person.

You need to know your major characters intimately, inside and out; you really can't know too much about them. But you don't have to reveal all these details to readers, only the most striking ones; keep the other information for your eyes only – and, believe me, it will seep subtly into your characters.

Think of a character you want to develop, and write a detailed description. Follow these steps to build up the character:

✔ **Ethnicity:** Don't fall into the trap of making all your characters the same ethnic background – unless this is an essential part of the story for, say, historical reasons. Everyone is a mixture of different ancestry, and referring to your character's family tree can be helpful (see Chapter 3). The character's ethnicity informs many of the aspects detailed in the rest of this list.

✔ **Shape of the face:** Is it round, oval, square, heart shaped? What about special features: a dimpled chin, a high forehead? Think of bone structure too, such as high cheekbones or a jutting brow.

✔ **Eyes:** 'The windows to the soul', as the old saying goes. Are they pale or dark? Be exact about the colour – not just blue or brown, but grey-blue, ice-blue, chestnut-brown, amber, greeny-hazel.

Eye colour is seldom solid – many eyes have variations of colour in them. Most green eyes, for example, are a mixture of hazel and blue. Plus, eye colour is often associated with personality – dark, almost black eyes can be thought of as passionate or evil, pale blue eyes as cold, rich brown eyes as warm, and green eyes as fascinating or jealous. But no scientific basis exists for these ideas, and so don't fall foul of stereotypes. Playing against your readers' expectations can be great!

✔ **Eyebrows:** Are they arched or flat, or shaggy or plucked? Eyebrows are extremely important in conveying facial expressions, but in their resting state they also create an impression: flat eyebrows look nonchalant, arched ones surprised, and frowning ones displeased!

✔ **Hair:** As with eyes, be exact about colouring. Don't just say blond, but use ash-blond, tawny-blond or strawberry blond. Brown can range from almost black through chestnut to mouse. So many people dye their hair in many cultures that you shouldn't neglect to mention this fact. You can include streaks of grey to reveal age as well. Think of the texture of the hair and make it appropriate for the character's ethnicity.

✔ **Nose:** Can be small and snub, large and prominent, wide or narrow, and straight or curved. You can use the fact that, rightly or wrongly, people tend to associate different noses with different personality types: a small upturned nose can be seen as youthful or innocent, and a large Roman nose as powerful.

✔ **Mouth:** Lips can be full or thin, and the mouth wide or narrow. Does it turn up in a smile, pucker into a pout or turn down at the corners? The mouth gives away many expressions, but when at rest it creates a strong impression of the character's basic personality. And don't forget the character's teeth: are they small or large, well shaped or crooked; do they have a gap in the middle; are they gleaming white or yellowed? Deciding on a tiny detail can spark off a whole set of ideas about a character: for instance, white or yellow teeth can suggest whether a character is young or old, poor or wealthy, vain or modest, or has lived a hard or a pampered life.

✔ **Body type:** Is your character tall or short, thin or overweight, with wide or narrow shoulders, hips and waist? Think about whether the person is fit or unfit, and whether she exercises. Don't forget other aspects such as a long or short neck, long or short limbs. Consider posture as well: does the person hunch her shoulders or walk tall?

✔ **Hands:** These can give away so much about a person. Are the fingers long or short, and are the hands wide or narrow? Are the hands soft and smooth or covered with calluses? What about the fingernails: are they long and elegant or bitten down to the quick?

✔ **Presentation:** Think about how the person presents herself: is she tidy or untidy, natural or contrived, sharply dressed or casually chic? Remember to consider things such as make-up, nail varnish and hair gel.

✔ **Body markings:** Consider giving the character freckles, a mole, birthmark or scar, or perhaps a tattoo or piercing.

Nobody's perfect, and so make sure to give your major characters flaws. Plus, don't forget about the sound of their voices and what their handwriting looks like.

Your characters are going to change and develop with age and over time. Don't keep them static, but instead have great fun by having your protagonists change throughout the story. People have their hair cut, grow beards, put on weight, diet and lose weight again.

Rounding out minor characters

Minor characters are important, and so don't neglect them just because they're only in a story to perform a particular role – the policewoman who's needed to make an arrest, the doctor who's necessary to diagnose an illness, or the courier who delivers an all-important letter. Often, writers tend to give minor characters no attention and stereotype them, making them seem unreal and lacking in interest.

One of the things to remember is that in life people have no choice about who they sit next to on the bus, what the doctor looks like or who moves in next door. When writing fiction, don't fall into the trap of exercising too much control over what happens. Try breaking this sense of control with the following exercise – it's fun and can bring your characters instantly to life:

1. **Write down a list of a dozen or so possible names for a minor character.**
   Make the names as different as you can – some male, some female – using names from different nationalities if you like (if you then need the character

to speak, check out Chapter 6 where I discuss working with accents in dialogue). Consult newspapers and phone directories for ideas on interesting names.

2. **Think of a number of non-gender-specific physical characteristics a person can have.** Examples include red hair, a prominent nose, a gap between the front teeth and so on.

3. **Choose a minor character you need to make more interesting or haven't yet described.** Pick a name at random and then a physical characteristic from your two lists. So, your doctor may be called Zuzanna Kowalska and have thick glasses, and your lawyer is Jake Arbuthnot and sports a natty blond ponytail.

Getting Under a Character's Skin

Most characters are going to have a conflict between the way they appear on the outside and how they often feel inside. For example, someone who appears attractive and confident to others may be preoccupied with her body image or how she comes across to people.

To help you work through these sorts of issues, try the following exercise:

1. **Describe how your character feels about her body.**
2. **Write about a physical aspect that the person likes.**
3. **Write about a physical aspect that the character dislikes.**

Thinking about emotional make-up

In life, people have no control over certain aspects of their physicality and appearance, such as skin and eye colour, height, bone structure and inherited health problems. Other aspects, however, they can control – for example, weight, fitness, how they present themselves, how they do their hair, what they wear and so on. The same is true of your characters – they are given some physical aspects (by you!) but can change others.

Childhood events often influence how characters feel about their bodies and appearance as adults. For example, children who're overfed early in life often have weight problems far into adulthood. People sometimes also overeat to compensate for a lack of love and security in childhood, or perhaps they were simply never taught impulse control. If characters were called ugly when young, they may always have no self-confidence even when they turn out to be highly attractive to others.

People are often teased or bullied about aspects of themselves that make them stand out from the crowd. For example, I was constantly teased as a child for having bright red hair. I was told so many times that I must have a flaming temper that in the end I developed one – especially in response to all the teasing!

Write about three events from a character's childhood where people responded to her physical appearance. Then write about similar events happening to your character as an adult. Is your character's response the same, or has she changed? Can the adult laugh off comments that mortified her as a child, or does she react by being even more wounded?

Coping with sickness

One good way to reveal hidden aspects of your characters' personalities is to put them under stress and see how they react: for example, when ill or when they have an accident.

Try this exercise to explore what happens to your character when her body lets her down or has an accident:

- ✔ **Write about your character with a cold.** Does the person struggle on at work or retreat to bed; swallow endless potions or stoically refuse them; visit the pharmacy or general doctor or opt for alternative remedies?

- ✔ **Describe your character going to the hospital for diagnostic tests and afterwards.** Consider the person's response: growing impatient or displaying stoicism; making light of it to friends or endlessly going on about it; lying awake at night worrying or going into denial and appearing oddly cheerful?

- ✔ **Imagine that your character has a serious illness.** Write about the person being given the diagnosis and confiding this traumatic news to a partner, lover or close friend.

Constructing Characters' Activities

Your characters' physicality involves far more than simply what they look like. Characters need to be living, breathing people who eat, work and play. Writing how they do these activities is a great way into character.

Here are some useful ideas to try out. Write as specifically as you can about your character doing the following:

✔ **Cooking and eating a meal:** Consider how the person cooks: with a recipe book or winging it; with care or in haste; with enjoyment or boredom? Don't forget to include the kind of food your character likes eating.

✔ **Getting up in the morning:** Describe actions in detail as your character puts on clothes or make-up, has a shower and so on.

✔ **Working:** Think about what job the person has and how she does it. Be very specific about the details. For example, if she is a potter, what kinds of pots does she make, does she mould them by hand or use a wheel, what kinds of coloured glazes does she prefer? You may need to do some research to go into convincing detail.

✔ **Playing:** Describe an activity that the person enjoys doing, such as playing tennis or chess, dancing, fishing, shopping, swimming or any of a hundred possibilities. Go into physical detail: the sensation of the ball on the racquet or the chess piece in your character's hand; the movement of the body in time to the music; the feeling of a fish pulling on the line or of the fabric of a dress.

Take two characters and make them play a game together. Explore the relationship between the characters from the way they deal with winning and losing.

Surrounding Your Characters with Physical Objects

Giving due consideration to all the physical objects with which your characters surround themselves can really help you create their personalities.

Owning up to your characters' possessions

Follow these steps to build up a character via owned objects:

1. **Decide on the bits and pieces that your character deems important enough to carry around in a bag or in pockets.** List all the items and then pick three to describe in detail, including textures, colours and any sounds they make.

2. **Describe the character's favourite possessions.** Who gave the items to her and when? Write about an occasion when a character loses a valued possession and then about her finding it again.

3. **Choose an object that a character hates but can't get rid of.** Again, work out who gave it to her and why she feels the need to hang on to it. Write about what happens when she finally gets rid of it.

4. **Write about your character's desk at home or work.** Is it messy or tidy? What objects are on it, and are any of them personal?

5. **Describe your character's fridge and all its contents.** Remember to think about those things lurking at the back that never get eaten!

Choosing what to wear

Characters' clothes give away a great deal of information about them. Some people are slaves to fashion, whereas others don't care what people think of their appearance. Remember that people often dress and present themselves very differently at work, in the privacy of their home and when socialising.

Describe in detail the contents of a character's wardrobe, including different footwear and the following:

- ✔ Never-worn clothes
- ✔ Tried and trusted favourites
- ✔ Pieces for special occasions
- ✔ Forgotten items hidden away
- ✔ Clothes that are now too big or too small
- ✔ Clothes with special memories attached

Describe what your character wears in the following situations:

- ✔ A best friend's wedding
- ✔ A Sunday evening at home
- ✔ An important meeting
- ✔ To meet an old friend

Think carefully before using brand names and labels in your story: do so only when it's absolutely necessary or essential to the plot. Apart from giving famous brands free advertising, what's high fashion today can be totally passé tomorrow and quickly make your story seem dated.

Chapter 6

Developing Your Dialogue-Writing Skills

In This Chapter

▷ Using accents, dialects and speech quirks

▷ Handling group dialogue

▷ Speaking in sparkling monologues

*A*s you build up your characters, you need to pay attention to how they speak. Developing an individual voice and vocabulary for characters is an important way of revealing information about them, sometimes even conveying personal aspects that the characters themselves aren't consciously aware of. Characters can give themselves away through the words they use, slips of the tongue, how they respond to what's said to them and the tone in which they reply.

Dialogue is the voice of your character speaking directly, and so it's also a great tool for showing concrete details about where your character comes from, how old he is, whether he's outgoing or shy, and whether this tendency changes in different contexts. You can also reveal information about characters' education, jobs and social status through any specialised vocabulary or jargon they use. Plus, your writing improves noticeably if you can develop the ability to convey foreign accents, dialect and slang for appropriate characters and so render the sound of their speech more accurately.

In this chapter, I provide lots of dialogue-writing tips and techniques to help in these areas. Most of the time you'll be writing conventional conversations between two people, but I don't neglect group exchanges and monologues.

For much more on dialogue, including how to use it to create drama and how to write realistic exchanges complete with interruptions and so on, flip to dramatic Chapter 4.

Conveying Individuality and Character through Dialogue

As a writer, your task (if you choose to accept it) is to create convincing dialogue and therefore individual, believable characters. To do so you need to develop one of the most useful but also difficult skills when writing dialogue: using different accents, dialects, slang and speech quirks.

The need to create credible dialogue is particularly acute in certain genres. For example, when you're writing historical fiction you need to capture something of the way people spoke at the time, and if you're writing science fiction or fantasy you need to find convincing ways to make different cultures speak, or even invent imaginary languages, such as in JRR Tolkien's *The Lord of the Rings* (1954).

But you don't need to travel in time and space to worry about this aspect of writing. In today's multicultural societies, any contemporary story seems contrived and false without some characters who don't speak Standard English with Received Pronunciation. Plus, speech has become more informal over the years, and nowadays many people use slang and local idioms more freely.

The way people speak depends on their country or region of origin, education and where they live now. In addition, characters need to have their own individual ways of speaking, with different phrases and mannerisms.

Feeling for foreign accents

Finding ways to convey an accent isn't easy. In this section I talk about a couple of the easier approaches before showing how you can use some more subtle ways to improve your dialogue.

The simplest method, if you don't feel able to tackle accents, is just to write a line like, 'He said in a strong guttural accent'. Or you can be more specific; for example, saying that the character rolled his 'r's. However, without some reminder or trace of an accent in the dialogue itself, readers are likely to forget and not hear the accent in their heads.

Some writers therefore prefer to use phonetics to convey the way a person speaks. For example, if you want to render the voice of a character who speaks with an American accent, you can put 'Bawn Street' instead of 'Bond Street';

or to convey an Australian accident, you can write 'Australhlian'. Similarly, Germans notoriously tend to use 'v' instead of 'w', and 'z' instead of 'th', and Japanese people have trouble with 'l' and tend to say 'r' instead.

One problem with this approach is that the text can quickly become hard to read and understand. Readers spend a great deal of effort trying to work out what on earth the character is saying and have difficulty hearing how the speech is meant to sound (which rather defeats the purpose of using phonetics). Another problem is that it can all too easily look as if you're making fun of the character, and can even seem stereotypical, one-dimensional and racist!

A more subtle approach is to select a few words in a sentence and make clear how the character pronounces them. This technique acts to remind readers that the character has an accent, without making the rest of the speech unintelligible.

You can start using heavier phonetics and then lighten up once the reader has 'got' the voice in his head, just reminding him now and again.

Getting accents accurate

A difficulty with accents is that you need to know a little bit about the native language of the character whose dialogue you're writing in order to be able to convey accurately how that person speaks. You need to know not only how the character pronounces words, but also the kind of mistakes in grammar or sentence construction that he's likely to make. These aspects depend on the grammatical structure of the character's native language and the sounds that are used.

You can't be an expert in a wide range of languages – in fact you may not be an expert in any! If you do need to write about characters from different countries and cultures, the best thing to do is to get some help from people who know the language and culture inside out. Listen to the way that they speak, meet their friends and jot down words and phrases that they use. Don't be afraid to ask someone to help you, to make sure that you have it right.

People who aren't fluent in a language are often overly formal and avoid contractions, saying, for example, 'will not' for 'won't', 'is not' for 'isn't' and 'I am' for 'I'm'. Knowing this tendency can help you to convey a foreign accent better than anything.

Another useful approach is to use the fact that non-native speakers often make mistakes with common idioms. These may be subtle – 'let's play it by *the* ear' – or literal translations of comparable idioms from their own language; for example, the French for 'as easy as falling off a log' is 'as easy as putting one's fingers in one's nose' and 'to cost an arm and a leg' is 'to cost the eyes from the head'. In Polish, 'let sleeping dogs lie' is 'don't call the wolf out of the forest'. Occasionally, using a misplaced idiom can be convincing to show that a character isn't a native speaker – but don't overuse this approach.

Find a friend who speaks a foreign language that you don't know, and request some common words and phrases such as 'yes', 'no', 'thanks' and 'of course'. Ask how certain sounds are pronounced and the kinds of mistakes people may make when speaking English, and see whether that culture uses any interesting idioms. Now write a dialogue including one character of that nationality or background who doesn't speak English very well. Show it to your friend and get him to check and appraise it for you.

However you choose to convey a foreign accent, you need to beware of making your characters sound silly or using their accent or lack of knowledge of English for cheap humour.

Taking tips from the greats

Seeing how different writers render foreign accents can be helpful.

In *Two Caravans* (2007) Marina Lewycka's Ukrainian heroine is introduced to the repulsive Vulk, who's probably from 'one of those newly independent nations of the former Soviet Union'. Notice how she uses phonetics to let us hear his accent:

> 'Little flovver, the expense will be first to pay, and then you will be pay. Nothing to discuss. No problema . . . Exact. You verk, you get passport. You no verk, you no passport.'
>
> —*Marina Lewycka (Two Caravans, Penguin, 2008, first published 2007)*

Sometimes, you may want to write passages where the characters are all speaking in a different language but you need to write it in English. To get around this problem, some writers introduce a handful of common words from the character's native language into the conversation.

Ernest Hemingway frequently puts in common Spanish words such as *nada* and *mañana* to show that the characters are speaking Spanish, and writes sentences such as, '"Hombre, there are bodegas open all night long"' (Ernest Hemingway, 'A Clean, Well-lighted Place', 1933, Scribner's Magazine).

In Diane Johnson's 1998 novel *Le Divorce,* the author uses simple expressions such as *de rien* and *c'est gentil* to remind readers that the characters are speaking French. She even uses a little bit of Franglais, as in '"Monsieur, excuse me for deranging you"'. (Diane Johnson, *Le Divorce*, Plume, 1998).

In French, *déranger* means to disturb and is an example of what linguists call a 'false friend', a word that sounds the same but means something completely different.

Some of the errors people speaking a foreign language make are due to cultural differences. In Xiaolu Guo's 2007 *A Concise Chinese–English Dictionary for Lovers,* for example, when offered a cup of tea or coffee, the character says, '"No, I don't want anything wet,"' without adding a 'thank you'. She goes on to say, '"The food you cook is disgusting. Why nobody tell you?"', her directness creating the impression of extreme rudeness (Xiaolu Guo, *A Concise Chinese–English Dictionary for Lovers,* Chatto & Windus, 2007).

Dealing with dialect

Regional accents can be problematic, and you have many of the same options that I describe in the preceding section when conveying foreign accents. You can just go for it, even writing a whole narrative or part of the narrative in a strong regional accent, as Anthony Cartwright does in *The Afterglow* (2004) or James Kelman in *How Late It Was, How Late* (1994), in which case you can make the dialect as light or as heavy as you like.

Picking a few words to render in non-Received Pronunciation (standard English) usually works best, however, in order just to remind readers from time to time without making the dialogue difficult to read.

Here are some illustrative examples of how professional writers handle dialects.

Emily Brontë doesn't leave anything to the imagination here:

> 'What are ye for?' he shouted. 'T' maister's down i' t' fowld. Go round by th' end o' t' laith, if ye went to spake to him.'
>
> —*Emily Brontë (Wuthering Heights, Penguin, 2003, first published 1847)*

Again, careful attention to phonetics tells us exactly what a Black Country accent sounds like:

> 'Ay got much on here today, son. Wharrum gonna do is put the rest o this lot on Banksy's line this after. Yow an im . . . wossisnaeme . . . yer dispatch mon?'
>
> —*Anthony Cartwright (The Afterglow, Tindal Street Press, 2004)*

Phonetics and the rhythms of speech show how people spoke in rural Ireland:

> 'Well, Jaysus,' said my father, 'there's Mr Fine himself coming out of our house. I wonder what he was looking for. I wonder does he have rats?'

And a few lines later:

> 'Just splendidly, yes, indeed,' said Mr Fine. 'How are you both? We were terrible shocked and anxious . . .'
>
> —*Sebastian Barry (The Secret Scripture, Faber & Faber, 2008)*

Also look at the way that Annie Proulx beautifully conveys a Wyoming accent, copying the local people's grammar and speech patterns exactly:

> 'Yah . . . I'll tell you, on Tin Head's ranch things went wrong . . . calves was born with three legs, his kids was piebald . . . Tin Head never finished nothing he started.'
>
> —*Annie Proulx ('The Half-Skinned Steer', from the collection Close Range: Wyoming Stories, Scribner, 1999)*

Accents that are too strong can end up sounding comic. Stella Gibbons parodies rural accents and attitudes in her novel *Cold Comfort Farm*. Notice the way in which she exaggerates the accent to create a comic effect:

> ''Tes *frittenin*' for them to see their preacher among them like any simple soul,' he whispered . . . 'Nay. 'Tes a fearful torment and a groanin' to my soul's marrow.'
>
> —*Stella Gibbons (Cold Comfort Farm, Longmans, 1932)*

Talk to someone with a strong regional accent and practise different ways of conveying it. Ask a friend to read it back to you and see how accurate it sounds!

Nailing down your use of slang

Slang is the use of informal words and phrases that are more common in speech than writing. In Britain, words and phrases such as gobsmacked, zonked, chinwag, knees up, off your trolley, taking the piss and tickety-boo are all slang expressions.

Slang changes and evolves all the time and is often used by particular groups of people. You need to know what kind of slang is appropriate to your choice of characters. Remember that the fluid and ever-changing nature of slang is a potential danger for the writer – because slang very quickly becomes outdated and thus will date your fiction if you're not careful!

Look at the following two quotes and notice how the author makes the meaning of the slang words clear by the context they are in:

> Dean: 'If you kiss a fugly she'll have a baby every time. You only need to look at 'em for too long and you'll put a bun in their oven, I swear. They're rancid, man, stay well away.'

And:

> Jordan: 'My mum's trying to get me in another school but no one wants me, innit. I don't even care man, school's shit anyway.'

> —*Stephen Kelman (Pigeon English, Bloomsbury, 2011)*

Sometimes you can make unusual spellings do the job of creating an accent – here some of the words are written as they would be in a text message:

> 'Shudn't b callin us Pakis, innit, you dirrty gora' . . . 'Call me or any a ma bredrens a Paki again an I'ma mash u an yo family. In't dat da truth, Pakis?'

> —*Gautam Malkani (Londonstani, Fourth Estate, 2006)*

Write a dialogue in which one of the characters uses slang expressions. Again, you'll need to listen to people speaking to make sure you've got it right!

Swearing off

Many writers use frequent swear-words in slang, because the characters would genuinely use them in speech. If characters really speak this way, then that's fine – though you may not need to use as many swear-words as the characters themselves to create the right impression. As speech has become more and more colloquial, so more people use swear-words in contexts where they would formerly have been shocking. Do remember though that swear-words become less and less powerful the more they are used, so you might want to limit their use to situations where you want to shock.

James Kelman won the Man Booker Prize in 1994 with his novel *How Late It Was, How Late*, narrated by a Glaswegian drunk. Not everyone was impressed with this choice and one of the reviewers counted the number of 'f' words in the book, which came to over 4,000. Many people found the book unreadable!

Getting quirky with speech quirks

Many people have particular ways of speaking that are often separate from their accents or regional dialects. Such quirks depend not only on the characters' age, education and background, but also on the work that they do (different ways of speaking are appropriate in different jobs). Teenagers often speak very differently at home than with their peers. People also acquire a fair amount of work-related jargon that can slip over into their ordinary everyday speech.

Clichéd phrases such as 'at the end of the day', 'I personally', 'it's not rocket science' and 'at this moment in time' are often used in speech and can be appropriate for a particular character. But be wary of using these too often.

Examples of characters in fiction with favourite phrases that function as speech quirks are Jay Gatsby's 'old sport' in F Scott Fitzgerald's *The Great Gatsby* (1952) and Mr Micawber's 'something will turn up' in Dickens's novel *David Copperfield* (1850), among many others.

Think carefully about the way your characters speak, and note down your decisions in the following areas to keep handy:

- ✔ Tone of voice
- ✔ Speed of speaking
- ✔ Choice of words
- ✔ Particular favourite phrases

You can use quirks to make a character's dialogue individual. This can be extremely useful when a number of people are present in a scene, because you can use the individual ways of speaking to distinguish the characters. (See the later section 'Don't All Shout at Once! Coping with Crowds' for more on dialogue and groups.)

Don't overdo speech quirks. Mistakes can be a useful way of making characters' individual voices stand out, and can sometimes be funny or endearing, but they can also become irritating if overused. You want to keep your dialogue easy to read, so that readers can concentrate on the story instead of getting bogged down in trying to work out what people are trying to say.

Impediments

Some characters in fiction have speech impediments such as stuttering, lisping (for example, Violet Elizabeth Bott in Richmal Crompton's Just William stories (1921–1970) – "'I'll thcream and thcream and thcream until I'm sick'") and Tolstoy's character Denisov, who can't pronounce 'r' and replaces it with 'w':

> Denisov first went to the barrier and announced: "As the adve'sawies have wefused a weconciliation, please pwoceed. Take your pistols, and at the word *thwee* begin to advance. O-ne! T-wo! Thwee!"
>
> —*Leo Tolstoy (War and Peace, translated by Louise and Aylmer Maude, Macmillan, 1971, first published 1869)*

Speech slip-ups

Many people make mistakes in speech, and this can be useful when creating dialogue. Although speech errors may be genuine mistakes, and so are useful for adding humour, creating embarrassment or conveying nervousness, they're particularly interesting in the way they sometimes give away unconscious messages about what the character is thinking.

Here are three specific types you may want to include in your writing:

- ✔ **Spoonerism:** Mixing up two syllables from different words within one phrase, and named after the Reverend William Archibald Spooner. An apocryphal example is, 'Is it kisstomary to cuss the bride?'

- ✔ **Malapropism:** Replacing an intended word with one that sounds similar but has a very different meaning, named after Mrs Malaprop in Sheridan's 1775 play *The Rivals*. An example is Mrs Malaprop's '*illiterate* him quite from your memory' (instead of 'obliterate').

- ✔ **Freudian slip:** This refers not to a silky undergarment worn by Sigmund, but a slip of the tongue caused by subconscious association. A character uses the wrong word in a sentence, thus showing what he's really thinking about. An example of a Freudian slip, probably invented, is: 'If it's not one thing, it's your mother!'

Write a dialogue in which a character's use of the wrong word unwittingly reveals something to another character – and to the readers. You may like to invent a spoonerism, malapropism or new word of your own and include it in the dialogue or add it to an existing story.

Intonation

An important feature of speech is how the voice rises and falls. Generally, the voice rises at the end of a sentence when asking a question or when someone's excited, and flattens when people are making statements.

A recent phenomenon in speech is the rise of *uptalk* among young people, where the voice rises after lots of phrases. Uptalk is usually conveyed on the page by using a question mark where no question exists; for example: 'So, we went to the park? And it was, like, amazing? And Fred was there, and he was, like, "Hi"?'

You can also leave out a question mark where you'd normally put one, to show that the character isn't happy about being questioned; for example, 'What' or 'Why would I do that'. This allows you to show that the person isn't asking a question but exclaiming or protesting.

Don't All Shout at Once!
Coping with Crowds

Sometimes you have to compose dialogue involving three or more people. This situation presents particular problems, because you can't rely entirely on 'he said' and 'she said' to distinguish speakers. You can, of course, refer to people's names, but this quickly gets repetitive and cumbersome – particularly when you're writing a conversation involving large groups and crowds, such as during meetings, social events, family gatherings or meals.

A better idea is to use subtle speech quirks so that readers easily grasp who's speaking at any one time (see the preceding section for ideas). You can also use references to people's body language, gestures that they're making and other observations to break up the dialogue in such a way that readers can follow what's going on.

To improve your crowd scenes markedly, give every character a name so that you don't have to keep referring to 'the man standing on the left of the man with the big nose' or 'the woman with the brown handbag whom he'd seen standing by the door earlier'. Otherwise you end up giving readers far too much to remember, and their eyes start to glaze over!

You need just a few lines to set up the crowd scene and introduce the characters who are present, but as always you need to focus on the important lines of dialogue that are spoken rather than writing lots of banter for the sake of it.

Write a scene with at least four characters and use individual speech patterns to make clear who's speaking.

Producing Effective Speeches and Monologues

Occasionally, you need to have a character make a long speech or impart a lot of information; for example, when he's briefing people on a task. Speeches and monologues are difficult to write well, because they are all in one voice and can become monotonous, and because readers always have difficulty taking in too much information simultaneously.

When you need to convey a long speech or piece of dialogue, try to relay only snatches of it or weave in descriptions and the emotions of the character who's listening. For example, your character may be angry or upset when listening, and therefore hears just part of what's being said. You can also try having a number of characters with different agendas present, who share the imparting of information and who disagree with one another – John le Carré does this brilliantly in his 1989 novel *The Russia House* when Barley is being interrogated by the secret services.

Imparting information

From time to time you're inevitably going to need to write a scene where one person is listening to another. You can use several techniques to make this situation interesting for readers:

- ✔ Your character doesn't have to listen passively. He can ask questions, be thinking about other things and observe what's going on around him.

- ✔ *Reported speech* (which, unlike direct speech, doesn't use quotation marks but instead sets out the words as, say, 'John said that . . . ') is useful for conveying the gist of what's going on, leaving you to just come out with a few choice phrases or the most important parts of what's being said in direct speech.

- ✔ The listening character can react emotionally to what he's being told – he may be afraid, angry or irritated. He may also be bored, of course, but remember that boredom in a character is often very boring for readers too.

Reported speech is extremely useful for summarising long passages of dialogue and highlighting the most significant parts of it. In reported speech you drop quote marks and work the dialogue into your sentences. For example, in a standard piece of direct piece of speech you'd write:

Nishma said, 'It's raining. I've been travelling for hours.'

But in reported speech this becomes:

Nishma said it was raining and that she had been travelling for hours.

Reported speech loses many of the idiosyncrasies and characteristics of the individual character's voice, and so try to mix passages of reported speech with the occasional actual speech of the character. For example:

Nishma said that it was raining and that she had been travelling for hours. 'I'm, like, totally drenched,' she said.

1. **Write a passage of reported speech.**

2. **Edit it down to be as short as possible while still conveying the important points.**

3. **Add in some pieces of direct speech to liven it up.**

Interviewing and making presentations

Finding a way of making an interview or presentation visual is just as useful in fiction as in real life. Describe the room, the characters and the atmosphere, and employ visual props in the presentation itself.

Include only the essential information; you don't need to convey the whole presentation just because it would've been that way in reality. Summarising most of the interview or presentation may be the best way forward, with only the crucial parts, which are necessary to reveal aspects of the character and to follow the plot, expressed directly in speech.

Going it alone: Interior monologues

A long *internal monologue* (the direct thoughts and feelings of the character) can be fun to read, but only if the writer has captured a genuinely original and interesting voice, or a gripping situation is going on outside the character while he's thinking. Otherwise, long internal passages of thought tend to slow down your story and can drive readers away entirely.

In the early 20th century, writers like Virginia Woolf and James Joyce pioneered a technique known as stream of consciousness where the characters' thoughts and feelings were expressed in their own words in an uninterrupted stream, sometimes without much in the way of punctuation. Look at the opening of Woolf's 1925 novel *Mrs Dalloway* or the famous monologue by Molly right at the end of James Joyce's 1922 novel *Ulysses* to see how this works.

Chapter 7

Conveying Characters' Thoughts in Style

*Y*ou hear and even read a lot of nonsense today about books and the written word being 'sooooo last century' because of the challenges posed by electronic media. But well-written prose still does one thing more effectively than any other form does: it can reveal a character's thoughts and feelings in a wonderfully direct and efficient manner. In this chapter, I look at the different ways in which you can convey your characters' thoughts and feelings to readers – including the incredibly useful free indirect style. I also describe some of the best approaches to getting a character's thoughts down clearly and stylishly on the page.

Exploring Ways to Set Down Characters' Thoughts

You can lay down your character's thoughts on the page in a number of different ways. In this section I discuss some of the options, using the same basic passage to examine the pro and cons of the different techniques. The crucial elements to aim for in your own work are clarity and believability, while not drawing too much distracting attention to your writing or making it too repetitive.

You sometimes see thoughts written out within speech marks as conventional dialogue, but with 'he thought' or 'she felt' instead of 'he said' or 'she said':

> 'Well,' she thought to herself, 'I wonder what I'll be having for dinner. I bet Jack forgot to buy the chicken this morning, and I know there isn't anything in the freezer. I'm really starving! Maybe I'd better pick something up on the way home.'

 This approach isn't always successful, because it seems contrived and unconvincing. It gives the impression that people think in complete, well-formed sentences, and so doesn't reflect the way they really think. It also tends to give the incorrect impression that the character is thinking aloud. The addition of the words 'to herself' also jars, because readers probably can't imagine who else the character could possibly be thinking to apart from herself.

Another technique is to use italics to reflect thoughts, but if you have long passages with a large number of thoughts this can look awkward on the page. For example, the passage would appear as follows:

> *Well*, she thought, *I wonder what I'll be having for dinner. I bet Jack forgot to buy the chicken this morning, and I know there isn't anything in the freezer. I'm really starving! Maybe I'd better pick something up on the way home.*

The italics can draw attention to the character's thoughts in an unhelpful way.

You can express thoughts simply by dropping the speech marks and the italics and just passing on the thoughts in ordinary prose:

> Well, she thought, I wonder what I'll be having for dinner. I bet Jack forgot to buy the chicken this morning, and I know there isn't anything in the freezer. I'm really starving! Maybe I'd better pick something up on the way home.

This technique draws less attention to itself, but make sure it doesn't confuse the reader.

Often writers convey thoughts in a way that's more similar to reported speech (see Chapter 6 for more information on reported speech):

> She wondered what she would be having for dinner. She was sure that Jack would have forgotten to buy the chicken that morning, and she knew there wasn't anything in the freezer. She was really starving. Maybe she'd better pick something up on the way home.

Or, you can drop the 'she thought' or 'she wondered' altogether and just convey the thoughts directly in what's called free indirect style:

> What would she be having for dinner? Jack would have forgotten to buy the chicken this morning, and there wasn't anything in the freezer. She was starving! Maybe she'd better pick something up on the way home.

The beauty of this technique is that it gives the impression of the character's thoughts while the character is thinking them, but doesn't disturb the prose or draw undue attention to itself. This technique is wonderfully useful, and I discuss it in more detail in the later section 'Enjoying the Flexibility of Free Indirect Style'.

However you decide to convey your characters' thoughts, it helps if you tend to use the same method throughout your story. If you use different methods, for example sometimes using quote marks or italics and sometimes not, the reader will start to become confused as to when a character is thinking and talking aloud.

Dramatising Characters' Thoughts and Feelings Effectively

No other narrative form can reveal a character's inner thoughts and feelings (known as introspection, internal dialogue, interior monologue or self-talk) as directly and convincingly as written fiction can. On stage, characters have to voice their thoughts aloud in the form of the soliloquy, as Shakespeare's Hamlet famously does in his 'to be or not to be' speech. On film, a character's thoughts can only be known directly through voice-over (or occasionally, for humorous effect, in subtitles, as in Woody Allen's great *Annie Hall* of 1977). People accept these artificial techniques on stage or in film, although they can sometimes seem rather contrived.

As anyone who's ever tried meditation or mindfulness training knows, a person's mind is a seething mess of incoherent thoughts and feelings, some of them happening simultaneously, some fighting with one another and some repeating themselves in an endless loop. Certain writers have tried to convey this so-called stream of consciousness as a character's thoughts come to mind, – this technique was most famously used by James Joyce in his 1922 novel *Ulysses* – but a more popular approach is to organise your character's thoughts in such a way as to reveal only the important ones.

You can use a variety of techniques to reflect the interior world of the character effectively, and in this section I discuss a few common approaches.

Thinking in the real world

One obvious approach to conveying the character's thoughts and feelings directly to readers in fiction and narrative non-fiction is to employ letters, diaries and other forms of written communication. The problem with writing a long passage of a character's thoughts and feelings is that it can become monotonous and undramatic. A page or more of internal musings gives the impression that nothing's happening in the story except what's inside the character's head – readers lose all sense of the outside world.

In reality, people are usually thinking while doing a whole host of other activities. They may be walking, cooking, cleaning, staring out of the office window, sitting in a café, riding on a bus or train, taking a shower or combing their hair. Your writing improves considerably when you convey this sense of what's going on in the outside world while your characters are thinking their thoughts.

This exercise should help you to create a sense of the outside world while you are writing about your character's thoughts and feelings:

1. **Write about your character mulling over some problem, planning what to do later that day or reflecting on something that happened earlier.**

2. **Move on to write about what's going on around your character: describe any sights, sounds and smells.**

3. **Make the character do something active while she's thinking.**

4. **Weave the writing in steps 1 to 3 together into a coherent whole.**

This exercise will also help you to dramatise a passage of writing by creating actions for your character to perform while thinking through a dilemma:

1. **Write about your character trying to make a choice, such as whether to go to Paris for the weekend or not.**

2. **Describe what the character is doing as she ponders the choice, including dramatic actions that reflect her indecision: perhaps she packs and unpacks her suitcase, gets as far as the bus stop and then turns back, or rings and books her ticket and then cancels.**

Gesturing towards body language

Describing your character's feelings and emotions can be difficult. You can all too easily fall into the trap of saying 'he felt angry' or 'she felt sad', which doesn't really convey the emotions directly to readers. But you can get around this problem by using the techniques I present in this section.

Showing not telling

The golden rule of creative writing is to show your readers rather than tell them. Scientific research shows that emotions are felt and expressed in the body *before* they come into your conscious mind. This is why people often find themselves trembling with shock or tensing up with fury before they're able to recognise or control their emotions.

The best way convey characters' feelings is through their body language. If you're writing from the viewpoint of a character, describe what she notices about her bodily reactions to the emotion. If you're looking at a character from the outside, describe what she's doing. Writers are often afraid of being melodramatic by over-dramatising a character's physical reactions, but in fact people often react more dramatically in reality than you may think.

Here's a description from William Wharton's autobiographical account of his reaction on being told that several members of his family had been killed in a car accident. Notice how the physical actions are completely outside the character's control:

> I realise I'd better get off my feet or I'm going to fall down. I slump onto the floor with my head against the side of the couch, the way I watch baseball on television . . . I know I feel terrible. I can't stop shaking my head. It's totally involuntary.
>
> —*William Wharton (Wrongful Deaths, Granta, 1994)*

The physical details are telling. Later, after Wharton telephones his remaining daughter to give her the dreadful news, he writes: 'I put the phone back in the cradle the wrong way, then turn it around.' How well that small detail conveys the reality that even in the most terrible situations people distract themselves with trivial things.

If you doubt people's dramatic reactions, look at the body language of a footballer after scoring a goal or an athlete after winning a race. Look at photographs of people in extreme situations. In your own writing, try to describe what the character does in exact detail.

This exercise helps you to reveal a character's feelings without stating them directly. For both cases, concentrate on the character's physical response:

1. **Write about a character receiving bad news.**

2. **Write about the same character receiving good news.**

Being betrayed by actions

People often give away what they're thinking or feeling through small, involuntary physical actions and gestures. You can use this tendency in your own writing, for the main character whose thoughts readers are allowed to know from the inside – who can feel her body reacting – and also for characters that readers only view from the outside, perhaps through the observations of another character.

Here are some tips on how people can inadvertently give away their thoughts. Try using them in your own stories:

- ✔ People may find themselves salivating, making involuntary movements with their mouth or licking their lips while thinking about what they're going to eat later.

- ✔ People may make sharp jabbing motions with their knife while cooking or eating when they feel angry.

- ✔ People's eyes tend to look in the direction in which they want to go.

- ✔ People stare into space when they don't want to engage with something.

- ✔ People tend to fold their arms in front of them when feeling defensive. Less obviously, a woman may toy with a necklace or rest her knuckles at the base of her throat, while a man may fiddle with his watch or shirt cuffs, or adjust his tie.

People are used to picking up these clues in everyday life. They know the person who somehow never seems to have any change in her purse and who reluctantly peels out a note of the lowest possible denomination when asked to contribute to a joint meal; or the person who's always looking at herself in every mirror and stopping to pat her hair or adjust her clothing.

Tiny gestures can also give away physical intimacy or reveal that somebody's telling a lie. In Henry James's 1881 novel *The Portrait of a Lady,* Isabel walks into a room to see her husband sitting while Madame Merle is standing. On seeing Isabel, her husband suddenly jumps up, indicating that he's more comfortable with Mme Merle than with his wife. This scene is a turning point in the story, which gives away to Isabel that her husband and Mme Merle are lovers.

Another example is in Leo Tolstoy's *Anna Karenina* (1887), when Anna and her husband, Karenin, go to the races. Vronsky and his horse fall at the last fence and Anna 'began fluttering like a caged bird, at one moment getting up to go, at the next turning to Betsy'. Her distress reveals to Karenin that Vronsky is his wife's lover.

Revealing hidden emotions with subtlety

One advantage of using body language to convey feelings is that you don't need to spell out the emotions to your readers, because they're able to pick up what's going on themselves. If you say 'she was upset', readers aren't likely to feel upset, whereas if you describe the character's body language, they're more likely to feel the effect in their own bodies and thus experience the emotion directly.

Here's a passage that subtly conveys a character's feelings through unconscious actions, in this case fiddling with an object:

> 'Mrs. Robert Ferrars!' – was repeated by Marianne and her mother, in an accent of the utmost amazement; – and though Elinor could not speak, even <u>her</u> eyes were fixed on him [Edward Ferrars] with the same impatient wonder. He rose from his seat and walked to the window, apparently from not knowing what to do; took up a pair of scissors that lay there, and while spoiling both them and their sheath by cutting the latter to pieces as he spoke, said, in a hurried voice,
>
> 'Perhaps you do not know – you may not have heard that my brother is lately married to – to the youngest – to Miss Lucy Steele.'
>
> —*Jane Austen (Sense and Sensibility, Penguin, 1969, first published 1811)*

In this passage near the end of the novel, Elinor discovers that Lucy Steele is married not to Edward, as she feared, but to his brother Robert. This leaves Edward free to declare his love for Elinor. This act of cutting up the sheath that holds the scissors shows how distracted Edward is and the difficulty he experiences in expressing his feelings. It also could be seen symbolically as showing that he no longer needs to conceal his passion (Freud would certainly have had something to say about this!).

In the following pivotal scene from *The Remains of the Day*, Miss Kenton tries to take a book from Mr Stevens's grasp:

> She reached forward and began gently to release the volume from my grasp. I judged it best to look away while she did so, but with her person positioned so closely, this could only be achieved by my twisting my head away at a somewhat unnatural angle.
>
> —*Kazuo Ishiguro (The Remains of the Day, Faber and Faber, 1989)*

When she finally gets hold of the book, Miss Kenton discovers it to be a 'sentimental love story'. This scene is telling, because readers realise that Stevens and Miss Kenton are attracted to one another, but Stevens is unaware of this and is even trying to avoid the knowledge. The fact that the novel is a love story and that Stevens is looking for love in a book instead of right in front of his eyes adds to the poignancy of the scene.

Write a scene in which a character performs an unusual physical action (for example, fidgeting or doodling) that subtly reveals her unconscious thoughts and feelings.

Capturing a character's inner voice

In order to be able to convey a character's thoughts successfully, you need to know the details about how she speaks and thinks, such as the following:

- ✔ The vocabulary she uses
- ✔ Her thoughts on a wide range of issues
- ✔ What she's interested in
- ✔ What she notices and doesn't notice in the world outside
- ✔ Where she doesn't see things accurately but misinterprets them

This exercise will help you to find your character's authentic feelings, so that you can convey them more clearly in your story.

1. **Write a diary entry for your character, in which she pours out exactly what she thinks without any fear of anyone ever reading it. Allow her to rant and rave, repeat the same thing over and over, and state her honest opinions about other people and herself.**

2. **Place your character in a situation in one of your stories.**

3. **Weave some of the character's thoughts from the diary into this situation.**

Write a letter or an email from your character to a close friend, making sure to use the precise words and phrases that she'd use. This exercise will also help you to find your character's direct voice.

Enjoying the Flexibility of Free Indirect Style

Many writers use free indirect style instinctively, even if they don't know the technical term. *Free indirect style* is when the author/narrator merges her voice with the character's voice and takes on the character's way of expressing thoughts and feelings. It's an incredibly versatile approach and enables you as an author to get really close to your characters, even when you aren't writing in the first person. Also, very usefully, you don't need to keep writing 'she thought' or 'she felt', because the fact that the character is thinking is quite clear.

The problem with constantly writing 'he thought', 'she felt', 'he wondered' and so on is that it makes the reader aware that there is an author telling them these things. Free indirect style allows the reader to directly enter the character's consciousness.

Here are some examples to show you how free indirect style works.

In the following extract, Henry James explores the point of view of a young girl who doesn't fully understand what's going on around her. He uses free indirect style to let us know what Maisie is feeling. The word 'embarrassingly' is Maisie's comment (not the author's); Maisie is the embarrassed person:

> Mrs Waites was as safe as Clara Matilda, who was in heaven and yet, embarrassingly, also in Kensal Green where they had been together to see her little addled grave.
>
> —*Henry James (What Maisie Knew, Penguin, 1978, first published 1897)*

In the next quote, James Joyce uses free indirect style to give us a real sense of Lily's point of view. Of course Lily isn't literally run off her feet, but she would no doubt say she was if she were speaking:

> Lily, the caretaker's daughter, was literally run off her feet.
>
> —*James Joyce ('The Dead', in Dubliners, Everyman's Library, 1991, first published 1914)*

Here, Dennis Lehane uses free indirect style to help us to get to know the character. It's not the author but the character Sean who is thinking what's cool or not:

> Kids at the Looey and Dooey got to wear street clothes, which was cool, but they usually wore the same ones three out of five days, which wasn't.
>
> —*Dennis Lehane (Mystic River, Bantam, 2001)*

'It is a truth universally acknowledged' that free indirect style is extremely useful!

Jane Austen is a pioneer of free indirect style, which is one of the reasons why she's so successful and seems quite modern in comparison with many people writing at that time. Her use of this technique enables her to get right inside the heads of her characters and allows her to express exactly what they're thinking in the words that they'd use themselves.

Here's a great example in which the character Emma is thinking all these thoughts, but her voice is merged with that of the narrator:

Harriet was one of those, who, having once begun, would be always in love. And now, poor girl! she was considerably worse from this re-appearance of Mr. Elton . . . —his air as he walked by the house—the very sitting of his hat, being all in proof of how much he was in love!

—*Jane Austen (Emma, Collector's Library, CRW Publishing Ltd, 2003, first published 1815)*

In the final quote, the author uses free indirect style to convey Sylvie's most intimate thoughts and feelings so that we really experience the way she feels:

> She [Sylvie] wanted rid of him. He had delivered all three (three!) of her children and she did not like him one bit. Only a husband should see what he saw. Pawing and poking with his instruments in her most delicate and secretive places . . . Doctors for women should all be women themselves. Little chance of that.
>
> —*Kate Atkinson (Life After Life, Doubleday, 2013)*

Write a passage using free indirect style to convey a character's thoughts.

Chapter 8

Choosing and Using Different Points of View

*Y*ou may think that an event is an event is an event. If, say, a car crashes into a tree, that's about it . . . isn't it? Well, of course not! Anyone who's ever read witness accounts of accidents knows that people can see the same event in hugely different ways. To one witness the car is white, to another black. One remembers a maniac with the 'pedal to the metal' screeching on the wrong side of the road, whereas another recalls the driver pootling along at a steady 20 miles per hour. Plus, of course, the driver denies being on the phone and insists that the 'tree shouldn't have been there'!

In this chapter I explore the different points of view you can use in your fiction, and the advantages and disadvantages of each technique. In addition, I lead you through the often tricky process of employing a mix of voices and multiple viewpoints in a single work.

'From Where I'm Standing': The Importance of Taking a View

Some writers have difficulty choosing and, particularly, maintaining consistently their narrator's point of view and voice. But point of view is such an influential aspect of your writing that getting the decision and implementation right is extremely important. After all, as George Eliot writes in her 1874 novel *Middlemarch,* 'It is a narrow mind which cannot look at a subject from various points of view.'

You have many options for choosing a viewpoint, and your choice depends on what you want to achieve with your story, the events you're relating, the tone and atmosphere you're after, and your narrator's personality and interests. Your choice is a crucial factor in how successful or otherwise your final piece of writing is going to be.

Experimenting with Voices and Viewpoints

As a writer, in essence you have the following main options when you choose how to narrate your story:

- ✔ **First person:** Using 'I' as the narrator. This restricts the narrative to one *subjective viewpoint.* By this I mean that the reader can only know what the narrator knows. Check out the later section 'Using "I", the first-person voice' for details.

- ✔ **Second person:** Using 'you' as the focus of the narrative, although this always implies an 'I'. Flip to 'Using "you", the second-person voice', later in this chapter.

- ✔ **Third person:** Using 'he' or 'she' as the narrator, but restricting the point of view to only one character. For more, see the later section '"He said, she said": Using the third-person voice, limited to one character'.

- ✔ **Point of view of an outside character:** This person observes the action but isn't directly involved in it. The later section 'On the outside looking in: Employing an outside narrator' has more details.

- ✔ **Point of view of an *omniscient* (all-knowing) narrator:** This person is outside the story and sees and knows everything that's going on. 'Seeing everything with an omniscient narrator', later in the chapter, is the place to visit for more info.

- ✔ **Multiple subjective narrators:** When the story is told in turn by different narrators. (I cover this approach in the later section 'Adopting More Than One Viewpoint').

When you start thinking about a story, you're not always going to be clear which point of view to tell it from, and so a great idea is to try out different ways of writing it and explore different voices. Doing so can save you a great deal of trouble later on, because you can get some way into a story before realising that it isn't working and having to go back to the beginning and try again.

Think of this early stage like being an artist who starts with sketches and is trying out his colour palette. Just play around with different points of view and see which ones you like best. You may find that you connect immediately with one character but struggle with another, or discover that a character you originally intended to be unimportant makes the best narrator for your story.

I believe that the simplest way to tell your story is usually the best one. Writing a piece of fiction is hard enough without making things more complicated than you need to! A single-viewpoint character is almost always the best way to tell a short story and is best for many novels too.

You may realise, however, that you just can't tell the story you want with only one viewpoint. A novel, especially a longer one, gives you the scope to explore more than one character in depth. If you do decide to have more than one viewpoint in the story, you need to think carefully about how to handle the different voices (see the later section 'Adopting More Than One Viewpoint').

Figure 8-1 helps you with making choices about the different voices and viewpoints you can use in a story.

When you're thinking of embarking on a story, it's a good idea to try out all the possible points of view before you begin:

1. **Think about the main characters in your story and write down their names.**

2. **Invent your first scene – either the opening scene or a dramatic scene you've envisaged.**

3. **Write this scene from the point of view of each character in turn.**

4. **Bring in a new character, one you hadn't thought of, and write from that person's point of view.**

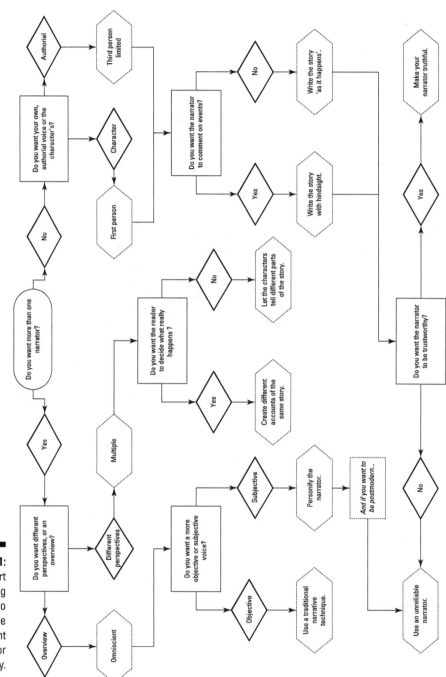

Figure 8-1:
Flowchart
showing
how to
choose the
right point
of view for
your story.

Using 'I', the first-person voice

The first-person voice is the simplest, most straightforward and easiest to understand of any writing style. You're used to telling a story in the first person, such as whenever you write a letter, relate your experiences to others, or write in a diary or journal.

It's all about me, Me, ME!

When writing fiction, bear in mind that the first-person voice is that of your character rather than of yourself. Therefore, you need to find the voice of your character – see some of the exercises in Chapter 7. You have to use the patterns of speech and the vocabulary of your character. This is easy if the character is quite similar to you, but difficult if the character's background and voice are different to yours.

A first-person narrator is almost always the main character or protagonist of the story. Most often, the character narrates the story as it happens. You also need to consider who the narrator is talking to – the story may be confessional, as if the character is writing in a diary for himself, or it may be conversational, as if the narrator is telling the story to someone else.

A major strength of this approach is that first-person narrators can be unreliable – they may be deliberately concealing something about themselves, be mentally unstable, have a faulty memory or not understand what's going on.

Examples of unreliable narrators include the one in Fyodor Dostoevsky's 1864 *Notes from Underground,* Engleby in Sebastian Faulks's novel of the same name and the butler Stevens in Kazuo Ishiguro's 1989 novel *The Remains of the Day.* Child narrators are also unreliable, because they're naive and don't necessarily understand what's going on in the adult world, such as Maisie in Henry James's 1897 *What Maisie Knew* or the child narrator in Emma Donoghue's 2010 *Room.*

You also have the option of having a character tell a story with hindsight – looking back on an event or period in his life. The story may begin something like, 'I am going to tell you the story of the year in which I turned 16 and fell in love for the first time. Although it is over 60 years ago, I still remember what happened as if it were yesterday.'

This technique allows the narrator to have more control over the way that he tells the story, because he may now understand things that he didn't at the time.

Stories told with hindsight often include phrases such as 'Had I known then what I know now, I would not . . . ' and 'José told me later that she had not gone to see Maria after all'. This gives you a flexibility that's not possible in a narrative that unfolds as it happens, in which readers can only know what the narrator knows at that time.

Here you get the chance to try out some different types of first-person narrative:

- ✔ **Confessional:** Write a page of a diary that your character keeps.

- ✔ **Conversational:** Compose a piece in which your character is narrating a story to someone else.

- ✔ **Unreliable:** Write a story in which your narrator isn't telling the truth or is holding back a crucial piece of information.

- ✔ **Retrospective:** Produce a piece in which your narrator tells the story with hindsight, relating something that happened a long time ago.

Playing with voices

Many novels have an effect by playing with the individual voices of the characters. Original, unusual voices have become fashionable, especially the voices of people who were previously 'written out of history' or whose views and voices were suppressed in the past. In the colonial era, it was the colonisers who wrote novels about life in India and Africa and viewed these cultures from the outside, while now novels are being written from the inside, sometimes using the language in ways that are very different from standard English. Novels are also being written from of the point of view of children, those with disabilities and those who were formerly ostracised.

Here's how some contemporary novels use the distinctive voices of their characters to explore different ways of thinking and being:

- ✔ Aravind Adiga's 2008 *The White Tiger:* written by an Indian character in the form of letters.

- ✔ Mark Haddon's 2003 *The Curious Incident of the Dog in the Night-Time:* written from the point of view of a 15-year-old boy with Asperger's.

- ✔ Peter Carey's 2000 *True History of the Kelly Gang:* written from the point of view of an Australian backwoodsman.

- ✔ Xiaolu Guo's 2007 *A Concise Chinese–English Dictionary for Lovers:* written from the point of view of a Chinese woman who arrives in London speaking quite poor English. Her English improves throughout the book as she learns to speak more fluently.

Write a piece in the style of a character with a very specific way of expressing himself. Don't hold back: see how far you can go while still being comprehensible.

Using 'you', the second-person voice

Some writers explore using the second-person voice (that is, 'you'). When you use 'you' (!), the narrative may be addressing readers or another character within the book. For example, in *The Reluctant Fundamentalist* (2007) by Mohsin Hamid, the story is addressed to an unknown person to whom the narrator talks about his life.

Of course, the 'you' implies an 'I' who's addressing someone, and so in this sense it's a form of first-person narrative.

Creating a long story using only 'you' is extremely difficult. Almost always, you find yourself slipping into 'I' at some point. However, you often find that the opening of a story addresses readers directly, inviting them into the narrative (as in the opening chapter of Michel Faber's *The Crimson Petal and the White* (2002) where the narrator invites the reader into the story).

The second-person voice is, of course, often used in poetry, especially to address the beloved in a love poem. You can also use it in love songs, letters, diaries and narratives in which the main character is addressing himself.

Write a short story in the second-person voice. Think about who the narrator is and to whom he's talking.

'He said, she said': Using the third-person voice, limited to one character

The third-person limited style is probably the most commonly used and yet the most difficult to handle of all the narrative voices. The problems stem partly from the fact that writers developed this point-of-view technique over a long period of time, and it can cover a wide range of styles.

Defining third-person limited

With the *third-person limited* technique, you pick one character, usually the protagonist, and write only from that person's point of view. You don't use the character's direct voice, however, but instead your own narrative voice to convey the character. In this style, you see only what he sees, hear only what he hears, know only what he knows, and go only where he's present – rather like first-person narration, which I describe earlier in 'Using "I", the first-person voice'.

Think of the difference between the first-person and third-person limited voices as being rather like the difference between being right inside the first-person narrator's head and sitting on the shoulder of the third-person narrator and seeing everything from his perspective.

In a third-person limited voice you can still know all the thoughts and feelings of your narrator, but as with first-person narration you can't know the thoughts and feelings of other characters directly. You can, however, make your narrator deduce what other characters are thinking from their body language, what they say and from what other people say about them.

Don't forget even for a moment that you've limited the point of view to your one character, because a common mistake is inadvertently including another character's thoughts or observations. This often happens when you want to reveal something about your main character – for example, you want to explain how stunning he looks, but realise that you can't reveal this fact from the character's own point of view without making him sound obnoxiously vain or self-obsessed. So, without realising, you slip out of the main character's head and into the head of his admirer just for a couple of sentences before going back again.

This mistake breaks the contract that you've set up with readers, and is usually offputtingly jarring. Even if readers don't notice specifically what's happened, they can feel that the narration isn't secure and sense that something's wrong; it interferes with their enjoyment. More astute or critical readers may even notice the actual error and feel irritated by it.

The golden rule is: when you're writing in third-person limited style, *never* change point of view within the story or scene. The clue's in the word 'limited'!

Trying on third-person limited for size

Have a go yourself at the third-person limited style. Let the following piece change and develop as much as you like as you write it:

1. **Write a piece about a personal memory in the first-person voice and in the present tense as if it's happening now (for example: 'I'm sitting on the beach with my bucket and spade . . . ').**

2. **Pick a random name that you like (for example, Claudia).**

3. **Rewrite the memory in the third-person limited point of view as if it happened to that character, this time in the past tense ('Claudia was sitting on the beach with her bucket and spade . . . ').**

Write a piece in the first person and then rewrite the same piece in the third-person limited. Ask yourself about the differences between the two pieces. Which do you find easiest and most comfortable to write?

On the outside looking in: Employing an outside narrator

While writing in the first person (see the earlier section 'Using "I", the first-person voice') you can create a more detached voice by using as the narrator a character who's outside the story or an observer of the events. Examples of this approach are Nick Carraway in Scott Fitzgerald's 1925 *The Great Gatsby* or Dr Watson in some of Sir Arthur Conan Doyle's Sherlock Holmes stories. This device creates a sense of mystery about the main character, because readers see that person only through the eyes of the narrator.

This narrator character is often telling the story with hindsight, and therefore has information that's unknown to the main characters. In this kind of story, the narrator frequently puts together what's happened from talking to other characters, from researching aspects of the story, and from using his imagination to reconstruct what must have happened. So you often find yourself using phrases such as the following:

- ✔ 'Jack told me later what had happened when Vladimir met Fatima.'

- ✔ 'I later realised why Fatima hadn't told Jack what Vladimir had done.'

- ✔ 'I imagine that the conversation between Jack and Fatima went like this.'

A great example of an outside narrator technique is used by W Somerset Maugham in *The Razor's Edge* (1944). This novel is narrated by the character of Somerset Maugham himself. He constantly finds himself, based on conversations that he has had with the main character Larry and others, reimagining whole scenes and conversations in vivid detail, although he can't possibly know all these details. This gives the effect of reading a fully dramatised novel while allowing the narrator character to comment on and interpret the events.

Another example is the character of Nick Jenkins in Anthony Powell's 12-volume novel *A Dance to the Music of Time,* published between 1951 and 1975. The novel spans about half a century, and although it's full of detailed portraits of other characters, such as the famously repulsive Widmerpool, readers discover almost nothing about Jenkins's own inner life – even major events such as his wife's miscarriage are only revealed in conversation with the other characters. This device enables the narrator to comment on and interpret events, while keeping the focus clearly on the other characters rather than himself.

Write a story told by a narrator who heard about the main events from another person. Think about how the events may have become distorted in the telling. Begin the narrative, 'Many years later, I was told what had really happened that day long ago when . . . '

Seeing everything with an omniscient narrator

The omniscient (all-knowing) narrator is the traditional 19th-century style of writing a narrative. Fyodor Dostoevsky's *The Brothers Karamazov* (1880) and Charles Dickens's *Our Mutual Friend* (1865) are good examples. The author is the narrator and knows everything about all the characters: what they think and feel, what happened to them in the past, and what will happen to them in the future. This kind of narrative may be highly suitable for large histori-cal epics, sagas and long novels with many characters, and it does offer the writer a huge amount of flexibility, but the problem is that it can seem too distant.

The omniscient narrator as a disembodied being who looks down from above and controls everything is now rather outmoded in literature. Today, writ-ers tend to avoid dealing in absolute truth, but instead prefer to accept that different people have different subjective views, and so they try to be more pluralistic in their approach.

Many contemporary writers have found a way of personifying their omniscient narrators. In his 2005 novel *The Book Thief,* now also a film, Markus Zusak made death into a character in the novel – death, of course, is omniscient. In *The Lovely Bones* (2002), also filmed, Alice Sebold kills off her main character at the end of the first chapter – she's then looking down from heaven and observing everything that happens to the other characters in the novel.

If you're writing an omniscient narrative, modern readers almost certainly need to know who that narrator is: perhaps a character in the future writing about what happened in the past, a self-conscious author writing the story, a history professor or a god-like or alien being. The identity doesn't matter as long as you give some explanation as to why the narrator knows what he knows.

Although the omniscient narrator can go into the heads of all the characters, in practice most narratives restrict this to only a few of the main characters. Readers have difficulty identifying closely with more than a handful of signifi-cant characters.

Some writers have tried to make the omniscient narrator a completely external observer who can't enter into the thoughts and feelings of the characters. This is a very difficult technique to pull off, because it's inevitably extremely distancing. If readers don't know what characters are thinking and feeling from the inside, they're generally unable to empathise with them and tend not to care what happens to them.

Write the beginning of a story of your own in the five styles discussed earlier in this chapter. See which ones work for you and which don't, and which you prefer. Being aware of the different styles will help you to avoid lurching from one to the other at different points in your story, which can be annoying for the reader!

Unusual omniscient narrators

Some writers have used the device of having an impossible narrator. For example, in José Eduardo Agualusa's *The Book of Chameleons* the narrator is a gecko. This lizard can climb over walls and ceilings and hear and observe everything that takes place. The lizard thus becomes a kind of omniscient narrator.

You can even refuse to let the reader know who is narrating the book, as Toni Morrison does in *Jazz.* It may be that the narrator is the book itself: there are hints on the very last page, when the book seems to confide in the reader and compare it to a lover: 'I have loved the way you hold me, how close you let me be to you. I like your fingers on and on, lifting, turning. I have watched your face for a long time now' (Vintage, 2005, first published 1992). It's a great example of an unusual, daring, really subtle use of the mysterious narrator.

It can be fun to explore unusual ways of telling a story. Try these:

1. **Write a story from the point of view of an inanimate object, giving this object at least a partial omniscience.**

2. **Write a story from the point of view of an omniscient character who is an extra-worldly being – an alien, an angel or a demon.**

Addressing the reader

In some more traditional omniscient narratives the narrator can step outside the story and make comments to the reader; for example, in the famous 'Reader, I married him' in Charlotte Brontë's *Jane Eyre.*

In *Vanity Fair* Thackeray stops his characters in the middle of the action to talk to readers:

We shall halt here, before Mrs Fussbudget sips her tea, and the motes of dust are still in the air, to consider now what we have learned about the wicked Mr Nogoodnik.

—*William Makepeace Thackeray (Vanity Fair: A Novel without a Hero, Penguin Classics, 2001, first published 1847–8)*

In *War and Peace* (1869), Tolstoy even takes out whole chapters from the story to expound upon his philosophy of history.

Nowadays, this kind of thing sounds very old-fashioned and so is best avoided. However, every rule is made to be broken, and in Clive Barker's 2007 novel *Mister B. Gone* the story begins and ends with the narrator, a devil, asking readers to 'burn this book'!

Five third-person narrative styles

Within a third-person narration you can have a huge range of distance between the narrator – and therefore the reader – and the characters, from being right outside the characters to being right inside them. Here are your options:

✔ A completely external viewpoint, where the characters are seen only from the outside, and their thoughts and feelings are unknown to the narrator:

> On a cold morning on 7th January 1966, a young girl in a red dress stepped out of a house in Mayfair and climbed into a cab. After waiting a few moments, the cab drove off and turned into Piccadilly, heading west.

✔ A traditional omniscient narration where the narrator can enter into the thoughts and feelings of the characters:

> On a cold January morning in 1966, Amanda Haycroft stepped anxiously out of her house in Mayfair and climbed into the cab, where the driver had been waiting with increasing irritation. She hesitated for some moments before telling him her destination. She was dreading her sister's wedding in Chelsea.

✔ A third-person limited narration where only one character's thoughts and feelings are entered into at any one time (note: the narrative voice remains the author's):

> Amanda left the house and stepped into the cab. The driver seemed irritated at having to wait so long, and she noticed him drumming his fingers on the wheel. She wondered if it was too late to change her mind, but knew that her sister would never forgive her if she did. She turned to the driver to tell him to go to Chelsea Town Hall.

✔ A close third-person limited narration where the character's voice merges with that of the author/narrator, often through use of free indirect style (see Chapter 7 for details):

> As she stepped into the cab, she saw the cabbie drumming his fingers on the wheel. It was too bad; after all, he was paid to wait. What to do? She could still change her mind: it wasn't too late to phone with her excuses; she didn't want to see Jo get married to that moron. But Jo would never forgive her if she wasn't there. Oh, to hell with it. 'Chelsea Town Hall,' she said.

✔ A completely internal stream-of-consciousness narration:

> This cab smells of cigarettes surely you're not meant to smoke in them any more why is that driver drumming on the wheel he's paid to wait the thought of Jo marrying that awful moron don't want to go but Jo would never forgive, never forget, would go on about it for ever, oh to hell with it, better get on. 'Chelsea Town Hall.' How weird that sounds.

Adopting More Than One Viewpoint

The modern solution to the problems of using an omniscient narrator is to use multiple narrators for your story. By putting together several different accounts of the same story you can give readers much more information than when using a single viewpoint.

Curiously, this technique goes back to many early novels that were written as an exchange of letters and therefore had two viewpoints. Jane Austen's 1871 *Lady Susan,* Pierre Choderlos de Laclos's 1782 *Dangerous Liaisons,* Samuel Richardson's 1748 *Clarissa* and Tobias Smollett's 1771 *Humphry Clinker* are 18th-century examples of stories narrated by a number of fictional correspondents.

You can use multiple narrators in loads of different ways. The first choice you have to make is how many different viewpoints to include: most commonly writers use three or four viewpoints. Some books do go as far as having five or six, but readers usually have difficulty following more characters than this.

Choosing the number and type of narrators

When using multiple narrators, you also have the choice about the voice to use. You can have, for example, four different first-person narratives, in which case you need to create four different voices for the different characters. Or, you can write each part in third-person limited point of view (see the earlier section '"He said, she said": Using the third-person voice, limited to one character'), in which case the author's voice is dominant. Some narratives are a mixture of these voices, with some of the narrators being third-person limited and others first person, perhaps using letters and diaries for the first-person voice.

You can easily see how using multiple viewpoints creates more material for the story and also builds up a more complete picture. For example, you can write a story about a divorce. Part 1 is told from the point of view of the unfaithful wife. Part 2 is told from the point of view of the betrayed husband. Part 3 is told from the point of view of the lover. Finally, Part 4 is told from the point of view of the couple's child. By the author putting all four accounts together, readers get a more complete picture of what happened.

When telling a story like this, make sure that all the accounts are completely different from one another. If you just repeat the same scenes with slight variations, readers soon become bored.

Many contemporary novels use multiple narrators. Some of these, such as Paul Torday's 2006 *Salmon Fishing in the Yemen,* use many different styles to narrate the story: newspaper articles, interviews, diary entries. Jennifer Egan's 2010 *A Visit from the Goon Squad* is made up of 13 interconnected short stories. Each story can be read separately, but if you read them all together you see each story in context and find out more about the fate of the characters. Each chapter is written in a very different style, and one chapter is even written as a PowerPoint presentation.

For a list of other multiple-viewpoint novels, check out the nearby sidebar 'Who's speaking now?'.

Who's speaking now?

The easiest and, let's face it, most enjoyable way to get to grips with multiple viewpoints is to read how the experts do it.

Two viewpoints:

✔ Carol Shields *Happenstance*

✔ Gillian Flynn *Gone Girl*

✔ Audrey Niffenegger *The Time Traveller's Wife*

Three viewpoints:

✔ Carole Matthews *The Chocolate Lovers' Club*

✔ Kathryn Stockett *The Help*

Four viewpoints:

✔ Iain Pears *An Instance of the Fingerpost*

✔ Nick Hornby *A Long Way Down*

✔ Andrea Levy *Small Island*

✔ Naomi Wood *Mrs Hemingway*

Six viewpoints

✔ David Mitchell *Cloud Atlas*

Seven viewpoints

✔ Sebastian Faulks *A Week in December*

Eight viewpoints:

✔ Christos Tsiolkas *The Slap*

For a novel with 15 (yes, count them, 15!) viewpoints, read William Faulkner's *As I Lay Dying*.

Write a plan for a novel with multiple viewpoints. Think about the timeline of the story and how you're going to arrange the various viewpoints.

Balancing and structuring your viewpoints

Readers and writers instinctively like a sense of balance in a piece of writing. Wherever you have more than one viewpoint in the story, you need to think carefully about how you're going to organise the different viewpoints.

Aim for an equal balance of the different viewpoints, no matter how they're arranged. If you end up having four viewpoint characters and one of them occupies about 50 per cent of the length of the novel, the second one about 30 per cent, and the other two about 10 per cent each, readers start to feel that something isn't quite right. Readers obviously tend to identify most closely with the character who has the largest part of the novel, and therefore feel less interested in the more minor characters.

Handling multiple narrators

Here are some of the most common ways of organising multiple narrators:

- **Divide your story into different parts, with each part narrated by a different character.** This technique enables you to tell a complete story from one character's point of view and then give readers a second point of view, and then possibly a third or fourth, which gives a lot of additional information. Readers then have to review the initial story and see it in a different light.

- **Write alternate chapters/sections in the viewpoint of your different characters; preferably keep to the same order throughout your story.** To help, head each chapter or section with the name of the character who's narrating, to avoid readers becoming confused. William Faulkner uses this device in *As I Lay Dying* (1930). Similarly, without the dates and ages of the characters being given at the beginning of each section, Audrey Niffenegger's *The Time Traveller's Wife* (2003) would be almost incomprehensible.

  If you decide against using characters' names in chapter headings for some reason, consider starting each section or chapter with the narrating character's name, action or observation, so that readers are clear whose eyes they're meant to be viewing the scene through.

- **Alternate viewpoints on a scene-by-scene basis.** If you choose this option, keeping to a strict order is less important. Making your first switch early in the story is a good idea and, as with the preceding bullet point, clarify whose viewpoint you're in right from the first sentence.

  Have clear breaks between scenes, using three asterisks (***) to show you're starting a new scene.

Whichever way you decide to go, make it clear to the reader. Viewpoint shifts are always distracting to readers unless they're very clearly signalled. Getting out of one character's head and into another's is an effort for readers, and so you need to help them as much as possible. Establish a pattern clearly with headings for new chapters or parts, and if you're switching frequently from scene to scene set up a pattern early and then stick to it so that readers know what to expect.

If you find that you have a character's viewpoint that forms only a small part of the story, see whether you can change it to show the same information from the viewpoint of one of the major characters. You can do so using a number of devices:

- Through the main character's observations of the more minor character

- Through dialogue spoken by the minor character

- Through letters or diaries he writes

- Through what other people tell the main character about the person

Draw out a timeline for each character, so that you can see how the characters' voices are arranged. You'll also be able to spot any bad balances – for example, a long period in which readers don't hear at all from one of the characters, followed by rather a lot of one character's viewpoint in paragraphs bunched close together.

You can also play around by allowing readers a choice about the order in which they read the story. Reading a book in a different order changes the way that the plot works and therefore creates a different narrative.

Carol Shields divides her 1980 novel *Happenstance* into two halves. On the front cover is *Happenstance: The Wife's Story,* and on the other cover *Happenstance: The Husband's Story*. You can pick up the book either way and start reading the story, which is set over the same five days in the lives of Jack and Brenda Bowman. Brenda spends the week at a craft convention while Jack is left behind in their Chicago home with their two teenage children. If you read Brenda's story first, it changes the way you approach Jack's story, but if you choose to read Jack's story first, it changes the way you view Brenda's story. Effectively, you have two different novels; two different readers feel very differently depending on which way they choose to read the book.

Structuring multiple-viewpoint narratives

When writing multiple-viewpoint stories, fix a timeframe and structure right from the beginning. Even if you change the structure later, it gives you a framework to work with. I now take a look at some of your options.

Parallel narratives

In this structure you have separate parallel stories narrated in turn by different characters. These offer a different perspective on the same series of events. Obviously, some things happen to one character that don't form part of the other character's narrative, although you'll have some overlap.

Some examples of parallel narratives are the 1915 short story by Ryūnosuke Akutagawa, 'Rashomon' (made into a film in 1950 by Japanese director Akira Kurosawa), the 2004 Oscar-winning film *Crash* and the Booker prize-winning novel *The Luminaries* (2013) by Eleanor Catton.

Passing the baton

The narrative structure of Mary Shelley's 1818 *Frankenstein* is like a relay race with three runners who each pass the baton in a circle. It starts with the voyager Walton, who opens the novel with a series of letters to his sister, Mrs Saville; moves on to the narrative of Dr Frankenstein, who creates the monster; and then passes to the monster himself. The monster then relays the narrative back to Frankenstein's voice, and then to Walton and his letters to his sister.

Nestling stories within stories

In this technique, stories are fitted within stories rather like Russian dolls. It's not an easy technique to handle, but can produce startling results.

The simplest form of this structure is to use a frame for the story. Often in the frame the story is being narrated by one character to another character. From time to time in the narrative the story may revert back to the narrator, who's able to comment on what's happening.

Wuthering Heights (1847) by Emily Brontë is an example of such a structure. The outer frame of the story has Mr Lockwood, who hears the story from Nelly the housekeeper. Within Nelly's narrative are reports by Heathcliff and events that Nelly couldn't have witnessed. Also included are Catherine's diary and Isabella's letter to Nelly.

Cloud Atlas (2004) by David Mitchell has six stories, five of which are split in half so that you read the first half of each story moving into the central story, and the second half of each story as you move away towards the end. Each story fits inside the other, and each story connects in some way with the next one to create an ingenious and thought-provoking book.

Diane Setterfield's first novel *The Thirteenth Tale* (2006) also uses the Russian-doll structure. Margaret Lea is a biographer summoned to write the life story of Vida Winter, an author well known for inventing her past every time she's interviewed about a new novel. She reveals to Margaret that she's dying, and says she now wants to tell the truth, relating a story that echoes events in Margaret's own past.

Elif Shafak's *The Forty Rules of Love* (2010) tells the story of bored housewife Ella, who's given a book called *Sweet Blasphemy* to read by her fictional publisher. This tells the story of a wandering Persian Dervish, Shams of Tabriz, and his relationship with the great Sufi poet Rumi. The book interweaves Ella's quest to find love with Shams and Rumi's story, which is told by them both with a range of characters including Rumi's wife and sons. The story is narrated through first-person fragments, letters and emails.

In Margaret Atwood's novel *The Blind Assassin* (2000) the main narrative is interspersed with excerpts from a novel written by one of the main characters; this novel itself contains a science fiction story written by one of the characters.

Chapter 9

Creating Complicated, Well-Rounded Characters

*T*he great characters from your favourite books are the ones that stay with you long after you finish reading: Fyodor Dostoevsky's agonised killer Raskolnikov from *Crime and Punishment* (1886); George Eliot's idealistic heroine from *Middlemarch* (1874), Dorothea Brooke; George Smiley, John le Carré's understated Cold War spy; or Susie Salmon, the dead narrator in Alice Sebold's *The Lovely Bones* (2002). These characters have power and longevity because they communicate and resonate with you, and most importantly because they have depth. Their authors create penetrating portrayals of fascinating, complicated characters that you return to again and again. After all, shallow characters are like superficial people: they tend to wear out their welcome in your home pretty quickly!

As you dig deeper into your literary creations you start to discover all kinds of aspects to their personalities and may well be surprised at what you find. You need to get to know your characters intimately, so that you can be confident about exactly what they say and do in any situation.

This process takes work, however, because creating realistically complicated characters is difficult. This chapter provides plenty of help as I explore the private, interior aspects of characters – their secret passions, unlikely friends, complex relationships, sexuality and less attractive aspects (the ones that people often hide). I provide loads of useful writing exercises too, so that you can improve your character-deepening skills.

You don't need to put everything you discover about your characters into your final story. But the more you know about them, the more real they seem to your readers. In addition, nobody's 100 per cent good or bad. Everyone's a mixture, and your characters need to be too – so don't forget to give them flaws and foibles as well as hidden strengths.

Adding Layers to Your Characters

With this heading, I'm not talking about dressing up your characters in warm clothes (like a concerned grandma!). No, the focus of this section is on psychological layers.

Everyone knows that people present only certain aspects of themselves in public. The rest, they hide away. Some parts are so well hidden that they're repressed and remain unknown even to the individual. One of your tasks as a writer is to reveal these hidden depths to readers.

To help with this aim, I describe creating characters with depth by considering their basic needs and pastimes as well as relationships with family and friends. I also show the value of subtly revealing character through contradictions.

Revealing depth through experiences

Although people may think that they know themselves well, in fact they seldom do. Like everyone, you're aware of how you're likely to think and feel in the ordinary circumstances that make up your day-to-day life, but you don't know how you'll react if something completely out of the ordinary happens.

For example, how do you think you'd behave if an aeroplane you were on crash-landed on a mountain top? Sorry to put you off your dinner, but would you set off down the mountain and hack through the jungle to a small village to get help? Would you curl up in the snow and wait to die? Would you eat the dead passengers in order to survive? And would you even be prepared to kill injured passengers in order to eat them? If I'm completely honest, I don't have a clue how I'd react, and I hope I never have to find out!

Such nightmarish crises are the stuff of fiction. You don't need a situation as extreme as this one to test your characters out, but every piece of fiction gives your characters a challenge or a choice, and their responses reveal who they really are.

Try this exercise to go deeper and deeper into one of your characters – perhaps a character you don't know very well yet, or one you are struggling with. Try not to think too hard about each step – just write what comes to you first:

1. **Write about a character as she presents herself to someone she wants to impress.**

2. **Move on to create a scene featuring your character in the privacy of her home.**

3. **Write about your character's secret desires.**

4. **Write about something in your character's past that influenced one of these desires.**

Remembering basic human needs

All people have a basic motivation to optimise their well-being, minimise physical pain and maximise pleasure. These deep-seated human desires underlie the motivation of all characters in fiction as well.

The psychologist Abraham Maslow created the concept of a *hierarchy of needs,* which he used to explain human motivation. He describes five stages, which you can put to use in your writing, moving from lowest (most basic) to highest:

- ✔ **Physiological:** Food and water, shelter, sleep and sex.
- ✔ **Safety:** Personal and financial security and health.
- ✔ **Belongingness and love:** Friendship, family and intimate relationships.
- ✔ **Esteem:** Admiration and respect from others.
- ✔ **Self-actualisation and self-transcendence:** Fulfilment through achievement in life.

Take one of your characters and see which of these basic needs she has achieved. What does your character want now, and what's preventing her from achieving it?

A character's motivation is the engine of any story. If a character lacks motivation, the story is as aimless as the character. A character who doesn't know what she wants is successful in fiction only if she's sufficiently well drawn that readers can see what she doesn't see.

Try this exercise to help you understand the power of motivation:

1. **Write a piece in which your character goes for an aimless walk.**

2. **Write a piece in which your character is walking to a meeting.**

You probably find that the second piece is much more interesting, although sometimes the sheer boredom of writing the first forces you to invent plot developments that may surprise you!

Of course, people can also be perverse and seem to want the very opposite of what's good for them – the father of psychoanalysis, Sigmund Freud (1856–1939), even decided that people have a 'death wish', to explain their often perverse behaviour. Sometimes, people find getting what they want is terrifying, because then they have no more excuses for not feeling happy or fulfilled, and nothing more to aim for. Surprisingly, people often get within reach of achieving their lifelong goal and then mess it up.

In the following exercise, examine a character's unexpected dilemma, creating emotions and responses that surprise the person herself:

1. **Write a scene in which your character is about to get what she wants, but does something to prevent this happening just before she succeeds.**

2. **Write a scene in which your character does get what she wants, only to discover that it's not what she desired after all.**

Looking at different areas of your character's life

Everyone's life has many different aspects. A character normally has a family life, friends and social groups, as well as a working life.

This exercise will help you to look at all the different areas of your character's life:

1. **Divide a page into four quarters:** Label these 'family', 'friends', 'hobbies' and 'work'. Put as many people as you can in each box.

2. **In the family box, include all your character's family:** Parents, grandparents, brothers and sisters, aunts and uncles, cousins. A great approach is to carry out the family tree exercise in Chapter 3 first.

3. **For the friends box, write in names from friends' from different areas of the character's life:** School friends; friends from college or university; friends from previous jobs and careers; friends among neighbours, in societies and clubs, and through chance meetings.

4. **For the work box, put in your character's colleagues, rivals, bosses and employees.**

5. **For the hobbies box, put in any friends who are connected with your character's hobbies:** Fellow artists, sports team-mates, a friend you go to the cinema with.

Now develop the 'friends' part of the exercise above:

1. **Draw a mind map of all your character's friends, including all the areas in the preceding exercise.**

2. **Invent a friend for your character from each one of these categories. Think about why they became friends, what they have in common and in which ways they're different.**

Depicting different kinds of friendship

People's different friends often reveal different aspects of their personalities and can illustrate something they'd like to be themselves. Aristotle identified three basic types of friendship:

- ✔ **Friendships of utility:** Formed between you and people who are useful to you in some way. For example, the neighbours who feed your cat while you're away, in exchange for you taking in their post; the mother who shares your school run; the man in the pub who gives you racing tips in exchange for you buying him a drink. These friendships usually die as soon as one or other person is no longer useful.

- ✔ **Friendships of pleasure:** Relationships between you and those whose company you enjoy. These can be people involved with interests and activities that you both enjoy; for example, playing sports together, having lunch, or attending concerts or the cinema.

- ✔ **Friendships of the good:** Based on mutual respect and admiration, these tend to last much longer than the first two types of friendship. They're often based on sharing the same goals and values, and may result in a lifetime bond. They're essential to people's happiness.

Write about friends for your character who fall into each one of these categories. Think about the tasks the utility friends perform for one another, the activities the pleasure friends share and the qualities the good friends admire in one another.

Friendships develop and change with time. You lose touch with some friends and gain new ones. Some friends just drift away, while others are lost after some crisis or betrayal. The same is true for your characters. To explore this:

1. **Select one of your character's friends.** Write about the complete friendship, by writing six significant moments from the start of the friendship to the present moment or the end of the relationship. Think about how many years are between these six moments.

2. **Write a scene in which your character first meets her childhood friend, and then write a scene later on.** Does she still want to be friends with that kind of person or not? If not, why?

3. **Write about someone your character fell out with a long time ago, and then write about her seeing the person again.** How does she feel? What does this response reveal about your character?

Sometimes friends are carefully chosen: you admire something about them, are attracted to their company, feel good when you're with them and share their interests. Other times friendships develop by accident: you meet someone by chance or in unusual or unexpected circumstances.

People's friends are not always predictable and people come together for all kinds of reasons. Think about somebody unexpected with whom your character becomes friends. Write the scene where they meet and then a scene later on after they're friends. This exercise can help you create an unlikely friend for your character – these characters can be very useful!

Exploiting friends in your fiction

In a story, friends can be useful in a number of ways. They can:

- ✔ Act as a foil to the main character
- ✔ Act as someone for the main character to confide in
- ✔ Pass on information to the main character
- ✔ Support the main character and help her; or get in the way, accidentally or deliberately

Friends can be your biggest help and support – but we all know those so-called friends who constantly undermine you! Try this exercise to think about both these options:

1. **Divide a page into six sections.**

2. **Think of three friends to support your character in what she's trying to achieve, and then three friends who deliberately or unconsciously hinder her.**

3. **Write the scenes in which these friends help or hinder your character.**

People who hinder your character may be trying to be helpful, and the person who helps most may be the one who tells her what she doesn't want to hear. Friends aren't always really friends. No doubt you can think of friends who you don't really like and sometimes want to drop but don't know how to without being hurtful. Occasionally, these friends can act in surprising and hurtful ways.

Try this exercise to help develop this theme. Think about how the characters met, what your main character is getting out of the relationship and why she has tolerated bad behaviour. Then write about a toxic friendship. Why is your character involved with this person, and what happens if she tries to end the friendship?

Bringing different friends together

Different friends from different parts of your life meeting up can produce fireworks or a damp squib. They may get on with one another or clash dreadfully (which is awful in real life, but fictional gold!).

People often reveal different aspects of themselves to different people and behave very differently with different friends. As a result, problems can arise when two groups of friends collide. Characters can feel highly uncomfortable when friends and colleagues from different areas of their life come together.

Write a piece in which two different friends of your character unexpectedly arrive at the same time. Do they get on, or do they take an instant dislike to one another? Write the dialogue between the three characters, and pay attention to their body language too.

Workplace relationships

Most people spend a great deal of their time at work – unless they are unemployed, in which case they may spend a great deal of time looking for work. Don't neglect this important aspect of a character's life. A character's work can give a great deal of information about a character and provide a useful foil to her home or personal life.

You need to create a network of relationships at work as well as in your character's private life. Remember that while we choose friends, we don't choose our work colleagues, so often people at work don't get along so well. Also, there are power relationships and rivalries at work that help to complicate the picture.

Remember: every workplace has its odd characters, people who don't seem to fit in or who defy stereotypes. Write about one of these characters – they can liven up the dullest scene!

You can reveal a great deal about a character by showing how she behaves with her boss, her colleagues and her subordinates.

Think about your character's work colleagues: overall boss, line manager, personal assistant, if appropriate, and a selection of colleagues and then:

- ✔ Write a scene in the workplace featuring conflict between your main character and one of her colleagues.
- ✔ Write a scene where your character has to assert her authority over an employee.
- ✔ Write about a meeting where a decision is taken that your character doesn't agree with.

In each case, think about your character's feelings and reactions. Does she enjoy power, or hate exerting it? How does she react when things don't go her way?

Although some colleagues can become friends, most people tend to keep their work and private lives slightly separate to avoid problems when these people meet. However, remember that when the worlds of work and home collide there can be fireworks!

Passing the time with hobbies and interests

Everyone enjoys different social or private activities, even the most socially awkward, isolated characters. Social activities often involve a large network of friends who share the same interest.

People's private hobbies and interests are often quite unexpected, and so don't be afraid to undercut readers' expectations. Perhaps the chief executive of a large company goes home to his mansion to play with his train set every night, or a surgeon is obsessed with his garden and has planted obscure French roses with exotic names, or a successful musician has a room dedicated to his guinea pigs!

Invent a surprising hobby for one of your characters and write about it. What hidden aspect of your character do you think it reveals? In what way does it make her feel secure or fulfilled?

Many people collect objects that have a certain meaning for them: books, ornaments, coins, medals and stamps, postcards, thimbles, paintings, china and even bottle tops. Such collections can start in childhood and become more sophisticated as the character grows up.

1. **Write about a collection of objects your character kept as a child.**

2. **Write about a collection of something similar your character has as an adult.**

You may find, for instance, that your character collected coins when young but now has a portfolio of stocks and shares; or she collected pebbles from the beach and now is a geologist with a rare collection of minerals.

To help you really get to know your character, make a list of her favourite things (you may be surprised at the ideas this exercises sparks):

- ✔ Animal
- ✔ Book
- ✔ Childhood object she still possesses
- ✔ Drink
- ✔ Food
- ✔ Painting
- ✔ Piece of clothing
- ✔ Piece of furniture
- ✔ Piece of jewellery
- ✔ Piece of music
- ✔ Place
- ✔ Smell

Confounding expectations and creating contradictions

Humans are pretty notorious for making assumptions about other people based on their initial superficial impression. They forget that the checkout girl with a working-class accent may be saving up for her PhD, or that a super-fit Olympic athlete is so afraid of flying that he has to travel ahead of the rest of the team by rail.

Your characters need to have contradictions to be believable. Remember that these contradictions may well show more about the other characters through their expectations of your character than about the character herself.

Write a piece about a character that reveals something unexpected – a characteristic that's the opposite of what you expect. For example, read the nearby sidebar 'Perfect Penny'.

One great way to depict contradictions and reveal a lot about your character is by using their attitude towards money: people who are normally tight with money can suddenly be generous, and the other way around.

How characters handle money is often influenced by their childhoods, their parents' attitude to money, whether they were wealthy or poor, and so on. Money is so fundamental to people's lives and involves so many daily

---

Perfect Penny

I used to know someone at work who seemed completely in control of her life. She was always immaculately dressed and had everything ready for every meeting, with never a sense of being harassed or rushed. Occasionally, her husband would appear when she left the office – he was a highly successful cardiologist, extremely handsome and charming. She had two daughters who were high achievers at school, where they achieved A grades in everything, and went on to gain places at top universities.

At some stage I lost contact with Perfect Penny. Then one day an old friend rang me to say that she'd bumped into her in the supermarket. To her astonishment, Perfect Penny said that she and her husband had been leading separate existences for years. They both had lovers but had waited until the children were grown up before separating, because they didn't want to disrupt their education. Despite this, Penny revealed that one of the daughters had a boyfriend with a job on a farm in Australia and had gone to join him instead of taking up her university place, while the other one had dropped out of her physics degree to become a massage therapist.

transactions that it's a great way to reveal character through showing and not telling. Remember that people's attitude towards money can be unexpected. For example, some people are very generous with money, but then run into trouble when they get short. Other people count every penny and hate to spend unless it's absolutely necessary – but may therefore have funds to help out in a crisis.

Have a go at writing the following five scenes. In each case, think about the character's thoughts, feelings and responses. Does she tell anyone? What does she do with the money? What consequences does this choice have?

- ✔ Describe your character finding a £10 note in the street.
- ✔ Describe your character losing a bag containing £100.
- ✔ Describe your character winning £1,000 in the lottery.
- ✔ Describe your character losing £10,000 in a business transaction.
- ✔ Describe your character inheriting £100,000 from a relative.

Adapt these amounts to fit in with the society and status of the world of your novel.

Try these exercises to help explore your characters' attitude to money (remember to show not tell):

- ✔ **Describe your character passing a beggar in the street, revealing what she does and the way she does it.**
- ✔ **Describe your character having a row with someone over money.**

Depicting Sexuality and Gender

Sexual identity is one of the most important aspects of human beings. From their earliest years, people are socialised as girls or boys and expected to behave in accordance with those different roles.

Many psychologists believe that the real differences in the psychological make-up of men and women are small, and that most of the differences are caused by people's social roles and the expectations that are placed on them. For example, many women hide their more aggressive or assertive tendencies because they've been taught that they should be passive, whereas men are often expected to conceal their more emotional or sensitive responses.

To create genuinely complex characters, remember that everyone is a mixture of what are considered male and female aspects. Women can be thoughtless and uncaring and afraid of commitment, just as men are often stereotypically thought to be. Similarly, men can be as caring and nurturing as women.

Beware of turning characters into superficial gender stereotypes. Not all men are interested in football and not all women in fashion and shopping!

Men and women are, however, physically different (what do you mean, you hadn't noticed!), and as a writer you need to remain aware of this and how it affects your characters' behaviour. For example, women are often more afraid for their physical safety than men are in the outside world, whereas men are less likely to be fearful. Most men are physically stronger than most women, which potentially gives them more power in intimate relationships if they choose to abuse this situation.

Writing from the point of view of a character of the opposite sex can be so intimidating that some writers never do it, but it's worth having a go! Write a scene from the point of view of a character of the opposite sex to yourself. Be conscious of the person's physicality and thoughts.

Risking the wrath of your grandmother: Writing about sex

One of the most difficult things any writer can do is write about sex. It's such a personal and intimate area that authors often feel uncomfortable at the thought of other people reading what they write. Sometimes this reluctance is because you imagine that readers will think that you've done everything you describe yourself, as well as the horrible possibility that your boss – or even worse, your grandmother – will discover the book and read what you've written! It could put you, her or both of you into years of therapy!

But unless you're writing specifically for the erotic market, you don't need to give too many anatomical details. After all, most people know the physical facts of what happens when people have sex – they don't need to have it spelled out as if they're reading a DIY manual!

What's interesting in sex scenes is what's going on emotionally between the characters and how the experience changes their relationship. Characters are often at their most open and vulnerable when having sex and may reveal different aspects of themselves to those they show in everyday life. A character who seems shy and timid on the outside may turn out to be surprisingly uninhibited in bed, and people who appear confident and attractive may reveal themselves to be ashamed of their bodies or unable to let themselves go.

The build-up and the aftermath are just as important as the sex itself, if not more so. Plus, remember that sex isn't always perfect: the earth doesn't always move! Sex can be funny, sad, awkward, routine, unpleasant and surprising, and sometimes all these in turn. The golden rule to writing sex scenes is: *less is more!*

Here are some examples of ways in which you can approach writing about sex indirectly. In *For Whom the Bell Tolls,* Hemingway makes clear that a couple are making love, without any need for description at all, just the following dialogue:

> 'Maria.'
>
> 'Yes.'
>
> 'Maria.'
>
> 'Yes.'
>
> 'Maria.'
>
> 'Oh, yes. Please.'
>
> —*Ernest Hemingway (For Whom the Bell Tolls, Jonathan Cape, 1941)*

What works so beautifully in the dialogue is that we hear the tenderness between the characters – when you are in love, there's nothing so beautiful as your lover's name. And we can imagine exactly what's happening, without any need to have it described.

In his novel *The End of the Affair,* Graham Greene also hints indirectly. His characters make love on the floor of the room below the one where Sarah's husband, Henry, is ill in bed:

> When the moment came, I had to put my hand gently over her mouth to deaden that strange sad angry cry of abandonment, for fear Henry should hear it overhead.
>
> —*Graham Greene (The End of the Affair, William Heinemann, 1951)*

Here the reader realises without having it spelled out that Sarah has had an orgasm – something she later reveals she never experienced with her husband.

In his debut novel, *Asboville*, Danny Rhodes has his character remembering making love to his girlfriend the night before, with his thoughts and feelings now interwoven with little memories of the previous day:

> . . . the smell of her . . . the heat building . . . as she stiffened under him, made tiny noises in her throat . . . the way their bodies shook and how she'd held on to him as it happened . . .
>
> —*Danny Rhodes (Asboville, Maia, 2006)*

This technique works beautifully because the book was aimed at teenagers and a graphic sex scene would have been inappropriate for that audience.

Try out these techniques for yourself with the following exercise:

- ✔ Write a sex scene using only the dialogue between the characters.
- ✔ Write a dialogue between two characters after they've had sex.
- ✔ Write a sex scene that the character is recalling the following day.

Finding the right words

One big challenge for sex scenes is to find the right language. When you're writing a first-person narrative, obviously you need to use the words that the character herself would use, but even for a third-person limited narrative, you should probably do the same unless it really jars with your own writing style (check out Chapter 8 for all about point-of-view voices).

In general, Latin terms sound over-formal or as if you're reading a medical textbook, words of Anglo-Saxon origin sound crude because they're used as swear words, and any euphemisms sound as if you're avoiding the issue, which of course you are! The problem is that language doesn't really have any neutral words for describing sexual organs, and so you have to make the best of the words that you do have, and use the ones that seem most appropriate in the context – usually, the ones the characters themselves would use.

Beware of using strange and often flowery metaphors: these usually confuse the readers completely. Sex has been compared to everything from exploding supernovae in distant galaxies, to exploring a deep nocturnal forest, to a spoon scraping the inside of a soft-boiled egg! More bad writing involves sex than pretty much any other subject.

Considering Other Ways to Add Character Depth

The fact is that people aren't always honest, open or, indeed, very on the ball about themselves – which makes real life tricky at times, but does provide fertile ground for your writing. You can use characters' lies to show truths about them, write about their secrets to reveal their insecurities or motivations, and use misunderstandings to complicate them and spice up your plots.

Employing lies, half-truths and evasions

One foolproof way to make your characters more interesting is to make them lie. People lie for all sorts of reasons: to escape punishment, to impress people, to placate them or shut them up, to seduce them, to get or keep a job, to avoid persecution, to make money, to feel better about themselves, to make others feel better.

Try this exercise to begin to explore some of the complexities that arise when characters tell lies:

1. **Take a character and have her lie for one of these secrets above.**

2. **Go on to make that person tell the lie to someone else.**

The great thing about lies in fiction is that they tend to escalate. You tell a small lie – for example, that you're a couple of years younger than you really are, that you don't have a boyfriend when you do, that you earn more or less money than you really do, that you can't go to a meeting because you're ill, when really you have a hangover, or that you tried to call somebody when you didn't. Then you have to keep on lying, because you can't admit that you didn't tell the truth initially. Sooner or later you're going to trip up or someone is going to find you out, and you have to face the consequences.

Try out for yourself the way that lies tend to get magnified with time – and have many unforeseen consequences:

1. **Give a small lie to one of your characters.**

2. **Write three further scenes in which she has to continue to lie, each one becoming more and more difficult.**

In Charles Cumming's 2001 novel *A Spy by Nature,* the protagonist, Alec Milius, is turned down by MI6 but given a job as an industrial spy. His role is to feed disinformation to a company's competitor. He becomes more and more deeply involved in a web of lies, distrust and betrayal, which has devastating consequences, and one small, seemingly inconsequential lie that he tells near the start of the novel returns to haunt him.

Everybody tells white lies because they don't want to upset people; much of human social life is lubricated by a series of lies about how wonderful friends look, how much that dress or jumper suits someone, how lovely it is to see someone you hate, how much you enjoyed a disgusting meal, and so on. The same is true for your characters.

They don't even need to lie directly: frequently, people omit to say things to give the wrong impression, and can phrase what they say in such a way as to indicate that they mean one thing when they mean the opposite. Characters surprisingly seldom tell direct, bald-faced lies!

Other forms of lying include the following (ensure that you master them all if you're writing a novel about politicians!). Think about how you can use them in your stories:

- **Being disingenuous or 'economical with the truth':** Pretending that you know less about something than you really do, or giving only part of the story, with the intent to deceive or mislead others.

- **Being evasive:** Failing to answer a question, acknowledging it without answering it, or answering a question with another question to avoid answering it. You can also change the subject or say something like, 'Let me think about it and come back to it later,' and then fail to do so.

- **Fabricating:** Saying something is true without knowing whether it is.

- **Exaggerating:** Making something bigger, better or worse than it really is, perhaps to make a story better, but also sometimes to mislead.

- **Lying to yourself:** People often reconstruct the past in such a way as to put their own behaviour in the best possible light. In the words of TS Eliot in his 1935 play *Murder in the Cathedral:* 'Humankind cannot bear very much reality.'

Of course, the truth is never clear. (Remember Pilate's enigmatic statement to Jesus in the Bible, 'What is truth?' (King James Bible, John, 18:38).) And I love the lines in Joseph Conrad's *Under Western Eyes* (1911), where an English teacher is talking to the mysterious Russian émigré Rasumov:

'How can you tell truth from lies?' he queried in his new, immovable manner.

'I don't know how you do it in Russia,' I began, rather nettled by his attitude. He interrupted me.

'In Russia, and in general everywhere – in a newspaper, for instance. The colour of the ink and the shapes of the letters are the same.'

—*Joseph Conrad (Under Western Eyes, Everyman's Library, 1991, first published 1911)*

Sharing and keeping secrets

Everyone has secrets: things that they'd never tell anyone, things they're ashamed of, things they won't admit even to themselves, and secrets that they share with only a few selected people. These can be family secrets, secrets between lovers and friends, professional secrets, and ones held by governments and corporations. Secrets can be damaging, but it's hard to imagine that people can ever be entirely open about everything. The secret things inside your soul are part of who you are.

Societies tread a narrow line between secrecy and privacy. When people invade your private self, it can feel like a violation. Many people live in oppressive societies where the state invades privacy in the name of security; even in the West this is the case, with the advent of increasingly sophisticated technology. This has been the subject of much spy fiction, such as the novels of John le Carré and Charles McCarry.

The secrets that a character holds can form the core of a piece of fiction. A character can be on a quest to uncover a family secret, or may hold a secret that she's afraid of revealing. Sometimes the secret coming out is a good thing for the character, sometimes it's a disaster and sometimes it's a mixture.

Try this exercise to see what happens when an aspect of a character's secret life is revealed to others. Describe a secret place and say what it means to the character. Then relate someone discovering that secret place: what effect does it have on your protagonist? I've used the example of a secret pace, but it could be a secret conversation that's overheard, or a secret letter that's found.

Here are some more fun ways to practise using secrets in your work:

- ✔ **Write a secret diary entry for your character.** Have her hide it and then suspect someone of having read it. How does she feel? How does the event affect what she writes in her diary in the future? Does she confront the suspect or try to find out for sure by some other means?

✔ **Think of an important object in your story – something that reveals something or gives away a secret.** Write a scene that includes this object, but conceal the object from readers in some way. Continue the exercise, now making clear what the important object is.

✔ **Write a conversation in which a character's unspoken thoughts are contrasted with what she says.** Consider the sort of things people think but never say, and why they never say them.

✔ **Write a scene including your main character and another character who has a secret.** Your main character doesn't know the other's secret. During the scene, drop in three clues as to what that secret may be: one at the start, one in the middle, one at the end. Don't be explicit. You can use a physical detail, a verbal comment, an action and so on. Your main character never does discover the secret in the scene.

✔ **Write about a character with a secret she covers up.** How does the secret and keeping it affect the person physically: do her actions, dress or mannerisms show that she's hiding something?

Secrets that characters don't know about themselves

You can let readers know things that the character isn't aware of through what she says – making use of Freudian slips or statements that give away more than the speaker knows – and through her dreams, which the person may fail to understand, though readers will!

Try out these ways of revealing to the reader things the character doesn't know about herself:

✔ Write a piece in which your character talks to someone who understands something the speaker doesn't.

✔ Write a dream revealing the character's secret fears or desires.

Secrets that everybody else knows

Sometimes characters can hang on to a secret, only to discover that people knew about it all the time.

Try out these exercises to explore what happens when a character has a secret or discovers what everyone else knew all along:

✔ **Think of an occasion when you discovered that other people knew something you thought they didn't.** How did they know? Then think of a fictional character in the same situation, drawing on your own emotions and experiences. Write about the secret being released: what happens then?

✔ **Imagine a character who lives in a fantasy world in at least one aspect of her life.** It can be to do with a relationship, with money, her appearance and so on. Write a scene in which this fantasy is shown and others react to it. What happened in the past to make this happen? Write a flashback scene.

✔ **Write about something your character did that was kept a secret for many years.** Then she finally reveals it. Did everyone else know? Does the secret matter any more? If not, why not?

Society's secrets and their impact

Some secrets are political, financial, business or environmental. The three biggest international areas of trade are arms, drugs and pornography, which all go on under the official radar. Fiction has often explored the dark underside of society, so don't be afraid to write about these areas if they interest you – and remember that hardly anyone can be untouched by the effects of drugs and pornography.

A character may come across another who is taking drugs or has been watching pornography. Try this exercise to see how they react: write a scene in which a secret has an impact on a character, possibly reflecting secrets in her own life.

Multiplying misunderstandings

Misunderstandings between your characters are great for creating layers and complications. Often these misunderstandings result from secrets, lies and other people's evasions.

In poorly realised fiction, a character simply overhears part of a conversation or hears a word wrongly and things end there. Make your writing deeper than that by understanding that misunderstandings often come about due to the naivety or blindness of characters. People often get things wrong because they want to – a classic example being the woman who misinterprets a friendly statement from a handsome man and thinks he's in love with her, because she'd like him to be.

Misunderstandings are often responsible for tragic events. They happen a great deal in romantic fiction as a way of keeping the lovers apart until the end of the story. Most of Shakespeare's tragedies and comedies revolve around misunderstandings of one kind or another, as do many of Jane Austen's novels.

In Jane Austen's *Emma* (1816), Emma mistakenly believes that her protégé, Harriet Smith, fell in love with Frank Churchill when he rescued her from the gypsies, and Harriet encourages Emma in this belief. But then to her horror Emma realises that Harriet is in love with someone else – and that in encouraging Harriet, she has made a 'most unfortunate – most deplorable mistake!'.

This misunderstanding arises because Emma is wilful and blind to the consequences of her actions.

In Ian McEwan's *Atonement,* Briony's misunderstanding of what she observes happening between Robbie and Cecilia in three key scenes – when she sees them by the fountain, when she reads the letter and when she eavesdrops on them in the library – leads to devastating consequences.

Briony's youth and innocence about the adult world – as well as her vivid imagination – cause the misunderstanding. As McEwan writes in the novel:

> It wasn't only wickedness and scheming that made people unhappy, it was confusion and misunderstanding; above all, it was the failure to grasp the simple truth that other people are as real as you.

> —*Ian McEwan (Atonement, Jonathan Cape, 2001)*

Both Emma and Briony make this mistake, using other characters for their amusement rather than seeing things from their point of view. Once they realise the impact of their behaviour, they are changed forever (see the section on the story's climax in Chapter 23).

Try this exercise to see how you can use misunderstandings and their impact to help your characters change and develop:

1. **Write a scene in which one of your characters misunderstands something that another character says or does.**

2. **Move on to write a scene that happens later, where this misunderstanding leads to another – even worse – one.**

3. **Write the scene where the misunderstanding from step 1 is resolved. Make the character realise which of her flaws caused the misunderstanding to happen.**

Part III
Painting the Picture with Description

Top five ways to help you describe the world of your story

- ✔ Create a sense of place by mapping out the world of your story in detail, so you know where all the major locations fit in and where your characters live, work and play.

- ✔ Use all the senses to hook your reader in and make him experience the world as vividly and directly as possible. Remember to use colour, sound and music, smell and taste.

- ✔ Describe your characters in action, not just statically. Remember to use strong verbs and keep the characters – and the story – moving.

- ✔ Use description to create suspense by weaving it into the action. Use the weather to reflect and evoke the characters' moods and build up tension, and create a sense of the uncanny.

- ✔ Use metaphors and similes to help create vivid images. The skilful use of symbols will add a layer of depth to your story, and don't neglect to use poetic devices such as paradox, personification and alliteration.

Check out www.dummies.com/extras/creativewritingexercises for an article on describing things afresh.

In this part . . .

- ✔ Find out how to set your story in a concrete reality – at a certain time in a specific place, whether that is past, present or future, at home or abroad.

- ✔ Grow your skills to describe the world that your characters inhabit, so that readers can visualise the scenes as they unfold, experience the action taking place, and hear, touch, smell, taste and feel the world and its objects.

- ✔ Use your powers of description in order to create suspense and drive your story forwards – even when you're describing feelings and situations that other people often fail to find words for. After all, you're a writer!

Chapter 10

Navigating the Locations in Your Stories

*E*very story has to take place somewhere – even if it's in the middle of nowhere! The location is an essential ingredient, and a story set on a remote island is sure to unfold differently to one played out in inner-city London. The story also takes place at a certain point in time, and that time becomes an intrinsic part of the story as well; a story set 200 years ago is going to be very different to the same story taking place today.

In some stories the location is so important that it becomes like a character: readers simply can't imagine the events taking place anywhere else (think of Graham Greene's seedy portrayal of Brighton in *Brighton Rock* (1938), the Yorkshire moors in Emily Brontë's *Wuthering Heights* (1847) or Gustave Flaubert's rural Normandy in his 1856 novel *Madame Bovary*). A story can't take place in a vacuum; without a strong sense of place, readers feel lost or distanced from the narrative.

A book with a strong sense of place takes readers out of their own world and into another reality. As I consider in this chapter, creating a sense of place is all about description and the way that the setting affects the characters. I discuss selecting a real location and inventing your own fantastical one, and – whichever way you choose to go – how to make it come alive through detail.

Choosing and Conveying a Setting

The setting for your piece of writing may be somewhere you know intimately, somewhere you need to discover or a place created entirely in your own imagination. (Travel to the later section 'Inventing Your Own World: Fantasy and Science Fiction' for details of the latter.) Whichever kind of setting you want to use, you need to know all the details so that you can communicate the location convincingly to your readers.

As the story unfolds, make sure that you never leave your readers without a sense of place. Always tell them where every scene is set. Take a look at the beginning of many novels and stories and you find that almost all give a vivid sense of place right from the start. So if your characters meet at a bar in the hotel, tell readers what the bar is like: modern and light, or dark and old fashioned; state the colour of the walls and whether the bar is crowded or empty. More than anything, convey what these details make the characters feel and how the setting affects the meeting.

Describing a place is hugely important for creating a mood. The location itself is less important than how your characters feel about it. They may love their home town and never want to leave, or they may hate it and be itching to get away to the big city – or they may, of course, feel both these emotions in turn.

You don't need to restrict every scene to whatever main location you choose. You can create impact and variety by taking characters to other contrasting locations. For example, if your novel is set in downtown Manhattan, take your characters out for a weekend on Long Island. If your story is set in a rural location, find a reason for your characters to go up to the city. The change of location can alter the mood of the story and change the pace dramatically.

You can give an ordinary story – whether a love story or a murder mystery – a new dynamic by setting it in an unusual location. A crime novel set in a sleepy rural town feels very different from one set in the slums of the big city, but if you set a crime novel on a transatlantic plane, it would have an extra dimension of claustrophobia and danger!

Making your characters feel at home

Nothing's wrong with setting a story in your home town – after all, it's the place you know best. But bear in mind that this may not always be the right place for the story that you want to tell, because where you set a story completely changes its nature. For example, imagine the differences inherent in a gay love affair set in contemporary San Francisco and the same story set in modern Uganda (with its brutal intolerance of such lifestyles).

Some authors unashamedly use a real place – think of James Joyce's 1922 *Ulysses,* which details many real locations in 1904 Dublin so accurately that every year on 16 June – the day when the events of the novel take place – fans of the novel retrace the route taken by the protagonist, Leopold Bloom. Other writers use real places as a basis but give them new names to disguise them – think of Thomas Hardy's Wessex, in which the town of Casterbridge is Dorchester, Melchester is Salisbury and, a little farther afield, Christminster is Oxford. But other writers invent their own worlds – such as Middle Earth with the countries Gondor and Mordor in JRR Tolkien's *The Hobbit* (1937) and *The Lord of the Rings* (1954), CS Lewis's Narnia (bordered by Archenland) and James Hilton's Shangri-La in *Lost Horizon* (1933).

Even when you're situating your story in a real place, you often need to make changes to specific street names and locations in order to protect yourself from libel. If you're writing about a corrupt official, a negligent doctor or an incompetent policeman, take care that you don't set the stories in a real place, or you can leave yourself open to legal action.

Houses can become as famous as characters in some stories. Famous fictional houses include *Wuthering Heights,* the house in Emily Brontë's 1847 novel of the same name; Manderley in Daphne du Maurier's *Rebecca* (1938); 221b Baker Street in the Sherlock Holmes novels and stories; and Blandings Castle in the PG Wodehouse stories. Everyone has special places connected with significant events that occurred in their lives, and these places occur in fiction too. I think of Humphrey Bogart as Rick saying 'We'll always have Paris' to Ingrid Bergman as Ilsa in the 1942 film *Casablanca,* and Varykino, the place where Yuri and Lara seek sanctuary in Boris Pasternak's *Dr Zhivago* (which was smuggled out of Soviet Russia and first published in the West in 1957).

Focusing on one location

Many writers use a single place as the location for a series of stories. This has the great advantage that readers get to see the world of the story from different perspectives and don't need to constantly adjust to new locations. Major characters in one story can appear as minor ones in another, helping the reader build up a complete picture of the location and its inhabitants.

Examples include Sherwood Anderson's *Winesburg, Ohio* (1919), 22 stories about life in a fictional small Midwestern town; Rohinton Mistry's *Tales from Firozsha Baag* (1987), 11 stories about the residents of an apartment complex in Mumbai; and VS Naipaul's *Miguel Street* (1959), consisting of stories about a number of characters living on Miguel Street in Port of Spain, Trinidad.

Describe a place of significance to a character in a story. Focus on the physical details and also any memories the place evokes for your narrator. Now describe the same place from a different perspective. How similar are the two accounts, and what do the different perspectives reveal about the characters?

A neutral, flat and over-detailed description of a place is unlikely to engage readers. What is important is the characters' reactions to the places that they find themselves in.

Bear this in mind as you try the next exercise.

This exercise will help you to explore how you can use a place to reveal your characters:

1. **Describe your character's home.**

   Start from the outside before writing about your character walking through the front door and through each room; describe how he feels about each one. Think about the following:

   - Which is your character's favourite room?

   - What would he most like to change about his home?

   - What objects does your character possess, and what memories do they connect with?

2. **Describe your character at home on a typical evening.**

   What activities does your character enjoy? Does he read, watch TV, phone friends, cook, play computer games, drink, take drugs, eat chocolate or shop online?

3. **Think of some other locations that feature in your character's life.**

   Think of key places where your character goes regularly: his workplace; the houses of friends; anywhere he visits daily, such as a café or wine bar, a library or swimming pool.

4. **Write a paragraph describing your character in each of these settings in turn.**

   Again, think about how your character feels in these different locations. A place is always more interesting to the reader if a character has a strong reaction to it.

Travelling to exotic lands . . . by book

If you decide to set your fiction in an exotic place, you need to do research in order to make your story convincing. If you've visited the location yourself, you have a head start, but remember to write down everything you can remember about this location before you begin. Describe the following aspects in particular:

- ✔ Events that happened, whether trivial or important
- ✔ Landmarks you visited
- ✔ Look and feel of the money
- ✔ Meals you ate
- ✔ Sights and smells you recall
- ✔ Sound of the language
- ✔ Times you felt afraid or elated

Nowadays you can easily research locations on the Internet. Plus, a huge number of guidebooks is available in which to look up information. However, none of this is a substitute for personal first-hand experience. For more on using the senses effectively in your writing, check out Chapter 11.

Of course, visiting every place that you describe in your writing is often not going to be practical or affordable. So if you really need to write about a location that you can't visit, try to track down someone who's been there. Make a list of all the things you need to know and write a scene you want to include as well, so that you know exactly what details you're looking for.

If you're writing a historical novel, you'll have trouble going back to the place as it was then (unless you have a time machine handy). Novelist Stef Penney's *The Tenderness of Wolves,* which won the 2006 Costa Prize for Book of the Year, is set in Canada in the 1860s. The author did all her research in London libraries and never visited Canada – but you'd never imagine that from reading the vivid descriptions in the book.

1. **Think of a place you've never visited that you may need to include in your novel.** It can be in a different country or just a location you haven't been to, such as a particular hotel, hospital or museum.

2. **Do as much research as you can.** Search out photographs on the Internet and see whether you can locate descriptions of these places written by other people.

3. **Write the scene describing the place.** How successful do think it is? When you show it to someone else, does it create the reaction you intended?

4. **Visit the place (if at all possible) and check out the reality against what you've written.** Can you spot any details that you could never have imagined? Does this have an impact on your story?

Creating a Location's Fine Detail

It's the little details that make a location come to life – an observation a character makes, a fleeting smell or sound or taste. A sense of clarity about the lie of the land and the relationship between one place and another also really helps. To help you get to grips with the minutiae of your location, I suggest you consult or create a map and work on including precise details to be as convincing as possible.

Using maps for realism

Maps are as useful to a fiction writer as they are to a navigator. If you're setting your story in a real place, get as detailed a map as you can. You can purchase small-scale maps for most locations. For cities, an A–Z street plan is ideal.

This exercise will help you create a physical sense of your character's world:

1. **Find a map of the country, city or town where your story takes place.** If this place is imaginary, draw a map yourself. Make it as detailed as you like.

2. **Choose the location where your character lives.** Make a note of the names of the streets, or invent them yourself.

3. **Lead your character on a walk through the neighbourhood.** Describe what he sees, hears and smells and all the sensations he experiences. Chapter 11 contains loads of tips on employing the senses.

4. **List all the major locations you need in your story and mark them on your map.** Consider places such as the school, the hospital, the library and the police station.

Although you have a map and know the exact location of everything in your story, don't fall into the trap of giving your reader a geography lesson. Exact distances in terms of miles or kilometres are less evocative than phrases such as 'an hour's walk' or 'half a day's drive'. Exact measurements are also off-putting because they're hard to visualise: 'The mountain behind the town was 4,000 metres high' isn't as easy to imagine as 'The mountain loomed over the town'.

Similarly, if you're describing a house or other building, you don't need to give the exact size of every room, the height of the ceiling and the dimensions of the fireplace. Impressions are stronger than facts.

Look at how Graham Greene cleverly maps out the town of Brighton in the second paragraph of his novel:

> For he had to stick closely to a programme: from ten to eleven Queen's Road and Castle Square, from eleven till twelve the Aquarium and Palace Pier, twelve till one the front between the Old Ship and West Pier, back for lunch between one and two in any restaurant he chose round the Castle Square, and after that he had to make his way all down the parade to the West Pier and then to the station by the Hove streets.

> —*Graham Greene (Brighton Rock, William Heinemann, 1938)*

Make your character map out his own town by planning his daily route or a walk he has to make to meet someone.

Imagining and recording the finer points

Small details create the most vivid impression of a place for readers. If you're visiting a location for your story, take a notebook with you. Jot down any place names and landmarks. Make notes of anything interesting you see and record descriptions of them.

You create a convincing sense of place not only through what you see, but also via the smells, the sounds, the taste of the food, and the feel of the heat of the sun or the cold of the icy air.

Take a look at how other writers create a sense of place. In the following, I like the way the author describes the history of this building and of Russia itself and the way the city has changed:

> I lived in one of the Moscow apartment blocks that were built as grand houses by doomed well-to-do merchants, just before the revolution. Like the city itself, it had been slapped about so much that it had come to look like several different buildings mashed together. An ugly lift had been fixed onto the outside and a fifth story added to the top, but it had kept the original swirling ironwork of its staircase.
>
> —*AD Miller (Snowdrops, Atlantic Books, 2011)*

In the following quote, the little detail of the sound of the grasshoppers snapping jolts you into the world of this story:

> That graveyard was about the loneliest place you could imagine. If I were to say it was going back to nature, you might get the idea that there was some sort of vitality about the place. But it was parched and sun-stricken. It was hard to imagine the grass had ever been green. Everywhere you stepped, little grasshoppers would fly out by the score, making that snap they do, like striking a match.
>
> —*Marilynne Robinson (Gilead, Farrar, Strauss and Giroux, 2004)*

Chapter 11 contains a number of exercises that help you use the senses effectively when communicating place and character.

Inventing Your Own World: Fantasy and Science Fiction

Just imagine the excitement (and the responsibility) of creating your very own world from scratch! You can invent new languages, colours which don't exist on earth, three-headed cats, talking worms and cities built on mile-high stilts. However, whatever you come up with will have to make sense in the world you have created in order to convince the reader.

If you're writing science fiction or fantasy, you can invent a world with as much richness and detail as you'd use in a real location. But make no mistake: creating an imaginary world is much more difficult than it sounds.

One way to get around the difficulties is to use a historic setting to give you ideas or to locate your writing in a place that's very similar to somewhere on earth. For example, Philip Pullman set part of *His Dark Materials* trilogy in a slightly different version of Oxford.

A completely alien universe or totally alternative reality in which *everything* is different can be quite exhausting to invent as well as confusing for readers. Imagine a world in which all the physical laws of nature are different, where the characters are made of a gaseous material, communicate telepathically through mathematical equations and don't experience emotions, and you soon see what I mean!

Here are certain kinds of imaginary worlds that writers have developed:

- ✔ **Alternative realities:** Can start with a historic event that ends differently; for example, in Robert Harris's novel *Fatherland* (1992), where he imagines a world in which the Nazis won the Second World War. Often you don't need to worry about explaining in detail how the world ended up differently – readers just need to know that it did.

- ✔ **Fantastical worlds:** Usually involve characters like humans who simply happen to live in an imaginary world different from this one.

- ✔ **Futuristic worlds:** Often involve new technology and contact with alien civilisations, but they can also be regressions to an earlier form of civilisation after some kind of apocalyptic event, as in Cormac McCarthy's *The Road* (2006) or Russell Hoban's *Riddley Walker* (1980).

When you're inventing an imaginary world, you need to think about the following aspects:

- ✔ Culture and religion
- ✔ Education methods
- ✔ History of your world
- ✔ Languages that are spoken
- ✔ Names the people are given
- ✔ Physical laws that apply
- ✔ Technology they have developed

The more you write about these things, the more convincing the details become for readers. You don't need to go to the lengths of JRR Tolkien, who adds an appendix and invents whole languages and mythologies, though without doubt this incredible effort is part of the reason that his story is so convincing.

Always make sure that you're clear about the rules of your world and that characters stick to them. This consideration is especially important if you're using magic or advanced technology. You need to foreshadow any revelations about such things earlier in the story, because nothing's worse than the character being trapped in some awful situation and then suddenly using a magical power or producing an advanced weapon to escape. Readers feel cheated.

Even if you've invented the entire history, mythology and geography of this imaginary world, you don't have to pass it all onto readers. In particular, avoid the characters in your story explaining it all to one another (they must already know it themselves!). As with so many aspects of writing fiction, less is more.

A historical place has more in common with a fantasy world than you'd imagine. Though you may have done a mountain of research and have all the facts at your fingertips, in the end you need to take a leap of the imagination to reconstruct the past for your readers. This is especially true if you're writing about issues that were hidden at the time, as prize-winning novelist Sarah Waters does in her novels *Tipping the Velvet* (1998), *Affinity* (1999) and *Fingersmith* (2002), where she explores lesbian relationships in Victorian times.

To help you with your world-creating skills, try this exercise:

1. **Draw a map of your world, whether it's a different version of our world or a totally imaginary one, a town or a continent.**

2. **Invent a language and create names for a few common objects.** Think of phrases that are common in that language, and some sounds or letters that don't exist.

3. **Invent a myth for your imaginary world, and then write it!**

Chapter 11

Appreciating the Power of the Senses

*I*n order to produce successful descriptions in your writing, you need to use all the senses to convey a convincing reality. Too many writers fall into the trap of writing visual descriptions while neglecting the information that comes to people through other senses. Yet sounds, smells, textures and tastes have just as strong an effect on readers and help them to imagine themselves in the scene that you're depicting.

Whenever you describe a scene in a story, avoid making it too static and too detailed. Readers aren't usually interested in long passages of description in which nothing happens. The trick is to weave description into action and highlight a few of the most vivid details, using them to imply the rest.

In this chapter I explore the different ways of using sensory information to make the world of your story more vibrant.

Creating a Colourful, Meaningful World

One of the most powerful descriptive tools you have is colour. Everyone reacts at a basic level to colours, which can have a direct physiological effect on people: bright red is exciting; deep blue and green are calming; certain shades of colour are warm, others cool. Because colours affect people's moods so strongly, you can use them in a deliberate way to reflect the emotions of the characters in your fiction.

When you choose clothes for your characters to wear, think of what people's colour choices reveal about their personalities and their mood that day. Bright colours normally indicate a confident, outgoing personality, whereas wearing dull shades may mean a character is shy and doesn't want to stand out.

Write down all the words that you associate with different colours. Fill a whole page for each of the following main colours if you can:

- ✔ **Primary colours:** Red, blue, yellow.

- ✔ **Secondary colours:** Purple, green, orange.

- ✔ **Other colours:** Black, white, pink, brown.

Now read on and compare what you've written with what colour theorists think.

Giving associations to colours

Here are some of the most common meanings and associations connected with colour. You can use these to create emotions in your characters – and your readers.

Some associations with colour are culture-specific. For example, black in the West is the colour of mourning and death, while in other cultures people wear white for mourning. Red is a lucky colour in Chinese and some other Asian cultures, and is often worn at weddings.

- ✔ **Red:** The colour of blood. It's an energetic colour and highly visible, standing out from the background, such as the pool of blood spreading across a white-tiled floor in a murder scene. Positively, red stands for energy, passion and love. Negatively, it stands for danger, anger and lust.

- ✔ **Blue:** The colour of the sea and sky, and associated positively with spirituality, wisdom and tranquillity. Negatively, it can connect with sadness, coldness and distance.

- ✔ **Yellow:** The colour of sunshine and of happiness, warmth and energy. Negatively, it's associated with jealousy, cowardice and illness.

- **Green:** The colour of nature, it can stand for fertility, harmony and growth. Green also stands for go! Negatively, it's associated with inexperience, envy, bad luck and ill health.

- **Orange:** A mixture of red and yellow, it's an energetic colour representing warmth and happiness. Orange is also the colour of autumn and so can be associated with sadness; for example, as a relationship ends with the falling leaves.

- **Purple:** Combines the stability of blue and the energy of red. It's associated with royalty, luxury, mystery and magic, but also with gloominess, overindulgence and artificiality.

- **Black:** As the absence of light, black in the West is associated with death and evil, although it's also a strong colour connected to sophistication and elegance. In other cultures, black can be associated with holiness and mystery.

- **White:** Associated with light, innocence and purity in many cultures, white is generally viewed positively. However, white is also associated with doctors and hospitals and is seen as clinical and sterile; and vast expanses of white snow can be hostile and blinding.

- **Brown:** The colour of earth, brown is associated with safety, security and friendliness. Negatively, it can be seen as dull, sad or dirty.

Remember that using colour to create simplistic divisions of good and bad or to create stereotypical characters is never a good idea. A key moment in the political awakening of Malcolm X was when he looked up the two words 'black' and 'white' in the dictionary, to find only negative associations connected with the word 'black', and positive associations with 'white'. Why not subvert your readers' expectations by having the hero wear black and his enemy white?

Of course, many different shades are possible within each colour, and these also have different meanings. A bright daffodil yellow feels very different to a dull yellowy green; a vibrant purple is a different colour to an insipid mauve. Pink can vary from the pale pastel associated with baby girls through sophisticated dusky pink to bright shocking pink; green can vary from pale yellowy green to a deep, dark colour. Some languages, for example Korean, have different words for yellow-green and blue-green and consider them to be completely different colours.

Colours also have personal associations and memories. For example, a child who last saw her mother wearing a pink dress may well associate that colour with death.

Colouring in scenes and characters

When describing a colour, be precise about the shade. Don't just say blue, because this colour can range from the palest turquoise to the deepest navy, with innumerable shades in between: peacock blue, sky blue, duck egg blue, lavender blue, marine blue, indigo. But beware of using terms so obscure that readers don't know what colour you mean!

Try out colour choices to see how using different colour palettes changes the mood of a scene:

1. **Write a scene in your story in which one colour dominates.**

2. **Choose an opposite, contrasting, colour and rewrite the scene using that colour instead.**

How does the choice of colour affect the mood of the scene? Does the scene turn out differently?

A great example of using colour in fiction is Charlotte Perkins-Gilman's classic 1892 story *The Yellow Wallpaper,* in which a woman is confined to a room by her husband, who is also a doctor, to treat her depression, but becomes obsessed with the paper on the walls:

> It is the strangest yellow, that wall-paper! It makes me think of all the yellow things I ever saw – not beautiful ones like buttercups, but old foul, bad yellow things. But there is something else about that paper – the smell! . . . The only thing I can think of that it is like is the colour of the paper! A yellow smell.
>
> —*Charlotte Perkins-Gilman (The Yellow Wallpaper, Virago, 2009, first published 1892)*

The colour yellow is sickly and unhealthy, reflecting the situation the character is living in and her psychological state.

Take a look at this extract of the description of the red room in which Jane Eyre is imprisoned at the start of Charlotte Brontë's 1847 novel:

> A bed supported on massive pillars of mahogany, hung with curtains of deep red damask, stood out like a tabernacle in the centre; the two large windows, with their blinds always drawn down, were half shrouded in festoons and falls of similar drapery; the carpet was red; the table at the foot of the bed was covered with a crimson cloth; the walls were a soft fawn colour with a blush of pink in it . . .
>
> —*Charlotte Brontë (Jane Eyre, Penguin, 2006, first published 1847)*

The colour red symbolises the passion young Jane feels in this scene, and also makes the room seemed claustrophobic, almost like the inside of a womb.

In this exercise, you can randomly mix up colours and emotions to explore beyond the stereotypes. Have fun and see which combinations work for you.

1. **Write a list of random emotions – love, hate, jealousy, sadness, anger, hope, despair, contempt and so on.**

2. **Make a list of colours.**

3. **Pair the items on the lists at random and then write about a character feeling the emotion and using that colour – pink despair, orange sadness, green anger!**

Listening to Sound and Music on the Page

Hearing is the sense that people often forget to use when writing fiction. Yet the world is full of sounds that can have a profound effect. Noise that people can't control, especially if it's loud, causes stress, and even in the most peaceful silence you can usually hear faint noises: the rustling of leaves in a gentle breeze, the distant sound of a bird or a vehicle moving far away. The absence of any sound at all is usually extremely disturbing.

Sensing scenic sounds

To develop your skills at communicating sounds in your writing, you won't be surprised to hear (!) that you have to practise listening.

Go somewhere outside your home and sit with your eyes closed for a while. Listen to all the sounds you can hear. Try to come up with words that describe the sounds.

Now write a piece of fiction in which you describe a place, paying particular attention to the sounds your character hears.

Using what you discover from that practice, try to translate the skills to the next exercise.

Write a scene in which your characters struggle to have a conversation against loud background noise – music in a club, drilling in the street outside or a baby screaming. How does the noise affect the characters and the course of the conversation? Remember not to constantly mention the sound itself – if you mention it initially and then show the characters struggling to speak or be understood, the reader should get the idea.

Not everyone can hear, or hear well. Think of including a character with a hearing difficulty in your story, and the effect that has on her life and that of others.

Making musical moments

You can use music for all sorts of powerful effects in your fiction:

- ✓ Music is great for fixing your story in a particular time period – you can find out which songs were popular at that time and have your characters hear or dance to them.

- ✓ Music is an excellent trigger for a flashback – your character can hear a piece of music being played through the open window of a house she's passing and be instantly transported back in time.

Write about a memory triggered by hearing a piece of music. Think of where the character was when she last heard that music and what it meant for her, including any images that come into the character's mind.

As you may find, describing the sound of music isn't easy – writers usually rely on their readers knowing the music they're referring to. This approach works with very well-known music, but not with everything.

The depth and abstract nature of much classical instrumental music (with its often highly personal interpretations) is perhaps the most difficult to describe, although EM Forster makes a good attempt in the following passage involving Beethoven's Fifth Symphony. Notice that he creates an impression of the music through the images that come into the character Helen's mind as she listens:

'No; look out for the part where you think you have done with the goblins and they come back,' breathed Helen, as the music started with a goblin walking quietly over the universe, from end to end. Others followed him. They were not aggressive creatures; it was that that made them so terrible to Helen. They merely observed in passing that there was no such thing as splendour or heroism in the world. After the interlude of elephants dancing, they returned and made the observation for the second time . . . Panic and emptiness! Panic and emptiness! The goblins were right.

—*EM Forster (Howard's End, Penguin Classics, 2000,*
first published 1910)

Music can play a central role in defining a character. In Nick Hornby's 1995 novel *High Fidelity,* Rob Fleming runs a record shop. He's constantly making lists of songs, and his record collection gives readers an insight into his personality. The songs he listens to also reflect his mood.

Music can also affect the way people work – which is why it's often used as background to assist people in performing particular tasks. Music can make you work harder in the gym or when out running, and can help you to get into a rhythm for repetitive work – singing has been used by chain gangs, cotton pickers and boatmen.

✔ Write about your character doing something while listening to a piece of music. How does the mood of the music influence the way she carries out the task? Perhaps slow music makes her do it dreamily, but music with a fast, angry rhythm forces her to work frenetically.

✔ Write about a character's favourite music when she was growing up, and how it made her feel. Describe your character listening to the music now, and how it makes her feel.

✔ Choose six pieces of music that reflect the different stages of your character's life – one from childhood, a song from early teenage years, a piece connected with the character's first love, a song she chooses for a big occasion such as a wedding, a song she connects with a special person and a piece she'd choose for her funeral.

Sparking Emotions with Smell

Research shows that smell is the most evocative of all the senses and the best at triggering memories. Think of the smell of freshly cut grass on a summer evening, the scent of seawater on your skin in the sunshine, the smell of freshly roasted coffee – or, less pleasantly, the odour of a student's bedroom after a 'lie-in' that's lasted two days!

Unpleasant smells are particularly powerful and can repel you instantly. I'll never forget the smell of the cabbage soup on the stairs of Raskolnikov's apartment block in Dostoyevsky's *Crime and Punishment* (1866), nor the list of foul smells from the opening chapter of the bestselling 1985 novel *Perfume:*

> the streets stank of manure, the courtyards of urine, the stairwells stank of mouldering wood and rat droppings, the kitchens of spoiled cabbage and mutton fat . . . The stench of sulphur rose from the chimneys, the stench of caustic lyes from the tanneries, and from the slaughterhouses came the stench of congealed blood.

> —*Patrick Süskind (Perfume, Diogenes, 1985, translated from the German by John E Woods, published in the UK by Penguin, 1986)*

Write two scenes in a story involving smells that your character experiences: the first about a smell the person loves and the second about one she hates. Don't overload the pieces with adjectives – try to find the telling word that is just right.

Tantalising with Taste and Food

Food is important to humans on many levels: emotionally, psychologically and socially. Everyone needs food to survive, and most people spend a great deal of time thinking about food, shopping for food, preparing food and eating it. Yet in some novels you'd think the characters never have to eat at all!

Describing the taste of food is one of the best ways to get your readers involved in the story. A well-written description of the sharp taste of a lemon can get your readers salivating, the sour taste of turned milk can make them wrinkle their noses, and the sweet taste of sugar or the succulence of roast meat can make them hungry.

Many writers have mixed writing fiction with describing food and even recipes. Here's just a taster menu to get your mouth watering:

✔ Laura Esquivel's bestselling 1989 debut novel, *Like Water for Chocolate*, is divided into 12 sections named after the months of the year. Each section begins with the recipe for a Mexican dish. The chapters outline the preparation of each dish and tie the meal to an event in the life of the main character, Tita.

✔ *The Debt to Pleasure* by John Lanchester (1996), formerly restaurant critic of the *Guardian* newspaper, is a novel that also contains recipes and mouth-watering descriptions of food.

✔ In *Gourmet Rhapsody* by Muriel Barbery (2009) the world's finest food critic is on his deathbed and seeks to savour one last perfect taste before he dies.

✔ Ernest Hemingway's *A Moveable Feast,* published posthumously in 1964, details the food and drink of 1920s Paris.

✔ *Chocolat* by Joanne Harris (1999) is about a single mother who sets up a chocolate shop in a small French town, incurring the disapproval of many of its inhabitants.

Explore the potential for using food in fiction with the following exercise. Remember to include the senses of touch, taste and smell:

1. **Write about your character preparing a meal.** Think about her favourite dishes and include a recipe.

2. **Move on to write about that character serving the meal to friends or family.** Do they like it? Does the meal go well?

You can reveal a great deal about your characters through the food they eat and the way they eat it. Is your character someone who goes into ecstasies about the way food is cooked, or is she the kind of person who doesn't care what she eats as long as it fills her stomach? A vegetarian is sure to have quite a different view of the world from a committed carnivore.

Family meal times are notoriously a great area for conflict, and a meal out in a restaurant provides characters with an opportunity for intense conversations:

1. **Write about two characters choosing a restaurant.** Make them disagree about their choice. What do their preferred meals reveal about their mood and personality?

2. **Describe the meals they choose.** Remember to detail the food they eat and the way they eat it, as well as writing down their conversation.

Food is also very important for marking special occasions: weddings and funerals, birthdays and anniversaries, and festivals such as Passover, Christmas and Eid.

Describe a feast for a big event. Put as much colour, flavour and texture into the scene as you can.

Feeling Your Way with Touch and Texture

The sense of touch is often neglected in fiction, perhaps because it's the hardest to describe. Yet touch and texture can quickly evoke a strong sensation in the reader.

Think of the pleasure to be found in the sensation of stroking a cat's fur, kneading fresh dough, running your hands over smooth silk and turning the crisp pages of a well-loved book. Think of the disgust caused by picking up a slimy slug in the garden, the discomfort of scraping your hand over rough concrete, the frisson caused by the tickling of a spider running up your arm or the pain of tight shoes pinching your feet.

It's the unexpected nature of some sensations that causes them to have such power – picking up something you think will be light that turns out to be extremely heavy, treading on a snail or a pin in the dark, biting into an olive when you thought it was a grape! With other sensations, the opposite is true – the expectation of a dentist's drill is often worse than the reality (especially if you've had a local anaesthetic!).

Your character goes into a dark room she's never entered before. Describe her feeling her way around, and the sensations she experiences as she touches the various objects in it.

Chapter 12

Getting Things Done: Describing Action and Activity

In This Chapter

▶ Revealing character through individual behaviour

▶ Creating exhilarating action scenes

▶ Doling out violence – responsibly

Descriptive writing isn't just about observing static objects such as a still life. You can also describe characters' movements, actions and activities. The more you keep people on the move, the more you can reveal about your characters and the better you can take the story forward.

As I show in this action-packed chapter, you communicate loads about your characters when you provide descriptions of what they do and how they do it. I demonstrate how actions can express feelings and emotions, depict people at work and play, and result in choices and further consequences: the very stuff of drama. In addition, to help you when you're writing scenes involving a large number of people, such as battles or demonstrations, I discuss ways of helping your readers to visualise an often confusing set of actions and keep them engaged throughout. I also show how taking care when picking your vocabulary allows you to add strength and specificity to your action scenes.

Watching Characters Tackling Everyday Tasks

People often have their own individual ways of carrying out tasks and activities. You can reveal a great deal about your characters through the things they do and the way they do them. In this section I cover characters mooching at home, working and relaxing. These three areas involve different pressures, emotions and states of mind, and so they provide different challenges to you as a writer.

You may need to make careful observations of how people carry out particular skilled tasks such as playing a sport, performing on a musical instrument or making a clay pot or piece of furniture.

Homing in on domestic life

Characters are most themselves when in the privacy of their own homes. Here they can let down their guard, say what they mean and do what they want – unless of course there are domestic tensions to explore!

It's helpful to try out different ways to get to know your character in his home environment.

Describe your character in his own home performing the following activities:

- ✔ Having a bath or shower, washing and drying his hair
- ✔ Making a cup of tea or coffee
- ✔ Relaxing in the evening – watching TV, reading a book, listening to music
- ✔ Cleaning and tidying his home, making the bed
- ✔ Trying to find something he's mislaid

Describe your character's actions in detail. Does he rush or do things slowly and carefully? Does he have any particular mannerisms? How does he interact with the people he lives with?

Working at creating a work life

Work takes up a great deal of most people's lives, and so don't neglect this aspect of your character's life. Fiction often explores the world of work – from Evelyn Waugh's 1938 *Scoop*, which is about journalism, to Nick Hornby's 1995 *High Fidelity* based around working in a second-hand record shop; from Richard Yates's *Revolutionary Road* (1961), where the main character works in the advertising industry, to Lauren Weisburger's *The Devil Wears Prada* (2003), which revolves around working for a fashion magazine . . . not to mention all the detective novels and spy fiction that are centred on the characters' jobs.

To find out what goes on in your character's working life, try this exercise. Remember that it helps if you think of specific tasks your character has to undertake, and whether he has concrete targets or goals:

- ✔ Write about a typical day in your character's working life. Select one particular task that he does regularly and describe it in detail.

- ✔ Describe your character in a meeting. Does he pay attention or fidget and think about other things? Does he have an agenda he wants to push through or is he content to let other people make decisions?

- ✔ Write down three things your character likes about his work and three things he hates about it. Do the positives outweigh the negatives?

- ✔ Think of an object that your character needs in relation to his work. Describe in detail your character handling it.

Arrange to do some research about your character's work if it's not a profession of which you have first-hand experience. If necessary, find someone in that job to talk to, and perhaps ask whether you can shadow him for a while.

Chilling out to reveal character at play

When your character isn't at work or at home, he may have time to play! Think of all the things your character enjoys doing – sports, hobbies or activities that help him relax. Many of these activities involve relationships with other people, so this can be a good way to explore such friendships.

To round out your character, write about him at play. Remember to explore his relationships with others who are involved too.

Write about your character doing three things he enjoys: a sport, a game, attending an event or whatever you like. Make sure that you describe your character's actions in as much detail as you can.

Writing Dramatic Action Scenes

Action scenes are notoriously difficult to write. One problem is that you sometimes find that you've distanced yourself from your character, and instead of seeing the scene impressionistically from his point of view, you find yourself suddenly adopting a bird's eye view in order to explain to readers what's happening. This is especially the case with set pieces such as fights and battles.

Here I suggest a few ways to improve your writing of an action scene, whether a fist-fight between two people or a battle featuring thousands.

Choosing the best words for action scenes

Describing physical actions in a great deal of logistical detail is often unhelpful. In hand-to-hand combat, the main character is likely to be aware of intense experiences such as the pressure on his throat or the pain in his arm as it's twisted backwards, but not of exactly what his opponent is doing.

Beware of writing passages along the following lines:

> He raised his right arm and positioned it at a 90-degree angle from his body while he moved his left leg backwards and twisted his foot outwards, shifting his weight from his left knee to his right ankle, before withdrawing his left fist and bringing it round in a semicircle to make contact with the left hand side of his opponent's chin.

Instead 'He swivelled around before throwing a left-handed punch to the chin' is perfectly adequate and much easier to visualise!

To write good action scenes, cut down on the adjectives and qualifying phrases and use strong verbs. 'He hurtled forwards' is more active than 'He moved forward rapidly', and 'She crunched onto the pavement' is stronger than 'She landed on the pavement with a crunch'. Keep this in mind when you try this exercise:

1. **Think of an action scene that you want to write.**

2. **Write down a list of standard verbs that you may want to use, such as 'went', 'put', 'took' and so on.**

3. **Write down all the different verbs you can use instead:**

   • **In place of 'went' (for example, in 'He went through the door'):** Strolled, ambled, careered, crashed, charged, scrambled, scurried, lurched, rushed, ran, hurried, hurtled, dashed, shot, disappeared, vanished.

   • **In place of 'put' (for example, in 'She put the mug on the table'):** Placed, positioned, rested, slammed, banged, flung, plonked, threw, tossed.

   • **In place of 'took' (for example, in 'He took the book she offered him'):** Seized, grasped, snatched, swiped, accepted.

4. **Write your action scene using as many strong verbs as possible.**

You can see the difference that strong verbs make in these two pieces:

She went into the room. The two men were standing by the window. She went over to them, taking the wine bottle from the table. She held it in front of her as the men came forward. One of them took a knife from his belt and held it in his right hand.

She rushed into the room. The two men were lounging by the window. She dashed over to them, snatching the wine bottle from the table. She brandished it in front of her as the men inched forward. One of them pulled a knife from his belt and gripped it with his right hand.

The second passage is clearly more effective. It is more precise and creates a much greater impression of movement and drama, helping the reader to visualise the scene.

 Use short sentences to create a more urgent rhythm in an action scene and give readers an impression that things are happening quickly. If you want to give a slow-motion effect, however, go right into the moment and do use longer sentences and more detail.

Controlling a huge cast

When you have a large number of people in a scene, such as in a battle, a demonstration or a panicking crowd of people, describing the scene with any clarity can be difficult.

 Avoid the temptation of trying to paint an overall picture of the whole chaotic event. Your main character is unlikely to see more than part of what's going on, and so a more effective option is to stick with what the person notices and experiences directly.

One problem with trying to describe fights is that they often happen between the main character and other characters who are unknown to him. This means that you can't refer to the others by name. You often find yourself writing things like 'the man who had been standing by the door when he came in' or 'the woman wearing a leather jacket and with the nose stud, whom he had noticed standing at the bar earlier', which makes the fight scene lengthy and confusing.

 To get around this problem, follow Raymond Chandler's approach and have your main character give the assailants a handle such as 'the brown man', 'the Indian' or 'mess-jacket', or refer to unusual physical characteristics such as green eyes or white hair.

A recent example of war fiction is *The Yellow Birds* by poet and Iraqi war veteran Kevin Powers. He manages to convey the full horror without going into gory or excessive detail:

> I shot him and he slumped over behind the wall. He was shot again by someone else and the bullet went through his chest and ricocheted, breaking a potted plant hanging from a window above the courtyard. Then he was shot again and he fell at a strange angle – backward over his bent legs – and most of the side of his face was gone and there was a lot of blood and it pooled around him in the dust.
>
> —*Kevin Powers (The Yellow Birds, Sceptre, 2012)*

Check out *For Whom the Bell Tolls* (1940) and *The Sun Also Rises* (1926) for more examples – Hemingway's writing about war is wonderfully vivid.

Portraying Violence and Its Effects

Extreme levels of violence have become much more acceptable in film and in fiction than used to be the case. This may be partly because as people become more and more distanced from violence and death they become more fascinated by it. People often read fiction to find out about things that they haven't experienced in life. Many people reach middle age without having experienced the death of anyone close to them, and so perhaps this explains the fascination for death in fiction, revealed in murder mysteries, books about serial killers and so on.

How graphically you portray violence depends on the genre you're writing in. Some detective novels and thrillers as well as true crime stories have quite explicit violence and gore, as do certain kinds of fantasy fiction and, of course, war stories. In other genres, violence plays only a small but important part of a narrative. For some guidance on when violence crosses over to become gratuitous, check out the nearby sidebar 'A punch too many'.

Violence is usually most effective with a build-up to it: the suspense and tension leading up to a violent action are often more disturbing than the violence itself.

In comic-book-style violence, the action is exaggerated and its true effect is glossed over. For example, in many films you see fights in which a single punch would break a person's jaw or cause permanent brain damage, and yet the characters go on trading blows for minutes on end and walk away with a few cuts or bruises. If you want to write more realistic violence, you need to research what weapons can do and the injuries that result.

A punch too many

Gratuitous violence is violence that's not necessary to the plot of the story or the development of the characters, or is unnecessarily gory or sadistic. Violence is also gratuitous when it's greater than what's needed to achieve the character's purpose – someone may need to frighten or subdue his victims in order to steal, but need not necessarily injure or torture them. Be aware of the danger of making sexual violence pornographic or titillating.

Make sure that you include scenes of violence only when they're needed to explain what happens next. Of course, if a character sees or experiences something extremely violent and is disturbed or seriously injured by it, you need to describe the violence itself and its after-effects.

If, say, you plan to write scenes involving contact fighting, go and watch a martial arts class. Look at the body language, the gestures and the sounds when participants fall or receive a blow. Or, if you know or can find people who've taken part in military action, interview them about what it feels like.

In *Crime and Punishment,* Dostoyevsky describes Raskolnikov's horrific murder of his landlady with great economy. After a long build-up, the moment comes:

> He had not a minute more to lose. He pulled the axe quite out, swung it with both arms, scarcely conscious of himself, and almost without effort, almost mechanically, brought the blunt side down on her head. He seemed not to use his own strength in this. But as soon as he had once brought the axe down, his strength returned to him.
>
> —*Fyodor Dostoyevsky (Crime and Punishment, translated by Constance Garnett, Dover Publications 2001, first published 1866)*

Dostoyevsky's genius lies in the description of the old woman as she's struck. Notice how in the preceding quote the act happens mechanically, as if he's not thinking of the victim. All this changes when, in the next passage, we see the victim as a human being:

> The old woman was as always bareheaded. Her thin, light hair, streaked with grey, thickly smeared with grease, was plaited in a rat's tail and fastened by a broken horn comb which stood out on the nape of her neck. As she was so short, the blow fell on the very top of her skull. She cried out, but very faintly, and suddenly sank all of a heap on the floor, raising her hands to her head. In one hand she still held 'the pledge.' Then he

dealt her another and another blow with the blunt side and on the same spot. The blood gushed as from an overturned glass, the body fell back. He stepped back, let it fall, and at once bent over her face; she was dead. Her eyes seemed to be starting out of their sockets, the brow and the whole face were drawn and contorted convulsively.

—Fyodor Dostoyevsky (Crime and Punishment, translated by Constance Garnett, Dover Publications 2001, first published 1866)

But as so often happens in fiction – and in life – something unexpected then happens – something Raskolnikov hadn't planned for, which complicates the murder.

Write a scene where something violent happens. Keep it short. Remember to describe any particular detail that would stand out in the mind of either the perpetrator or the victim, depending on whose viewpoint you're using.

Hinting at something dreadful can be more effective than describing it in detail. In this extract from Ian McEwan's *Enduring Love,* the narrator is apprehensively approaching a man who's fallen from a hot air balloon. Note how McEwan creates the impression of something terrible that is only half-seen:

I tried to protect myself as I began to circle the corpse. It sat within a little indentation in the soil. I didn't see Logan dead until I saw his face, and what I saw I only glimpsed. Though the skin was intact, it was hardly a face at all, for the bone structure had shattered and I had the impression, before I looked away, of a radical, Picassoesque violation of perspective. Perhaps I only imagined the vertical arrangement of the eyes.

—Ian McEwan (Enduring Love, Jonathan Cape, 1997)

Write about your character trying to look and yet not look at something repulsive – a mangled animal, an accident he passes by on the street, someone with a horrible disfigurement.

The aftermath of violence is as important as the violence itself. The scene may replay itself in the character's mind afterwards. He may be physically damaged and take time to heal. His relationships may be affected and he may be traumatised. If you fail to allow characters to respond emotionally to violence, your readers fail to respond too. Only in comic-book fiction are the heroes or detectives so hard-boiled that they don't respond to the sight of a mutilated corpse.

Write about the after-effects of physical violence on the character. Describe his body language, how he feels and what he wants to do in response.

Chapter 13

Building Character with Objects and Possessions

*I*n Thomas Pynchon's wild, blackly comic novel *V* (1963), a character called Rachel Owlglass has a peculiarly intense relationship with her MG car. She loves it – and when I say she loves it, I mean *really* loves it! Although the relationships your characters have with material things don't need to go that far, how the characters relate to objects is vital in creating and revealing their personalities and perhaps making changes in their lives over time. Therefore, one of the most important devices you have in your writing toolkit is the skill to describe and employ physical items effectively.

I cover using objects in all kinds of ways in Chapter 2, but here I focus specifically on employing objects and possessions to give personality to your characters, including the symbolic and representational values attached to items, how they can act as subtle clues to character and their role in triggering memories (something I also touch upon in Chapter 3).

Giving Your Characters Significant Possessions

The kinds of items people own and the way they feel about them show a great deal about their character. Some people are careful with their possessions, keeping them organised, neat and tidy, while others are chaotic and careless. You can make use of this reality to construct believable three-dimensional characters.

In this section I show not only how you can define characters by their possessions, but also how objects can possess them.

Choosing objects to use

Look around your home at all the different kinds of objects you possess – kitchen tools, crockery, books, music, ornaments, clothes, furnishings, bathroom products. Plus, consider what you carry around in your bag or pocket. Examine the contents of your bedside drawer and your desk. Look at the things you want to keep and the things you intend to take to the charity shop. Rummage in the back of your wardrobe for items you've forgotten all about.

Now you're ready to start thinking about all the objects that belong to your main character.

Imagine walking through your character's home room by room, and make a list of the possessions. Be precise, and bear in mind what each choice reveals about the character. To help, here are some questions to ask:

- Is the bed linen plain or floral, and does she have sheets made of silk?
- Is the furniture old or modern?
- What about paintings, ornaments, books, CDs?
- Does the character have items she's sentimentally attached to that don't otherwise fit in?
- Does she have souvenirs from visited places or gifts from people she used to love?

Pick a handful of these objects and describe them in detail:

- Write about your character handling the objects.
- Write some of these items into a scene in your story.

People acquire possessions all the time: they shop, receive gifts, find things left behind in their home, are left things in wills, swap things with others. You can reveal quite a lot about your character through her reactions to all these objects:

- Write about your character shopping for a particular item:
  - How does she go about it: enter shops at random and try out dozens of items, or plan first?
  - Is she fussy about getting exactly what she wants or does she fall for a completely different item and buy that instead?
  - Does she end up with several items or none?

✔ Write about one of your characters receiving a gift that she likes. Then write about her receiving a gift she doesn't like.

✔ Write about your character finding something on the street or in her house:

- Does she like it?

- Does she decide to keep it?

- Does she decide to hand it in somewhere or find out who its owner is?

✔ Write about your character receiving a strange object in a will.

✔ Write about your character exchanging a possession with someone else. Is she happy with the exchange?

In Dostoyevsky's 1869 novel *The Idiot*, Prince Myshkin exchanges his simple tin cross for Rogozhin's golden one, becoming 'brothers'. This exchange symbolises a mysterious and yet unequal connection between the characters, who are in many ways opposites of one another.

Owning objects (and being owned by them)

Possessing objects can be a trap. Characters can become so attached to them that they're unable to move on in their lives – think of fanatical collectors or people who hoard things, from newspapers to old pieces of wrapping paper and even plastic bags. For such people, the loss of a possession can seem a blow at first but may also represent a form of freedom.

You can't take it with you

Historical attitudes to possessions are interesting and can provide insights you can use to depict your characters' psychological relationships to objects.

In ancient Egypt, people were buried with significant objects, because the belief was that these would be needed on the journey to or in the afterlife. People often cling on to things as if they'll protect them. But as this passage from the New Testament reminds: 'For we brought nothing into this world, and it is certain we can carry nothing out' (*King James Bible*, 1 Timothy 6:7).

Letting go of material things can be frightening when it's seen as a step in the direction of the ultimate loss: death. But it can also be a step towards maturity and away from materialism. In either case, such an event has a powerful effect on your characters.

In his 1996 short story 'The Clothes They Stood Up In', Alan Bennett writes about a couple who come back from a night out at the opera to discover that everything has been stolen from their flat, right down to the toilet paper. The couple discover some surprising things about themselves as a result, and the event is ultimately liberating.

Find out about your character's attitude to possessions through the following exercise:

- ✔ Write about your character losing everything; it can be a dream or a fantasy. How does your character react? What does the person feel?

- ✔ Write about your character giving away something that she values. Explore why she does it and what this action means for her.

Remembering to Use Objects to Spark Memories!

I just spotted a copy of Proust's *Remembrance of Things Past* (1913-1927) on my bookshelf, and it reminds me to talk about how objects can trigger memories! Objects are incredibly useful for this purpose, not least because flashbacks work best when something concrete reminds the character of what happened earlier. You can use possessions and objects to connect characters to the past and convey information about their earlier lives: a shell on the mantelpiece collected at the beach on a childhood holiday; a painting inherited from a grandfather; a ring that belonged to a mother.

Finding an object from the past is an obvious way to take the character back in time. Discovering something in the attic, being given a gift that belonged to a parent or grandparent, and finding a childhood toy are all obvious ways of linking the present with the past. An object doesn't even have to be physically present to create a memory – another character can simply mention it.

In Henry Green's novel *Caught,* Trant is promised pork pie for dinner by his wife: 'This put Trant in mind of his sub officer who had made them a laughing stock the previous day, running about like a chicken that had its head cut off' (Harvill Press, 1943).

Quite why the pork pie reminds Trant of a headless chicken is a bit obscure – but people do think in peculiar, indirect ways. Sometimes an object can make a person think of another one that's connected in some way, however personal the association.

Try this exercise to explore ways of using objects to trigger memories and take the reader back to different times in a character's life:

1. **Divide your page into six sections.**

2. **Pick half a dozen objects in your character's home and write one in each box, making sure that each one relates to a different phase of your character's life.**

3. **Write a memory that each object triggers.**

Oh . . . and don't forget to flip to Chapter 3 for loads more on characters' memories.

Representing Characters: Objects as Symbols

You can add depth and subtlety to your fiction by using objects to symbolise a character. The object concerned can be something that the character values highly or is never seen without.

In William Golding's 1954 novel *Lord of the Flies,* Piggy's glasses represent intellect and the power of science – they're used to focus the sun's rays and make a fire. When they're broken, it implies that another link with civilisation has been lost. It also foreshadows something bad happening to Piggy, because the glasses are seen almost as an extension of Piggy himself.

Some objects almost become extensions of ourselves – you only need to look at how some people react to a minute scratch on their precious car! Find out more about your character through this exercise:

1. **Write about an object that your character is seldom seen without.** It can be a watch, mobile phone, purse, wallet, bag, piece of jewellery, an item of clothing, a cosmetic, a packet of tissues – anything your character feels lost without.

2. **Write about your character mislaying this object.** What does she do and how does she react? Does she find the object or learn to make do without it?

As well as using objects to help develop and identify main characters, you can also do so for minor ones. Giving characters a quirk helps readers to remember who they are. Some characters can become like objects: a businessman may look as shiny and perfect as his new mobile phone, or an artist as scruffy and paint-splattered as his brush and palette!

1. **Choose an object and write a list of its qualities.**

2. **Write about a character who has as many of the qualities in your list as possible.**

Same object, different meaning

Physical objects may be solid and unchanging, but that doesn't mean that their meanings remain consistent – not at all. Different characters can relate differently to the same objects.

In George Eliot's novel *Middlemarch,* published in 1874, the sisters Dorothea and Celia go through their late mother's jewellery box. Dorothea disapproves of worldly things and gives Celia a beautiful amethyst necklace and cross, saying she won't take any jewellery. But then she sees an emerald ring and bracelet and talks of the symbolic importance of gemstones in the Bible's Book of Revelation, and decides to take them. The girls' discussion of the jewellery reveals their relationship with one another, and also shows that although Dorothea tries to be self-denying, it isn't her real nature, as becomes apparent when she later marries the dull, pedantic Casaubon – a terrible mistake – and subsequently falls for the much more suitable Ladislaw.

Write a scene in which two characters discuss possessions in such a way as to reveal something about the characters themselves. Make the objects symbolic.

Making use of magical objects and superstitions

In fantasy fiction, writers often use magical objects that connect to the character's personality. A magical sword can give the character power, a flying carpet or super-boots can enable the person to travel distances, a helmet or cloak of invisibility can enable her to escape detection, or a magical compass can help her find her way (a sort of supernatural GPS).

Magical objects you'd love to own

Here's a list of some famous magical objects that I hope get your creative juices flowing:

✔ **Excalibur:** Only the true king can draw the magical sword from the stone. Arthur uses it in battle and ultimately it's returned to the Lady of the Lake. Excalibur is the prototype of many magical swords found in much fantasy fiction, and has been wielded in the hands of young boys in imaginary fights to the death for centuries.

✔ **The One Ring:** JRR Tolkien's magic ring has the power to corrupt even the best human being and is a symbol of evil. It confers invisibility on the wearer, like many magic rings in Celtic mythology, which would be incredibly useful were it not for the Ring's dark side.

✔ **Magic or flying carpet:** *One Thousand and One Nights,* a collection of Arabic tales, features a carpet that transports the characters almost instantly to where they want to go – which would be as useful today as it was then!

✔ **Seven-league boots:** This impressive footwear features in several European fairy stories, including 'Jack the Giant Killer'.

The character wearing the boots can cover 7 leagues (some 3 miles) in one stride, so travels huge distances with incredible speed (again enormously helpful!).

✔ **Helmet of invisibility:** In Greek mythology Perseus receives the helmet from Athena when he goes to kill the Gorgon Medusa. The helmet enables the user to become invisible to other supernatural entities. Wagner also uses a magic helmet called the Tarnhelm in his opera *Das Rheingold,* part of a 14-hour, four-opera cycle. (If Wagner's not your thing, put on the helmet and you can slip out unnoticed!)

✔ **Magic wands:** Wizards and witches use these to cast spells – they can be made of wood, ivory, stone, iron or precious metal. In JK Rowling's Harry Potter books, the wand chooses its owner.

✔ **Seeing stone or crystal ball:** Enables the person who looks into it to see into the future or the past, or over long distances. Seeing stones called *palantíri* play an important role in Tolkien's *The Lord of the Rings.* No fortune-teller is complete without one.

Write about a magical object your character wants to possess.

Although these objects are literally magical in fairy stories and fantasy worlds, remember that you can also give your characters lucky charms or objects that they feel help or protect them. People often imbue ordinary objects with symbolic and magical powers:

✔ Losing a piece of jewellery such as an engagement ring can be incredibly upsetting: a character may feel that it means a relationship will break up.

✔ Breaking something – especially a mirror – is often considered unlucky, whereas a character may think that finding a coin will bring her good fortune.

✔ Losing her car keys or mobile phone can make your character feel completely powerless, because it removes her ability to travel somewhere or make contact with people.

Write about your character losing an object that she values or considers lucky. Think about what that object symbolises for her.

Many people feel superstitious about items of clothing that belonged to someone else. Some spend enormous sums of money buying dresses or jewellery once owned by famous people, whereas others refuse to wear clothes that belonged to a dead person. In a scientific experiment, people were offered £10 to wear a jumper. However, when told that it had belonged to infamous serial killer Fred West, almost everyone refused.

Try this exercise to explore how your character feels about objects that belong to other people. Remember that some people are happy or even proud to wear second-hand clothes while for others it would be unthinkable, and that some people care a great deal about where something came from while others have no curiosity at all:

✔ Write about your character wearing or handling something that belongs to someone she loves.

✔ Write about your character wearing something or handling something that belongs to someone she hates.

Getting (metaphorically) emotional

You can use objects to represent your character's emotions in a subtle manner. Instead of writing that your character is angry, have her looking at a statue or painting of an angry animal, deity or person. Instead of writing that she's sad, depict her standing by a fountain with a weeping nymph or creature.

In Thomas Hardy's 1872 novel *A Pair of Blue Eyes,* Henry Knight tries to retrieve his hat from the edge of a cliff, and finds himself suspended by his arms:

> . . . opposite Knight's eyes was an imbedded fossil, standing forth in low relief from the rock. It was a creature with eyes. The eyes, dead and turned to stone, were even now regarding him. It was one of the early crustaceans called Trilobites. Separated by millions of years in their lives, Knight and this underling seemed to have met in their place of death.
>
> —*Thomas Hardy (A Pair of Blue Eyes, Wordsworth Classics, 1995,*
> *first published 1872)*

This fossilised creature represents Knight's own death staring him in the face.

Write a scene in which an object similarly reflects the character's hopes or fears.

You can also describe emotions in terms of objects, using the objects as metaphors. For example, you can compare a character's delight to the discovery of a shiny golden egg, or her horror to seeing a dead bird.

Write a list of random emotions. Then describe each one in terms of an object, as in the preceding examples.

Experiencing unexpected meetings with objects

The emotional impact of encountering unfamiliar or unexpected objects can convey a great deal of information about your character's personality. This technique is effective for finding ways to surprise your character with her own feelings.

Coming into contact with a famous painting or statue that the person hasn't seen before can trigger surprising emotions in your character. For example, she may be visiting a foreign city and wander into a gallery where she unexpectedly comes upon a world-famous masterpiece. A painting, clock, bust or statue may be entirely new to your character, yet something about it forms an instant connection. The scene in a painting may show a place she knows and misses; or the pose or facial expression of a statue can symbolise her mental state. Her mood may well change completely because of this encounter and colour her subsequent conversation, meeting or event, which can in turn have a significant impact on the plot (for more on objects and plot, check out Chapter 2).

Exploring an object that your character doesn't find aesthetically attractive yet still wants to be around can be interesting. For example, an ugly ornament or garden gnome owned by a parent and hated in childhood may represent a happy memory when seen in an antique shop 40 years later – the character may even want to buy it!

✔ Write a scene in which your protagonist encounters a familiar object unexpectedly. Perhaps it's in a gallery, or something left at a friend's house and subsequently forgotten.

✔ Write about your character visiting a gallery or museum and encountering a work for the first time. She's instantly affected by it.

✔ Write about something of value to your character that she doesn't find useful or beautiful. Why won't she get rid of it? Why does she have it in the first place?

✔ Write about your character seeing a name or photograph she's not expecting – in a newspaper, an advert or even a graveyard!

Creating Clues to Your Character

You can use objects to reveal clues about different aspects of your character. Think of how Sir Arthur Conan Doyle in his Sherlock Holmes stories has his master detective deduce enormous amounts about characters from the objects they possess.

In the modern world, people often don't pay attention to small things. They're all too busy getting things done and so lose the habit of focusing on the details. As a writer, you need to slow down and pay attention, just like Sherlock Holmes does.

Notice things. Look for the small details. Make notes so you don't forget.

When you're writing, you become a kind of Sherlock Holmes in reverse. You need to sow clues about your character into your writing so that readers can deduce things about your characters subtly, without you needing to spell them out.

Focusing on what you can reveal about your character through the objects, write about the following objects:

✔ Your character's favourite toy

✔ Your character's favourite item of clothing

✔ Your character's most treasured possession

Using objects to stand in for aspects of your characters

Objects can allude to many aspects of a character. Readers see a character with a lot of books as an intellectual, and one surrounded by mess and clutter as having a disorganised mind.

A character can be used as an object by some characters – making use of another person as a means to an end is the great evil that overtakes many of the characters in Fyodor Dostoyevsky's novels and those of Henry James, as well as too many crime novels to mention!

In Henry James's *The Portrait of a Lady* (1881), Osmond is a collector who surrounds himself with precious objects. He doesn't love Isabel, but uses her as if she were another object for his collection. Objects can also represent traits that characters want to get rid of but can't (a common motif in fairy stories). In Oscar Wilde's *The Picture of Dorian Gray* (1880), the painting becomes uglier and more corrupted, while the increasingly sinful Dorian Gray himself remains handsome and young, unchanged by time. When his conscience hits, he stabs the portrait and so kills himself.

Write a scene from your story in which a character tries to get rid of an object she possesses, something that stands in for an aspect of herself. Make sure that getting rid of the object is much more difficult than it appears. Write about the object returning to the person in some unexpected way.

Abu Kasem slips up

In an old Persian tale, a wealthy miser, Abu Kasem, has a revolting pair of ancient slippers that he's too mean to replace. One day at the baths he finds a magnificent pair of slippers and thinks they've been left for him. The owner of the slippers is a magistrate and recognises the old pair that Abu Kasem leaves behind in their place. Angrily, he gives the miser a hefty fine.

Abu Kasem decides to get rid of the old slippers. First he throws them into the lake, but they end up being caught in the fishermen's nets and damaging them, so the fish escape. They're instantly recognised as the miser's and thrown back through his window, where they break some of his favourite glassware.

Abu Kasem then decides to bury the slippers in the garden, but is spotted by a neighbour who thinks he must be burying treasure. This is illegal in Islamic culture, because wealth should be kept in circulation to benefit everyone, so he is fined again. Time and again he tries to rid himself of the slippers, but everyone recognises them and returns them to him. In the end he's left impoverished with the revolting slippers his only remaining possession.

The moral of the story is that you can't easily rid yourself of aspects of your personality that you don't like, and that these traits can easily be your undoing.

Seeing things in the dark

At an unconscious level, people often see objects that aren't present: a shape in a cloud, an apparition on a dark night, in an unlit room. What a person 'sees' may reveal something about what's on her mind and show her fears, hopes and emotions. For example, if one of your characters sees a tree that looks like a skull, she may be afraid of death.

Have a go at this exercise, which involves the famous inkblot test (search for 'Rorschach test' online to view examples). Some psychologists use this test to examine a person's personality and emotional functioning. You can use it to kick-start some creative thinking – and reveal what different characters might be thinking.

1. **Look at an inkblot, see what objects you can make out and decide what your character would see.**

2. **Move on to write a scene where a second character sees something completely different.**

3. **Write a scene in which the character sees something in a shadow, cloud, piece of material or wallpaper pattern.**

Objects also appear in dreams, where they can have a personal or symbolic meaning:

- They can be things the character sees or handles in the course of the day.

- They can be items the person possesses or wants to possess.

- They can be things the character had completely forgotten.

You can use objects in dreams to make vague longings or fears more concrete. When you do this exercise, think about just what the objects mean for the character, and remember that in dreams, one thing can change into another, either from something bad to good, or the other way round:

1. **Write about an object in your character's dream.**

2. **Transform it into another object.**

Chapter 14

Using Description to Create Atmosphere and . . . and . . . Suspense!

> *I felt that I breathed an atmosphere of sorrow.*
>
> —Edgar Allan Poe *(The Fall of the House of Usher, 1839)*

*F*ew writers can create a chilling mood as effectively as Edgar Allan Poe. As the above quote implies, some of his characters seem to exude atmosphere from their very person.

Precise, evocative description is key to the way a story works. Although some people think of description as a kind of padding between the exciting bits of a fictional narrative, nothing's further from the truth. Description aids the creation of mood, atmosphere and tension.

Description allows you as the writer to offer a window into your character's thoughts, feelings and inner world. People sense and experience the world differently, in their own unique way; effective descriptive writing provides readers with a great deal of information about your characters as well as the world outside them, which is all essential to conveying a convincing, persuasive atmosphere.

In this chapter, I explore different ways of employing description to create atmosphere and suspense. You can use events, objects, the weather and the seasons to reflect the character's own circumstances, internal struggles, fears and hopes. You can also use description to prepare readers, often unconsciously, for what's in store for the characters.

Adding Ambience and Atmosphere

Mood is crucial to creating atmosphere and suspense in your story. Just think about how film-makers use music to create a sense of unease and tension in viewers. You need to create a similar effect with words and images for your readers; every piece of description that you write needs to produce an emotional response in readers.

In this section I cover the importance of using the right words and phrases to set the mood, as well as ways to reveal character subtly by describing objects, places and people.

Choosing your words carefully

You can create very different effects according to the adjectives you use when describing a person, a location or an object. Your selection is often down to the feeling you want to convey. For example, long, mournful-sounding words will create a very different impression to short, crisp ones, apart from the meaning of the words themselves.

Think about the precise words that evoke exactly the meaning you want. Don't swamp your prose with too many adjectives, but work on finding a few well-chosen ones that produce the desired effect. For example, I can't forget the 'sour' smell of Millbank prison in Sarah Water's 1999 novel *Affinity,* or the 'granite' sky in Daphne du Maurier's 1936 novel *Jamaica Inn,* or the 'wine-dark' sea of Homer's *The Odyssey.* More usual words fail to evoke a feeling in the reader, while the word that is spot-on will.

Creating an atmosphere is all about the feelings it evokes in the characters and the readers. Try describing somewhere you know and the feelings it evokes in you, before doing the same for the characters in your story:

1. **Find a postcard or photograph of a place you know.** Describe the memories and feelings it evokes in you.

2. **Use a postcard or photograph of a place in your story – or that's similar to a place in the story, if you're writing about somewhere imaginary.** Similar to step 1, describe the memories and feelings it evokes in the character.

Enhancing character and atmosphere with description

Always relate description in your story to a character's feelings and thoughts, so that the passage constantly gives your reader information about the character, but in a more subtle manner than writing 'he's anxious' or 'she's determined'. To do so, you can use the fact that different people can perceive the same place completely differently. A character who is anxious or depressed might think a place unpleasant, while someone who is happy might see only the good things about it.

Write about the same place from the point of view of three different characters. Make them respond emotionally to the place and also make them notice different details. Make sure that you reveal important things about your characters' mood and emotions through the words you choose and details you highlight.

Description is always more interesting when you weave it into action (something I discuss in more detail in Chapter 12). Work on finding ways to make your character's experience of something active – for example, have the character search frantically for an item under time pressure in order to describe the shambolic contents of a room; or make your description of a misty, murky, inhospitable landscape more interesting by requiring the character to cross it while inadequately dressed.

You can reveal aspects of characters by what they do and don't notice. For example, when a character sees a person or place that he knows well, he probably doesn't see the whole picture. What he does notice, however, are the things that have changed – and describing these objects or people can be really interesting to readers. If the character has lost weight, readers wonder why: is he ill or lovesick or has he just decided to get healthier? If a picture is missing from a wall, readers want to know who took it and why.

Describe the following, saying what's changed since your character last saw them:

- ✔ A person
- ✔ A place
- ✔ An object

Foreshadowing Events for Suspense

One of the best ways of shaping your plot and building suspense into your story is to plant subliminal details into the prose. These small details may seem irrelevant at the time, but are in fact an indication of events to come. Your character can observe these actions, gestures or words in others, or say or do them himself. For example, someone may drop an object out of a window from which he later jumps, or see a baby in a café just before discovering that his wife is pregnant.

Here I show how you can foreshadow events through objects (such as dead-eyed dolls) and events (such as an accident witnessed on the road), or through omens, warnings and prophecies. (Plus, don't forget that you can use the weather and dreams, as I cover in the later sections 'Working with the weather' and 'Creating suspense in your sleep: Dreams and premonitions' respectively.)

Describing things that your characters notice can give insight into their state of mind, and therefore what's likely to happen to them later:

1. **Write about a character walking to a meeting.** Describe what the person sees on the way and what happens in the meeting.

2. **Describe the character walking back the same way past exactly the same places after the meeting is over.** Again, describe what the person sees, but make sure to reveal that what he sees has changed according to what happened in the meeting and his feelings about it.

For example, if he was dreading the meeting, you could describe him noticing snarled-up traffic and an angry exchange on the way there, which would make the reader feel anxious about the meeting too. If the meeting goes well, on the way home he could notice a happy-looking couple and the flowers blooming in the park.

Omens and prophecies

Much fiction builds suspense and tension through the use of prophetic statements. Look at many of the classical myths. In Ancient Greece, Oedipus's parents are told that he'll one day kill his father and marry his mother. Therefore they abandon the child. But Oedipus survives and grows up not knowing the identity of his parents, which causes the very events his parents tried to prevent.

Similar prophecies are made to characters in Shakespeare's plays. In *Macbeth,* the three witches tell Macbeth what will happen to him – though not how the events will come about. In *Julius Caesar,* the soothsayer tells Caesar to 'Beware the Ides of March' – the date on which he is subsequently murdered.

In modern fiction, prophetic statements are more likely to be made by another character than by an oracle or god figure. A character may be told that he'll never amount to anything, or that he'll inherit a large sum of money if he behaves in a certain way (for example, marrying the right person). These statements change the character's attitude – some people go passively along with the declared fate, whereas others fight against it and do the opposite.

Owning omens

Omens are slightly different than prophecies in that they're objects or symbols that the characters see as signifying that something good or bad is going to happen. Many of these omens survive in superstitions: a black cat crossing your path, a single magpie, walking under a ladder, breaking a mirror.

If you're clever in your writing, you can phrase things so that readers don't realise the importance of the omen at the time it first appears. Perhaps a character mentions it in passing, but then the story moves on and readers forget – only to be reminded later when the foreshadowed event does indeed happen. This creates a shocking moment of revelation that can be atmospherically chilling.

In Leo Tolstoy's *Anna Karenina* (1873), on the day Anna meets her future lover, Vronsky, on the station platform, she sees a man accidentally killed by a train. Some of the bystanders think that the man threw himself under the wheels. Anna says 'It is a bad omen', as proves to be the case. Witnessing this event may have planted in Anna's mind the idea that this would be a foolproof way to kill herself.

In modern fiction, and to some extent in classical mythology, it's the character's response to the so-called omen that usually causes it to come true – or not. Therefore, when you create an omen or prophecy, readers must see how the character reacts to it and what he thinks about it. Omens work best when they're seen in actual events or objects rather than as vague feelings of unease.

Often, a modern character dismisses the omen as mere superstition – but it works away in his subconscious and may affect his actions and choices, thus altering and often foreshadowing what happens in the future. For example, a character may read his horoscope in the morning paper, which tells him that romance is in the air, but also to be wary of something going wrong at work. He's happy with his current partner and job, and dismisses the horoscope as irrelevant. However, at a meeting at work later that day, the character meets someone he's attracted to. The fact that he read that horoscope may make him behave differently towards this new person, thus leading to a new relationship but also the problems in the workplace that the horoscope foretold.

A large number of fortune-telling devices that were developed in the past are still around today, and you can use them in your writing to prophesy the future:

- Astronomical events such as comets, supernovae and meteors
- Books of divination such as the *I Ching*
- Casting lots, bones or sticks
- Crystal balls
- Dice or coins
- Flowers or fruit stones ('he loves me, he loves me not'; 'tinker, tailor, soldier, sailor')
- Horoscopes
- Lucky numbers (see the next section)
- Palm reading
- Playing cards
- Tarot cards
- Tea leaves

I predict (!) that you'll want to have a go at the following exercise in foreshadowing events for creepy suspense or brooding atmosphere:

1. **Write a scene in your story in which one or more characters use one of the above omens to predict what's going to happen to them.** Remember to describe the details of the process you choose. Think about how the characters react to the result, and whether they decide to accept it or defy it.

2. **Compose a scene in which a character encounters the chosen item but doesn't really pay any attention to it.** For example, perhaps he reads about an imminent event in the skies, but doesn't think about it or pay any attention. Or a minor character reads his palm or his tea leaves and dismisses the prophecy instantly.

3. **Jump ahead in your story and have whatever was predicted happen.** Remember to use description and atmosphere to build up to this event.

Living with lucky and unlucky numbers

You can use lucky and unlucky numbers as a way of foreshadowing good or bad events in your fiction. Numbers have long been associated with good and bad luck, and these superstitions survive into the modern world. The number 13 is considered unlucky by so many people that streets often don't have a number 13 and apartment blocks don't have a designated 13th floor. When the NASA scientists refused to be superstitious and elected to have an Apollo 13, that mission was a disaster – though fortunately the astronauts survived! Number 666 is also believed to be unlucky, because it's the 'number of the beast' in the Book of Revelation. In Japan, number 4 is unlucky, because one word for it sounds very similar to the word for death.

Make mine a placebo please!

If you're thinking that nobody believes in the power of prophecy these days, think again. In medicine, the *placebo effect* is well known – if patients are told that they're taking a powerful medicine, they tend to get better even if they're given a sugar pill. Complex clinical trials test whether any new medicine is better than a placebo. So strong is the placebo effect that recent research shows that people even respond when they're told that they're being given a placebo. Pills are apparently most effective when they're large and red!

Something called the *nocebo effect* also exists. A patient told that his medication may have severe side effects is more likely to experience these symptoms than someone who's told that the medicine is harmless. A patient given a prognosis of six months to live is more likely to die by that time than a patient with the same prognosis who's told that he has a lot of hope.

Lucky numbers tend to be more individual than unlucky ones. Many people choose their personal lucky numbers, possibly related to their date of birth, for their lottery tickets or pin numbers. Generally 2, 7 and 12 are considered to be lucky.

Try creating a lucky number for one of your characters, or even an unlucky one to add to the centuries of existing superstitions!

Be aware of the implications of using particular numbers in your description, unless you intend to give readers a subliminal message.

Anticipating the future with objects and events

You can use almost any object as a way of foreshadowing the future. If a character goes into a room and sees fading flowers, readers expect something to end or go wrong. If you describe a tree about to burst into leaf, it implies hope or that things are going to take a turn for the better. Of course, your writing can be made more exciting and unpredictable if you sometimes subvert these expectations.

In horror fiction, objects such as dolls, puppets and masks are used to create a sense of unease and foreboding. Items considered unlucky are broken mirrors, anything that's cracked or spilt, shoes on the table, opening an umbrella indoors, taking off your wedding ring and upside-down horseshoes.

Because they rely on the visual, horror films often use the device of foreshadowing an event using an object. If, in a film, you see a character using a sharp knife in the kitchen, you can be fairly certain someone will be stabbed with it later in the film – unless it's a red herring of course!

In Dostoyevsky's *The Idiot* (1868), when Prince Myshkin visits Rogozhin's apartment he sees a knife and picks it up. The knife is described in enough detail that readers won't forget it: 'It was a plainlooking knife, with a bone handle, a blade about eight inches long, and broad in proportion, it did not clasp.' Rogozhin takes the knife and puts it in a book. Later, the knife is used to injure and kill.

In the same way, you can have a character observe a small incident that fore-shadows a future event. For example, your character may see the following:

- ✔ **A person missing a train, early in the story:** Later on, the character misses the train himself, or a flight, or something really important.

- ✔ **A couple arguing in the street, seen through the window of a bus:** Later in the story, your character has a terrible row with someone he was close to.

- ✔ **A couple who have just been married, standing outside a registry office:** Later in the story, a main character gets married.

Try this exercise to practise using objects and incidents to foreshadow what happens in your story. The more varied the objects and incidents are, the more fun you will have with this exercise:

1. **Keep a notebook with you.** As you go about your day, jot down small incidents that you observe that are similar to the ones in the preceding list.

2. **Give each one a number.** Keep going until you have 12 incidents.

3. **Roll two dice to select a number and then write this incident into your story.** Does it fit? Can you make use of it to foreshadow something you plan to happen later or make something happen later because of this incident?

   If this incident doesn't fit then skip to another one on your list and try again until you find one that does!

Writing in All Weathers and All Year Round

You won't be surprised to hear that using the weather is a great way to create atmosphere, mood and suspense. Therefore don't leave storms and showers, heatwaves and droughts, to meteorologists.

In this section I discuss ways to use the weather, including the conditions and changes that come with the seasons and across times of the day, to create atmosphere in your writing.

Working with the weather

The weather is important in people's day-to-day lives. It changes plans, forms the basis of much small talk and affects the way people feel. The weather is such a basic part of human consciousness that it should really form part of every scene and story. It's like a background atmosphere to all the action (and sometimes dramatically takes centre stage).

I don't mean that you need to spend a huge amount of time describing all the details. Saying something like 'When Shakira left the house, it was still raining' is often sufficient, or 'It had turned cold, and Fred went back to fetch his coat'. Of course, the rain or the cold can influence the story in more ways than you, the writer, first intend. Shakira's bicycle may slip on the wet streets. Fred may notice something is amiss when he picks up his coat. Fred's forgetfulness, of course, may also foreshadow him forgetting something important later.

'Here comes the rain again!' Weather and mood

Undoubtedly, the weather affects people's moods. People tend to feel happy on bright, sunny days, and sad or depressed when it's cold and rainy (so a character stating that he loves the rain can be inadvertently revealing something about his self-image). A storm brewing makes the characters feel tense, and a howling wind makes them jittery. Severe cold can freeze people's emotions as well as their bodies. Extreme heat and cold can also exacerbate illness or even kill a person.

You can also create weather in your fiction that reflects the way you want your characters to feel.

Try out using the weather in different ways to change the mood in your story, and affect the way your characters feel:

1. **Write a scene that takes place in particular weather – a hot summer's afternoon, perhaps, or a gloomy winter's evening.** Make sure that the weather reflects the mood, and see whether you can find any ways of increasing the drama in the weather or the mood, or in both.

2. **Rewrite the scene, keeping the mood the same but changing the weather.** This time, make the weather in contrast to the mood – so, gloomy mood but gorgeous weather, or jubilant mood but dark and foreboding skies.

Of course, the weather isn't always extreme, and you don't want to fall prey to clichés when tying the weather to atmosphere. Avoid the tendency to go for baking hot or freezing cold and the rain always coming down in torrents.

You can create more subtle effects by using less extreme forms of weather. It may be sunny but with a cold breeze, or overcast but hot. Drizzle can be more effective in conveying atmosphere than heavy rain. You can also keep the weather changing, sometimes in line with the characters' changing feelings.

Clouds can be useful for creating atmosphere and suspense too. Large, threatening clouds are different from the small, fluffy clouds you see on a summer's day. Some clouds are good for predicting the weather: mackerel skies indicate a front coming and a change, and anvil-shaped clouds may precede a thunderstorm.

I'm sure that, like most people, you often wish the weather was different. In winter you imagine and long for the warmth of summer and for light evenings, but in the middle of a heatwave you find yourself yearning for the cold of winter. So weather can exist in a character's mind as well as outside.

Write a scene in which the character is in a very hot (or cold) place. Then write some more, staying in the scene but having the character move to a cold (or hot) place, either in his imagination (a memory, perhaps) or in reality. Think about what happens when you have this transition in a scene: the dramatic effect and whether any contrasts are happening.

Sometimes a change in the weather can completely change the outcome of an event. A sudden downpour can ruin the picnic and force everyone to find shelter, changing the dynamics of the group. A freak storm can cancel a flight and prevent an important meeting. A character can get lost in the fog.

You can use a change in the weather to enable somebody to get what he wants, or to prevent him from doing so, often through the changes in atmosphere and emotion that the weather provokes:

1. **Write a short scene in which a character wants something emotional or physical from another character.**

2. **Continue writing the scene in which something in the weather makes it possible for the character to get what he wants from the other character.**

3. **Write the scene again, using the weather to get in the way.**

'Turned out nice again!' Weather and the future

You can use weather forecasting as a way of foreshadowing the future, especially if a storm is coming. Remember that the weather forecast can turn out to be wrong, hence creating an element of surprise.

Don't underestimate the power of the weather: it can change history. Battles have been lost and won due to bad weather, and the Russian winter defeated Napoleon in the 19th century and Hitler's German army in the 20th. Freak weather events can postpone or destroy lives. The weather can also foreshadow human events. The UK storm of 1987 preceded a stock-market crash, and the unseasonably fine weather on 31 March 1990 encouraged riots in London, which ended the unpopular poll tax.

If you're writing fantasy or science fiction, you may also want to think about the weather conditions in your fantasy world or on your alien planet and how they affect your society. In Poul Anderson's 1954 science fiction story 'The Big Rain', the explorers visit a planet where it never stops raining, and they all end up going mad!

Many novels have used weather events as a backdrop. For example, the long, hot summer of 1976 in England gives a familiar world an unfamiliar twist in Maggie O'Farrell's 2013 novel *Instructions for a Heatwave.* Normal life continues but everything becomes slightly affected and unpredictable, and the heatwave is a catalyst for major life events. Ian McEwan also set *The Cement Garden* (1978) in the baking-hot summer of 1976. Similarly, in his 2001 novel *Atonement,* set in wartime, the suffocatingly hot weather helps build tension between the characters.

At the end of AS Byatt's 1990 novel *Possession,* the great storm of October 1987 in the southern UK strikes and a power cut plunges the characters back into a world like that of the 19th century.

John Steinbeck's 1939 novel *The Grapes of Wrath* is set during the dust bowl era of the 1930s and opens with a chilling description of the dust and wind.

Understanding pathetic fallacy

This term, coined by the art critic John Ruskin, refers to the tendency in much romantic poetry to ascribe human emotions to things in nature, such as referring to brooding clouds or laughing brooks. It later came to mean the way that writers use the weather to reflect the character's emotional state.

Wuthering Heights by Emily Brontë is full of instances of this technique. She frequently uses storms to mirror and foreshadow dramatic events. Lockwood is trapped in a snowstorm before the scene in which he has the nightmare, it's a wild and windy night when Mr Earnshaw dies, and a violent thunderstorm happens on the night when Heathcliff leaves Wuthering Heights.

Dickens also frequently uses the weather to give atmosphere to his novels. *Bleak House* opens with a description of the fog:

> Fog everywhere. Fog up the river, where it flows among green aits and meadows; fog down the river, where it rolls defiled among the tiers of shipping and the waterside pollutions of a great (and dirty) city. Fog on the Essex marshes, fog on the Kentish heights. Fog creeping into the cabooses of collier-brigs; fog lying out on the yards and hovering in the rigging of great ships; fog drooping on the gunwales of barges and small boats. Fog in the eyes and throats of ancient Greenwich pensioners, wheezing by the firesides of their wards; fog in the stem and bowl of the afternoon pipe of the wrathful skipper, down in his close cabin; fog cruelly pinching the toes and fingers of his shivering little 'prentice boy on deck. Chance people on the bridges peeping over the parapets into a nether sky of fog, with fog all round them, as if they were up in a balloon and hanging in the misty clouds.
>
> —*Charles Dickens (Bleak House, Penguin Classics 2003,*
> *first published 1852-1853)*

But the fog isn't just a physical phenomenon – it represents the impenetrable processes of the court of Chancery, which forms the subject of the novel:

> hard by Temple Bar, in Lincoln's Inn Hall, at the very heart of the fog, sits the Lord High Chancellor in his High Court of Chancery.
>
> —*Charles Dickens (Bleak House, Penguin Classics 2003,*
> *first published 1852-1853)*

See if you can use the weather to reflect a theme in your story, and create the right atmosphere. Write about some weather that represents a theme in your story. Describe the weather in great detail, as Dickens does.

'Is it morning already?' Time of day

You can use the time of day to help create the atmosphere for your scene. A bright, sunny morning feels very different to a dark, cloudy evening. As everyone knows, problems that seem insurmountable in the middle of the night often appear quite manageable in the bright light of morning.

Explore changing the time of day to see how the atmosphere changes and how your character will react:

✔ Write about your character at different times of the day. Is he a morning person or an evening person? When does he feel at his best and most productive?

✔ Write about your character making an important decision at different times: in the morning, the middle of the day, the evening and during the night. At which time does he make the best decision and why?

Using the seasons

The changing seasons of the year can be a useful way in fiction of showing the passing of time and also creating a mood for your story. If your novel starts in the spring and ends in winter, it has a very different feel to a novel that begins in winter and ends in spring.

If you're writing a short story, think about the best season of the year in which to set it. If you're writing a novel, see whether you can set it over an entire year. Think about the best season in which to start and end it.

Look at how Hemingway uses the autumn and rain as a symbol of death in his 1929 novel *A Farewell to Arms,* which begins and ends with the rain:

> In the fall when the rains came the leaves all fell from the chestnut trees and the branches were bare and the trunks black with rain. The vineyards were thin and bare-branched too and all the country wet and brown and dead with the autumn.

> —*Ernest Hemingway (A Farewell to Arms, Jonathan Cape, 1929)*

In contrast, the ending of John Williams's novel 1965 novel *Stoner* takes place in late spring or early summer. The dying man observes

> a richness and a sheen upon the leaves of the huge elm tree in his back yard . . . A thickness was in the air, a heaviness that crowded the sweet odours of grass and leaf and flower, mingling and holding them suspended. He breathed again, deeply; he heard the rasping of his breath and felt the sweetness of the summer gather in his lungs.

> —*John Williams (Stoner, Vintage Classics, 2012, first published 1965)*

The coming of summer represents the character's acceptance of his death and the fact that life goes on after he's gone.

Write the same scene taking place in each different season. Remember to describe the background and the weather. Notice how the weather and season influence the characters and what happens in the scene, and see which version you prefer.

The seasons in ancient Greece

The Greek myth of Persephone is a pre-scientific attempt to explain the seasons that has been much repeated in literature. Persephone, the daughter of Demeter, the goddess of the harvest, is taken to the Underworld by Hades. Demeter is so stricken with grief that she withdraws and the world is overcome with autumn and winter.

While in the underworld, Persephone eats 6 of the 12 pomegranate seeds given to her by Hades, and because of this she's forced to spend half the year, from then on, in the Underworld, which is why the world experiences autumn and winter. For the other half of the year Persephone is permitted to be in the mortal realm with Demeter, and as a result the world has spring and summer.

Characters have their own individual responses to the seasons. For example:

✔ A character's baby dies in spring. On the way to the funeral she sees masses of daffodils everywhere. For the rest of her life, she's unable to see daffodils in the spring without recalling her grief.

✔ A character is very pale skinned and hates the summer. In hot, sunny weather he has to plaster himself with sun cream and wear a wide-brimmed hat. He hates beaches and sunbathing and is always happy when autumn arrives.

Your character's response to the weather and the seasons can tell the reader a great deal about him. Write about your character's favourite season. Describe how he likes to spend his time. Write about him looking forward to the season, and then what happens to him when it comes.

Handling the Uncanny

One certain way to inject an atmosphere of tension and foreboding into a story is to introduce an element of the uncanny – the weird, strange or unsettling. Fiction has often ventured into this territory, probably because human beings aren't nearly as rational as they think they are and still believe in unseen forces. Children often believe that inanimate objects can have emotions and come to life, and these feelings persist into adulthood, so that many people feel squeamish about ripping up a photograph of a person or cutting the head off a doll.

When you write fiction, you're often allowing subconscious aspects of yourself to find expression, and as a result you may find uncanny events or objects creeping into your work. Real people and fictional characters often project onto external objects emotions they're feeling. How often have you cursed a 'beastly' table that you stubbed your toe on, or a 'stupid' lid that won't unscrew properly? In children's stories, and in horror fiction, objects frequently come to life.

Children also have feelings of being more powerful than they are, and that their hostile thoughts can injure someone. You can use this persistent feeling in your writing. Even as an adult, you may still find that if in a fit of temper you wish someone would die, you start worrying that he will, or that if you hear of a person sticking pins in an effigy of a person, something bad will happen. If something bad does happen to the target of your malevolent thoughts, you can feel responsible even though you know at one level that this is completely irrational. Perhaps it's a form of guilt for having bad thoughts.

In reverse, people often attribute to others feelings that they possess but don't want to admit to. According to Sigmund Freud, dread of the 'evil eye' – a malevolent look that many cultures believe able to cause injury or misfortune to the recipient – arises because people project onto others the envy they'd have felt in their place. So, someone who achieves success may feel that other people want to attack and bring him down. A sense of paranoia is very common in horror fiction.

The uncanny can also come out of things that aren't seen or understood properly – things glimpsed through a half-open door, shapes in the dark. The whole essence of the uncanny is that it's ambiguous. Look at a masterpiece such as Henry James's 1898 *The Turn of the Screw*. Possibly the apparent ghosts are real, but equally the stressed governess may be imagining everything.

It can be hard to create a feeling of the uncanny – the secret is usually to keep the reader thinking that there is a rational explanation up to the very last moment. Write a scene in which you create a feeling of the uncanny. Go slowly, stretch things out and keep them real until you reach a point where the character realises that he's seeing something impossible. Then let readers see how the character reacts.

Seeing ghosts

Even if you're not writing fiction in a specific horror or ghost story genre, you can still introduce an element of the uncanny to create tension. For example, a character may see a person in a crowd who looks like someone who died recently. In reality, this happens quite commonly, although the person concerned may feel as though he's going mad, or has seen a ghost, or even that the person is still alive.

Alternatively, a character may see a face at a window that frightens him. Later on, if you like, you can give a rational explanation . . . and then perhaps undermine that reassurance at the very end to unsettling effect.

Try out this exercise to play with your reader's expectations:

1. **Write a story or scene in which a character sees something he thinks is impossible.**

2. **Make sure there is a rational explanation that sets your character's mind at rest.**

3. **Now write about something else eerie happening that echoes the first incident and throws the character into confusion again.**

Dabbling in doubles

A common theme in fiction is that of the double; I don't mean a large drink (though there are many of those too!), but a character who's the same as the main character but also different. Sometimes the double takes on opposite aspects to the main character as in the *Strange Case of Dr Jekyll and Mr Hyde* by Robert Louis Stevenson, first published in 1886.

I'll never forget the bizarre experience of opening my Sunday colour supplement and seeing a photo of someone who looked uncannily like me! Think about how your character reacts to seeing a double. Now make him meet that double, or see him in a different context. You can make it clear there is something uncanny going on – or make it all coincidence:

1. **Write about your character seeing someone who looks like him, has the same name as him or who someone confuses with him.**

2. **Move on to write a second incident in which the identities of the two characters are further confused.**

Conjuring up curious coincidences

People often have a sense of the uncanny when coincidences occur. They can accept one or two coincidences, but if coincidences keep on building up, at a certain point people become frightened.

Try out this exercise to explore how your character reacts to a series of coincidences:

1. **Pick a number between 10 and 100.** Think of a specific day in the life of a character that you're working on in which that number appears – it can be the number of a house he visits, a seat number in the theatre, the number in the queue waiting for a doctor or whatever you like.

2. **Write about that number appearing again in something completely different.** Make sure your character notices the coincidence and thinks about how curious it is.

3. **Write about the number appearing for a third time.** How does the character now start to interpret the number? What meaning does he find and how does he feel?

Receiving visions and visitations

In the past, people believed that ghosts and spirits of the departed visit and communicate with the living. Nowadays, most people dismiss this as superstition – and yet if pressed many people claim to have seen or heard a ghost or the voice of someone they loved who died.

The appearance of a ghost or hallucination in fiction usually reveals to the character something he suspects but doesn't know, or something that will happen in the future.

Shakespeare's plays are full of ghosts: the ghost of Hamlet's father, who tells Hamlet that he was murdered, something Hamlet may have suspected, thus setting in train the events of the play; Banquo's ghost in *Macbeth*, who may represent Macbeth's guilt at what he has done.

In Charles Dickens's 1843 novel *A Christmas Carol,* the ghost of Christmas Yet to Come shows the miser Scrooge that his employee's son, Tiny Tim, is dead because his father can't afford to feed the family properly. He then shows Scrooge his own neglected grave. When Scrooge awakes, he's determined to change and becomes generous and compassionate.

In Susan Hill's 1983 book *The Woman in Black,* a mysterious ghost haunts a small English town. Her appearance always precedes the death of a child. The narrator, Kipps, uncovers the story of a woman, Jennet, who was forced to give up her child. At the end of the story, Kipps spots the ghost of the woman again, foreshadowing another terrible event.

Try out a ghost in your own story – you don't have to keep it if it doesn't fit – or you can make it happen when your character is under the influence of medication, drink or drugs! Write a scene in which a character sees a ghost. How does he react? What does it change about his attitude to life or to other characters in the story?

Creating suspense in your sleep: Dreams and premonitions

Dreams are a powerful device used in fiction to create atmosphere, to reveal characters' hopes and fears, and to foreshadow the future. Because we all have dreams every night – even though we may not remember them – we are all familiar with this strange alternate state where the rules of the everyday world do not apply.

Dreams and visions

Writers often use dreams in fiction to foreshadow events. In biblical and ancient times, the interpretation of dreams was considered an important art, because people thought that dreams could predict the future. This belief has persisted into modern times, and people still feel that their dreams can sometimes predict future events.

You can also undercut the expected associations, however, by depicting your character having dreams that show the opposite of what will happen; for example, a character dreaming of failing an exam and then finding that he has in fact passed. The stress and anxiety that a character feels causes him to dream about what he fears happening rather than what really will happen.

You encounter many examples of dreams foreshadowing events in Shakespeare, such as Calpurnia's dream in *Julius Caesar,* which goes:

> . . . she saw my statue,
>
> Which, like a fountain with an hundred spouts,
>
> Did run pure blood.
>
> —*William Shakespeare (Julius Caesar, Wordsworth Classics 1992,*
> *first performed 1599*

In Tolstoy's *Anna Karenina* (1877), Anna's fate is foreshadowed not only by the event at the train station (see the earlier section 'Owning omens'), but also by a series of dreams in which she sees the sinister figure of a railway worker tapping the joints between the carriages. These dreams reinforce the earlier event and prevent readers from forgetting it, as well as creating an uneasy feeling about what may happen. At the end of the novel, readers fully understand the significance of both the dreams and the event itself.

Dreams can foreshadow the future in the sense that they reveal what the character wants to happen. Readers know, therefore, that the person is likely to do everything to make the dreamed-of event happen. Dreams can also reveal the obstacles the character fears will get in the way, thus preparing readers for when these occur later in the story. I look at more aspects of dreams in fiction in Chapter 15.

Remember that in dreams, events do not follow one another logically and the strangest things can happen. Making use of these facts can help you to create the weird atmosphere of a dream, and disturb the character and the reader. Write a dream for your character that foreshadows something you have planned to happen in the future.

Premonitions

A *premonition* is a feeling of anxiety or apprehension, an intuition about what may happen in the future. To experience a vague feeling of anxiety is fairly common and often occurs because people know subconsciously that they should have done something more to prepare for a future event. However, some people have a very strong feeling that they shouldn't do something or that something bad is about to happen, which can be quite overwhelming and feel almost supernatural.

In your writing, you make any premonition powerful by having it triggered by something the character sees, hears or smells. Readers pay much more attention when the feeling is powerful, plus you retain narrative credibility because the character is far more likely to change his course of action if the feeling is strong.

Try this exercise to explore the power of a premonition. Remember to describe the atmosphere in detail and to use what the character sees to reflect his emotions:

1. **Write about a situation in which your character has a premonition.**

2. **Jump ahead: will what he fears happening come true, and what are the implications for your story if it does?**

Chapter 15

Managing Metaphors, Similes and Symbols

*M*etaphors, symbols and similes are all around you – in everyday con-versation, scientific enquiry and across the media, like (dare I say) a plague of locusts. But they're also valuable writing devices that allow you to communicate strong messages to your readers and create layers under the surface of your fiction, thus making your work more profound. So, without doubt, at some points in your writing you're sure to want to use these power-ful literary tools.

Metaphors, similes and symbols aren't easy to handle, though. If you use them obviously, they draw too much attention to themselves, and as the writer you can appear to be jumping up and shouting, 'Look how clever I am!' This is very off-putting: it takes readers out of the story and makes them look at the writing itself as words on a page, instead of enjoying the effect the story has on them. Clunky metaphors and similes and over-obvious symbols destroy the very effect you're trying to create.

If you employ these tools well, however, your readers don't notice that you're using them at all unless they go back and study the work in detail. Readers simply find a powerful picture in their minds or sense something running beneath the surface without quite knowing why. In this chapter I look at ways in which you can use these literary devices to give your fiction more depth.

Employing Metaphors to Deepen Your Writing

A *metaphor* is a figure of speech in which you talk of one thing in terms of another. Writing a good metaphor is all about finding the similarities in difference, and also avoiding the attraction of clichés. As I describe in this section, metaphors can be huge (controlling) or tiny (one word).

Successful metaphors conjure up mental pictures for readers that are vivid and sometimes unforgettable. Therefore, one great advantage is that metaphors can achieve concisely in a word or phrase what may otherwise take you many words or even sentences to convey.

Don't mix your metaphors! A *mixed metaphor* is when you combine two different metaphors in the same sentence, with often comical or nonsensical results, such as 'burning the midnight oil at both ends' or 'the headless chickens came home to roost with a bang'!

Entering the world of the metaphor

People use metaphors informally all the time when speaking and dealing with concepts: phrases such as 'time is money' or 'life is a journey' are common examples.

But more importantly, metaphors often determine the way that people think about the objects and events evoked. For example, 'time is money' implies that you don't want to 'waste' time because it's a scarce resource that may 'run out'. Thinking of life as a journey makes you feel as if you need to have a destination, and makes you fear that you may get lost on the way.

Often, common metaphors involve the senses:

- ✔ You can receive a 'warm' reception or be 'frozen' with fear.
- ✔ A task is 'hard' to achieve, things 'go smoothly' or people 'feel rough'.
- ✔ Remarks can be 'colourful', books receive a 'glowing' review and meetings produce a 'wide spectrum' of ideas.
- ✔ People have great 'taste' in art and things end on a 'sour' note.
- ✔ Some people have the 'sweet smell' of success but others 'reek' of failure.

Even scientists use metaphors to try to explain the world around them. They refer to light as travelling as a 'wave' or a 'particle', even though this model doesn't quite fit reality, to the 'solar system' model of the atom, and in medicine to the model of warfare, with diseases 'attacking' the body and the immune system 'defending' it.

The best way of coming up with good metaphors is to carry a notebook with you and jot down anything that occurs to you that can be a good comparison. Don't try to force metaphors – they either come or they don't. Look out for effective metaphors when you're reading, so that you can discover which ones work well and which ones don't.

Here are some metaphors I really like:

- ✔ 'She stared at a motorboat making white frothy scars on the chalky-blue sea' (Deborah Levy, *Swimming Home,* And Other Stories, 2011)

- ✔ 'All flesh is grass' (*King James Bible,* Isaiah 40:6)

- ✔ 'I am the vine, you are the branches' (*King James Bible,* John 15:5)

- ✔ 'The rain came down in long knitting needles' (Enid Bagnold, *National Velvet,* William Morrow & Company, 1935)

- ✔ 'The rock became an unbroken carpet of tiny, ecstatic spiders' (Tove Jansson, *The Summer Book,* translated by Thomas Teal, Random House, 1974)

Try out the following exercise that helps you to come up with some fresh and original metaphors. You may end up with some bizarre comparisons; the kettle of anguish or the sausage of happiness! Of course you'll only want to use the ones that work.

1. **Make two lists: the first of 12 random objects that you number from 1 to 12, and the second of 12 random emotions that you again number from 1 to 12.**

2. **Throw two dice and add up the total.**

3. **Select the object from the list of objects with the same number as the dice total.**

4. **Throw the two dice again, add up the total and select the relevant emotion from your list of emotions.**

5. **Pick the three weird comparisons you like best and work them into metaphors to include in a piece of your writing.**

Finding a controlling metaphor

A *controlling metaphor* is one you use throughout a whole work, usually an allegory, parable or fable.

Take these lines from Shakespeare's *As You Like It:*

> All the world's a stage,
>
> And all the men and women merely players;
>
> They have their exits and their entrances,
>
> And one man in his time plays many parts.
>
> —*William Shakespeare (As You Like It, Wordsworth Classics, 1993,*
> *First performed 1623)*

Shakespeare uses this extended metaphor to show how people are born and die and change throughout their lives, performing many roles. He uses the same metaphor again at the end of his tragedy *Macbeth,* in which his character compares life to 'a poor player, that struts and frets his hour upon the stage, and then is heard no more' *(Macbeth, Wordsworth Classics, 1992, first performed 1611).*

Whenever a piece of fiction uses a controlling metaphor like this one, the writer is suggesting two interpretations of the work:

- ✔ A literal one, which is obvious and usually applies to the characters in the story. In the *As You Like It* metaphor this is the level at which the character speaks the words in the play to make his point.

- ✔ A symbolic one, whose meaning is usually more profound and universal. In the Shakespeare quotes, this is a deeper reflection on the meaning of life.

Stretching out with allegories

An *allegory* is an extended metaphor that almost always has a moral or spiritual lesson in it.

An early example that's quite well known is Plato's allegory of the cave. He writes of a group of people who've lived chained to the wall of a cave in which they see shadows projected from the light of the fire. He uses this allegory to show that people's earthly lives are like these prisoners', whereas the true reality is as distant from them as the world outside the cave is to the prisoners.

Animal Farm by George Orwell (1945) is an example of a modern allegory. The animals on the farm overthrow the humans and take over. They start off with good intentions, stating that, 'All animals are equal.' But the pigs eventually take control, saying that, 'All animals are equal, but some are more equal than others.' The book is an allegory for what happened in Stalin's Russia, where communism started off with good intentions but became as terrible as the Tsarist regime that preceded it.

Similarly, Arthur Miller's 1953 play *The Crucible* about the witch trials in Salem in 1692 is an allegory of McCarthyism in the US in the 1950s, when the US government blacklisted alleged communists.

Write an outline for a story that's an allegory of a historical event. Make sure the main events are close parallels, but beware of following the actual event so slavishly that your story is cramped. Also, try not to be too heavy-handed with your allegory and make its meaning too obvious; a little ambiguity here can work wonders.

Parading your skill at parables, fables and fairy tales

A *parable* is an extended metaphor telling a story to make a particular point. Parables are most often associated with Jesus's teaching in the Bible. His parables are often hard to understand at first glance, because they tend to challenge or overturn people's usual way of understanding things.

In the parable of the workers in the vineyard (Matthew 20: 1–16), the landowner goes out early in the morning to hire labourers for his vineyard. He agrees to pay them 1 denarius a day (a very generous wage in those times). In the middle of the day, he sees men standing idle and hires them to work too, and later in the day, at the last minute, he hires more. When he comes to pay them, the people who've worked the whole day for 1 denarius are horrified when they find that everyone, including those who were hired late in the day, is being paid the same. They complain to the landowner, but he says that he's been fair to everyone in paying them what was promised.

This parable often irritates readers. People tend to think that it's extremely unfair and make comments like, 'There weren't unions in those days!' But they're missing the whole point of the parable, which is about the kingdom of heaven and unconditional love. The payment of a denarius isn't about receiving money, but is a symbol of God's love, which is equal for everyone.

Fables work in a similar way to parables, in that they make a moral point, except that they usually use animals, plants or mythical creatures, while parables usually involve people.

One of my favourite fables is a famous one by Aesop. An old man is riding his donkey, with his son walking along beside him. They pass people on the road who comment that the old man is mean to make his son walk, and so they swap over. The next people they encounter comment that the son is a lazy good-for-nothing to make his father walk, and so they both get on the donkey. They're then criticised for overburdening the poor donkey, and so they get off and walk, at which point they're mocked for not making use of the animal. The moral of the tale is that in trying to please everyone you end up pleasing no one, including yourself!

Fairy stories also work at more than one level. In his classic book *The Uses of Enchantment* (1976), child psychoanalyst Bruno Bettelheim interprets many fairy stories. He points out that talking animals are usually a symbol of the character's instinctive side. The sleeping beauty pricking her finger on the spindle is a symbol of menstruation – her parent's attempt to prevent this is an attempt to prevent their beloved only child from growing up.

Many contemporary authors rewrite ancient myths, fables and fairy stories, such as Angela Carter with *The Bloody Chamber and Other Stories* (1979) and Sara Maitland with *Far North and Other Dark Tales* (2008). Such stories that give a new spin to timeless tales are very satisfying to read.

Why not take a favourite fairy story, myth, fable or parable and re-tell it in a modern setting? For example, you could retell 'Rumpelstiltskin'. The princess, who has to spin straw into gold and escapes by guessing the strange creature's name, becomes a bank employee, who has to invest money to get enormous returns and guesses the right company to invest in with the help of a man she encounters on the street.

Avoiding metaphor clichés . . . like the plague!

A *cliché* is a metaphor that's so overused it's completely lost its effect. People sometimes refer to these as dead metaphors. For example, 'falling head over heels in love' no longer evokes the image of someone doing cartwheels, and 'fishing for compliments' doesn't make people think of dangling a fishing line in the water. Bank 'branches' don't make you picture trees, and 'running' for office doesn't make you imagine the candidate doing a sprint!

These phrases have become so much a part of everyday language that people can hardly do without them. As a result, no one can write without ever using a cliché. Don't become so paranoid about using clichés that your writing becomes self-conscious and over-wrought. Clichés can be useful because they're shorthand and everyone knows what they mean. Every writer uses some clichés in her writing, but as long as they're mixed in with new images as well it isn't a problem; just don't use nothing but clichés and weed out the most hackneyed ones.

Sometimes a word or an image catches on in the media and turns up everywhere, until people are completely sick to death of it. Look out for these words or phrases and avoid them when they get to the point of becoming clichés. A few years ago, everything was a 'double whammy' and last year everything was an 'omnishamble'.

Personifying: A heading that jumps for joy!

Personification is a kind of metaphor in which you give inanimate objects human emotions, feelings or intentions. People use personification all the time; for example, when saying that 'a house needs tender loving care', the 'table is waiting' for someone to put food on it or 'a kite is dancing gaily' in the wind.

Even science makes use of this technique when, for example, scientists say that gas 'seeks' an equilibrium or that genes are 'selfish'.

Personification is useful in fiction because it enables you to reflect the emotions the character feels in an indirect way. Instead of just writing that the character is joyful, when you say that she's looking at the trees dancing joyfully in the wind readers can feel her joy in what she sees and thinks, projected onto the world around her.

Write a passage of description from the point of view of one of your characters in which you personify an object in this way. You may want to write quite a few of these for practice, but in the final piece, don't go overboard; as with all these techniques, a little goes a long way!

Substituting Similes That Fit Like a Glove

With a *simile,* you say that something is *like* something else (such as 'cold as ice') rather than saying that it's the thing itself. When you use a simile, it's clear that you're comparing different things, but crucially that the things you're comparing aren't *exactly* the same and that limits apply to the comparison.

Appreciating the strength of a simile

Sometimes a simile can work as well as or better than a metaphor. (I discuss metaphors in the preceding sections.) You can reveal quite a lot about a character through what she compares something with.

A simile can be useful for revealing aspects of a character, because you can use it like a very short flashback into the past. For example, you can write that the day was 'as hot as the ones she remembered from her childhood in Singapore, when she used to stand sweating in the playground waiting for the school bus'. With a simple sentence like this, you can give an impression of the heat of the day and also a bit of biographical information about the character.

Write a simile like this the one in the preceding paragraph from the point of view of three of your characters while also giving information about their past.

Here are some similes I love:

- ✔ '[H]e looked about as inconspicuous as a tarantula on a slice of angel food' (Raymond Chandler, *Farewell, My Lovely,* Knopf, 1940)
- ✔ 'A sickly light, like yellow tinfoil, was slanting over the high walls into the jail yard' (George Orwell, 'A Hanging', *The Adelphi,* 1931)
- ✔ 'He paused, and swallowed convulsively, like a Pekingese taking a pill' (PG Wodehouse, *The Code of the Woosters,* Herbert Jenkins, 1938)
- ✔ 'A hot wind was blowing around my head, the strands of my hair lifting and swirling in it, like ink spilled in water' (Margaret Atwood, *The Blind Assassin,* McClelland and Stewart, 2000)
- ✔ 'Elderly American ladies leaning on their canes listed toward me like towers of Pisa' (Vladimir Nabokov, *Lolita,* Olympia Press, 1955)

Making the best use of similes

Here are some invaluable tips for using similes:

- ✔ Keep them short and direct.
- ✔ Make them appropriate for the style and subject matter. For example, if you're writing a tense crime novel, don't slip into flowery prose.
- ✔ Surprise your readers by using an unexpected image (see the examples in the preceding section).

✔ Appeal to all the senses – don't just use visual similes.

✔ Don't use too many similes together in the same place.

✔ Make sure that your simile makes sense and the two things you're comparing share some similarity!

Try this exercise to practise writing similes. It helps if you think of what an object reminds you of and whether it might remind your character of something different:

1. **Pick half a dozen objects in your home.** Make them as varied and interesting as possible.

2. **Describe each one using a simile.** You don't have to stop with just one – think of as many things each object is 'like' as possible!

Standing for Something with Symbols

A *symbol* is an object that represents an idea, a belief or another object. Symbols are slightly different from signs, which are simpler, more direct and easier to understand. Street signs, for example, are necessarily simple, with red standing for stop and a wavy line meaning a bend in the road. Signs usually have only one meaning, while symbols are normally far more complex with many layers of meaning. Symbols can work at two levels:

✔ **Universal level:** Although some symbols are considered to be universal, their meaning can vary in different cultures. Escaping such symbols is difficult because you've absorbed them (often unconsciously) from other works of literature, art and your own experience.

✔ **Personal level:** Some objects are symbolic only to the individual concerned, because they represent something specific that happened in the person's life. These symbols are often connected with people or places from a person's past.

For more on symbols, check out the nearby sidebar 'Symbolising through the ages'.

Symbolising through the ages

Symbols have been used in storytelling and literature since ancient times. Mythology rests on the use of symbol: a cup isn't just a cup but a symbol of the womb and therefore of fertility; a sword can be a phallic symbol (though often it's just a sword!); a wheel is a symbol of the cycle of life and death and rebirth. The cross is a Christian symbol but also a more ancient symbol in which the vertical axis divides good from evil and the horizontal axis divides earth from heaven.

Modern art often plays with symbolism, attempting to uncover or undermine its power. For example, Belgian surrealist artist René Magritte's clever painting (called, in English, *The Treachery of Images*) features a pipe with the words *'Ceci n'est pas une pipe'* ('This is not a pipe'). At first viewers are confused, until they realise that of course it isn't a pipe – it's a *painting* of a pipe (merely a representation)!

One of the founders of psychoanalysis, Carl Jung, writes in his book *Symbols of Transformation* (1956) that a symbol is unclear and has many meanings; it points to something that's not easily defined and therefore not fully known. This mysterious nature of symbols is what gives them their power.

Language itself depends on symbols, because words themselves stand for objects, actions and so on. Therefore, literature is symbolic, which means that its meaning isn't simple or singular. The nature of symbols means that literature has what's sometimes called *surplus meaning:* exhausting or completely explaining the meaning of a piece of literature is impossible. Another reading or another reader can always produce new meanings or new shades of meaning (which is a boon to university humanities departments!).

Using universal symbols

Here, in no particular order, are some common or universal symbols:

- An egg
- A ring
- A butterfly
- A stone
- A snake
- A mirror
- The sea
- A mountain
- A key
- A heart

Write down a list of all the words that occur to you for each object in this list. Think of all the associations that the objects have for you, both good and bad. For example, for 'egg' I'd write: warm, white and yellow, Easter, chocolate, chicken, yolk, crack, fragile, broken, fried, omelette, sticky, painted, shell, and boiled egg and soldiers. For 'ring', I'd write: gold, wedding band, engagement, diamond, eternity, circle, happiness, bondage, slavery, and the One Ring.

Now write a scene or story that includes one of these symbolic objects. Make sure you include all the different levels of meaning.

Don't be tempted to overdo the use of symbols or make them too obvious. Symbols work best when they naturally occur in a story, so that readers may not realise their significance until later.

Here's an example of symbolism in a modern novel to illustrate what I mean. It helps if you read the passage twice, once just to enjoy it, and then again to think about any possible symbols in it:

> About half way between West Egg and New York the motor road hastily joins the railroad and runs beside it for a quarter of a mile, so as to shrink away from a certain desolate area of land. This is a valley of ashes – a fantastic farm where ashes grow like wheat into ridges and hills and grotesque gardens; where ashes take the forms of houses and chimneys and rising smoke and, finally, with a transcendent effort, of men who move dimly and already crumbling through the powdery air. Occasionally a line of gray cars crawls along an invisible track, gives out a ghastly creak, and comes to rest, and immediately the ash-gray men swarm up with leaden spades and stir up an impenetrable cloud, which screens their obscure operations from your sight.
>
> But above the gray land and the spasms of bleak dust which drift endlessly over it, you perceive, after a moment, the eyes of Doctor T. J. Eckleburg. The eyes of Doctor T. J. Eckleburg are blue and gigantic – their irises are one yard high. They look out of no face, but, instead, from a pair of enormous yellow spectacles which pass over a nonexistent nose. Evidently some wild wag of an oculist set them there to fatten his practice in the borough of Queens, and then sank down himself into eternal blindness, or forgot them and moved away. But his eyes, dimmed a little by many paintless days, under sun and rain, brood on over the solemn dumping ground.
>
> —*F Scott Fitzgerald (The Great Gatsby, Penguin Modern Classics, 2000,
> first published 1925)*

Many people see the eyes of Eckleburg as the eyes of God or of judgement. Because the eyes look out from no face they seem to represent the death of God, or at least of spiritual values, in the era Fitzgerald is writing about. Here are some clues that suggest this interpretation:

✔ A general rule of writing says not to include something in fiction unless it does something in the story; so symbolic importance is likely to apply to these eyes, which are mentioned several times. Later on, the relationship to God becomes more explicit when, underneath the gaze of these sightless eyes, Wilson says, 'God knows what you've been doing.' Also, I think that the valley of ashes is like the antithesis of the Garden of Eden, the paradise of the natural world that humans inherited and that industrialisation has at least partly destroyed.

✔ Two adjectives in this passage, 'transcendent' and 'eternal', are words usually used only in describing the divine. Their use, gently slipped in by Fitzgerald so that you may not notice them at first, inevitably makes you think subliminally of God. Also, the fact that the eyes are on a billboard advertising an optician prompts the thought that God has been replaced with capitalism.

The whole point is that you can enjoy the novel without noticing these things. Simply taking this passage as an example of atmospheric description (something I discuss in detail in Chapter 14) is fine. The symbols probably have an effect on you without you realising it. If you do become aware of them, however, you understand what a complex and profound work of fiction *The Great Gatsby* is, and you grasp the message of the novel more fully.

Investigating individual symbols

Sometimes in a piece of fiction you want to use an object that has a particular meaning for a character. Perhaps an object belonged to a character's grandmother and came from the house where the character spent her holidays as a child, and so this object represents the grandmother's affection and the carefree time of youth.

In Orson Welles's famous film *Citizen Kane* (1941), the character dies with the enigmatic word 'rosebud' on his lips. Welles later reveals that Rosebud was the trade name of the little sled Kane was playing with on the day when he was taken away from his home and his mother. The sled represents the safety of childhood and the love of his mother.

Try out this exercise to explore how you can use a personal symbol in your writing to help add depth to your character:

1. **Think of something that has individual symbolic importance for your character.** This could be an object, perhaps relating to a particular period in your character's life or a special character who gave it to her.

2. **Write about three occasions where this object appears in your story.**
These could include a memory, a time when the character sees or touches the object, and a time when the character wants or needs it.

Dreaming up some dream symbolism

You seldom dream directly about what's on your mind; instead your brain seems to need to protect you by concealing things in symbolic form. This process leads many people to see dreams as being full of symbols that can be interpreted and their meaning uncovered.

Dreams are useful in fiction because they're an effective way of revealing to readers aspects of the character that the person herself isn't aware of. You can use dreams to reveal anxieties, fears, desires and hopes, and they can create a powerful atmosphere in a story. A nightmare can produce a feeling of unease, and a beautiful dream can add tension by making readers wonder whether any of the character's dreams will be fulfilled.

Dreams can reveal to readers things that may have been and therefore make what happens even more painful. For instance, a character may dream of escape before being executed, or of being with her beloved before they are separated.

In George Orwell's *Nineteen Eighty-Four* (1949), Winston has several significant dreams: of the past and his guilt about what happened to his family, and of freedom, which helps motivate him to struggle against Big Brother. His dreams give a glimpse into his feelings and motivations in a world where he isn't allowed to experience these things. They show that some areas of human consciousness just can't be controlled.

Try this exercise to help you write a dream. I have tried to remove your conscious control of the exercise, just as you can't control a dream:

1. **Write about a character's dream.**

2. **Open a dictionary at random halfway through writing the dream, and introduce the first object that you encounter into your dream.**

3. **Make the dream change: if it's a pleasant dream, introduce something frightening; if it's a nightmare, change the dream into something less alarming.**

Dreams have a particular quality all of their own. Things that appear in dreams don't have to obey the natural laws. Consider using some of the following bizarre features in your writing:

- ✔ Broken objects can put themselves back together again.
- ✔ Dead people can return to life.
- ✔ People can fly, breathe underwater and transform themselves from one thing into another.
- ✔ Someone can look like one person, although you know in the dream that she's really someone else.

Don't overwrite your dreams or include too many of them. Keep them short and always make clear when a character is going into a dream and coming out of it again. Nothing is worse than reading a strange passage in a novel and thinking that you've suddenly been transported into a different genre before the character suddenly wakes up and you're told she was dreaming!

Keep a notebook by your bed and write down your dreams when you wake up. If you don't dream much, you'll probably find this exercise helps you to remember and record your dreams.

As you get used to recording your own dreams, you'll usually find it easier to write suitable dreams for your characters. Your mind is no doubt thinking of your writing project while you're asleep, and so sometimes your dreams turn out to be highly suitable!

Meanings of dreams

Psychoanalysis suggests that, when interpreted, certain dreams reveal hidden or repressed aspects of people. (Freud describes dreams as 'the royal road to the unconscious'.) In fact, some people believe that dreams can be interpreted to reveal *specific* meanings.

Whether you believe that dreams have meanings or not doesn't matter – your characters can believe (or disbelieve) in these meanings, which allows you to use dreams to reveal character or drive actions:

Common dream symbols

Some people think that certain items contain specific symbolic meanings. Try these out in your fictional dreams:

- ✔ **Animals:** Represent your habits or the unconscious part of your mind. Being chased by an animal may represent some hidden aggression. The type of animal you dream of gives you clues as to what the dream means.

✔ **Babies:** Mean a new start. The baby can represent an innocent part of yourself or that you need to be loved and cared for.

✔ **Food:** Represents all kinds of nourishment and can reveal that you may be 'hungry' for new information and insights. Different kinds of food can be symbolic: if you dream of spices, it may mean your life needs spicing up; an apple may mean temptation.

✔ **Houses:** Represent your mind. Different levels or rooms may relate to difference aspects of yourself. The basement often represents what's been neglected – things you aren't aware of in your waking life or your conscious mind. Bedrooms often relate to intimate thoughts and feelings. The higher levels of the house represent your intellect (so I hope you don't dream of a dusty attic full of nesting pigeons).

✔ **People:** Don't represent the people themselves, but different aspects of yourself.

✔ **Vehicles:** Represent ways of getting to your destination, though not necessarily in a literal way. The kind of vehicle you dream of and kind of journey you experience may indicate the degree of control that you feel you have and the obstacles you may face.

Delving into the deepest of meanings

Religions have used symbolic objects and actions to make sense of human experience since the first civilisations. Even today, as Western society becomes more secular, these symbols remain powerful. Many thinkers believe that symbols put people in touch with the spiritual part of themselves. Don't worry, I'm not getting all new-agey and mystical. But humans certainly don't understand every aspect of themselves and the world, and the human psyche can't (at least not yet!) be explained entirely in factual, scientific terms.

Writing fiction can be a way of creating meaning in an often chaotic and frightening world. Fiction obeys a pattern, and everything that happens in a story has a purpose and a meaning, just as people would like to see their lives having a purpose and a meaning. Fiction often has a moral – by identifying with a character, readers see and experience what making a certain choice or action would be like and can therefore avoid it. Using symbols in fiction helps us to connect with feelings of meaning and purpose.

Dostoyevsky, in *Crime and Punishment* (1866), shows what committing a murder is likely to be like, and the subsequent psychological effects. Dickens made people identify with the plight of the poor (particularly children) in Victorian England and thus brought about social and legal change. To some extent this tendency fell out of fashion for a time, as I discuss in the nearby sidebar 'Cynical or realistic? You decide'.

Cynical or realistic? You decide

Some contemporary writers react against what they see as moralising in literature (and the presumption that an author can lecture readers or change the world), creating instead a world-weary or even cynical view in which characters don't suffer pangs of guilt when they do something dreadful or where plot events happen at random. At first, these experiments had their impact because they subverted what the audience expected. In Samuel Beckett's theatrical masterpiece *Waiting for Godot* (1952), for example, early audiences were horrified that Godot never appeared! (Godot's name, of course, may well be symbolic, standing for an absent God (of the Old Testament – OT – perhaps), although Beckett claims it was simply a name he heard on a plane.)

Many people react with distaste or confusion to the postmodern, distanced kind of fiction. They don't want to read about people getting away with terrible deeds, even if that seems to happen in life. Most readers want to see generous acts in some way rewarded. Even though society and knowledge have changed hugely over the past centuries, human nature has probably altered little since ancient times; that's why the old stories are still read and re-read.

Allowing yourself to use symbols in your writing is the surest way to connect readers with the deeper, often hidden aspects of themselves, and to make a piece of fiction meaningful. Don't worry about whether you understand why symbols work – just trust that they do.

 Good fiction is symbolic not because the writer deliberately and self-consciously places symbols in it, but because symbols inevitably arise in your mind when you are deeply immersed in your writing. Writing description is the best way to allow this process to happen.

 Whenever you get stuck with your writing, write some passages of description. They may not stay in your final story – you may keep just a sentence or two – but almost inevitably something that acts as a symbol comes up and starts your story moving forwards again.

Chapter 16

Describing the Ineffable: Saying What Can't Be Said

I'm sure that you sometimes find yourself lost for words when talking to someone – even the most articulate person has that experience from time to time. People understand and it's quite acceptable. But for an author, it isn't. As a writer your job is to be able to find the necessary words, phrases and techniques to communicate anything, however complex, mysterious or personal. In fact, readers often turn to literature for that very reason: to read about and understand something that they can't put into words themselves.

At some point you're sure to find yourself unable to express what you want in plain prose. Perhaps the feelings you want to write about are too powerful or too subtle to explain – in other words, they're *ineffable*.

This problem isn't because you aren't a good enough writer or lack a large enough vocabulary. It's to do with the nature of language and the fact that humans don't wholly understand the world in which they live.

In this chapter I look at the tools writers use to communicate the ineffable, such as using the sound of language rather than its literal sense and employing techniques such as paradox and ambiguity that rely on their inherent impossibility for their effect.

Handling the Ineffable: When Words Fail

The following is a famous quote, but I don't agree with it. If Wittgenstein's words were true, many of the world's greatest works of literature would never have been written down!

> One must remain silent about what one cannot speak of.
>
> —*Ludwig Wittgenstein (Tractatus Logico-Philosophicus, translated Jeremy Hamand, 2014, first published in W Ostwald's Annalen der Naturphilosophie in 1921)*

The writer's art and perhaps even duty is to find ways to create as close an impression of experience as possible. In doing so, authors encounter a basic problem of all human experience: how do they know that their experience of something is the same as someone else's?

For example, when I perceive the colour red, I can't ever be certain sure that I'm experiencing the same colour as you. When I hear a particular sound, I can't be sure that you hear it the same way. And I don't know whether we experience the exact same sensory impression of physical things such as the stickiness of glue or the roughness of sandpaper. In some instances, people clearly don't have the same experience and reaction – I personally can't stand the sound of chalk squeaking on a blackboard, but it doesn't seem to bother some people. I also hate the taste of strawberry ice-cream or yoghurt (yuck!), but lots of people seem to love it.

In this section I examine this problem and the type of things I'm talking about, from the most down-to-earth experiences (like the disgusting nature of strawberry flavour!) to the highest concerns of life and death. I describe how literature can help you take the first hesitant steps towards conveying the ineffable.

Defining the difficulties of the inexpressible

In a sense, some of people's deepest experiences are the most personal but also the most common and universal. People can't describe their births and deaths, because they can't remember the first and won't be alive to relate the second. Other aspects of life in this regard are powerful emotions such as love or anger, religious experiences such as ecstasy or a feeling of oneness, and psychedelic or near-death experiences.

Conveying such experiences sounds like an insurmountable problem, but in fact literature is great at using language to express what can't be put into words. Writers have wrestled with this problem for centuries, finding literary devices to convey the things that seem impossible to convey with ordinary language – devices such as symbolism, metaphor and paradox. (For more on paradoxes, see the later section 'Playing with paradox'.)

Attempting to communicate subjective experiences

Here's something you may find helpful when you're trying to express the inexpressible in your writing. Philosophers use the term *qualia* to mean individual instances of conscious, subjective experience. These are by their nature impossible to communicate directly, but with skill and practice, you can communicate them in writing to give the reader the exact impression you wanted to convey.

When writers use a particularly vivid image, readers sometimes feel the experience as if it's happening to them. They may think, yes, that's exactly what it feels like to wade through thick mud, or to hear bells ringing in the distance on a frosty morning, or to feel the hot sun on your skin. More deeply, they may recall sharply what being in love for the first time was like or their feelings when they first realised that one day they would die.

As the preceding examples show, you can get an idea about something you haven't experienced by reading descriptions of it. A book can give you a good idea of what standing on top of Mount Everest is like, or crossing the Gobi desert or landing on the planet Mars. Mostly, you understand these experiences in terms of what you already know: for example, experiences of heat and cold and sand and snow in other contexts help you here.

Try out ways of describing something exactly. Think carefully about the words you use, and afterwards use a thesaurus to see if you can find more exact words than the ones you first used:

1. **Make a list of individual qualia.**

2. **Describe them in as much detail as you can.**

Consider for a moment the specific example of a scientist who knows everything possible about light and colour, such as the exact wavelength of red light and how it's transmitted. Yet he's blind and can never know what red actually *looks* like. Imagine that this scientist then has an operation that gives him sight. How does he interpret what he sees? Does all his knowledge about colour make any difference to his experience of seeing the colour red for the first time?

If you invent a world that's completely different from this one, you have no alternative but to describe it from scratch, step by step, which can be cumbersome or difficult. For this reason, most fantasy and science fiction writers make their worlds not too dissimilar from our own.

Revealing the Mysterious with Literary Devices

In poetry and prose, many literary devices are at your disposal to help you render as closely as possible various kinds of ineffable experience.

Defamiliarising to see the world anew

You can create a powerful effect in a piece of writing by stepping back and describing an everyday object as if you've never seen it before. In your day-to-day life, you become so used to looking at familiar objects that you don't always see them as they really are.

The purpose of *defamiliarisation* is to make people see and hear the world afresh, as if for the first time. This technique can challenge their way of perceiving the world and provide new insights into human perception and behaviour.

One example of defamiliarisation is when you've been away from home for a long time and come back to find that everything is the same yet different. A teenager who's been travelling for a year or at college finds that his previously beloved objects in his bedroom suddenly seem shabby and irrelevant. His parents may also seem different – older perhaps, and more vulnerable.

Writers use defamiliarisation deliberately to convey experiences we may not have had in a way that makes us identify with them. Tolstoy uses it to good effect in his 1886 story *Kholstomer,* narrated in part from the point of view of a horse, making us empathise with the animal. Modern writers have also used unusual narrators in order to see the world in a new way, such as in Mark Haddon's *The Curious Incident of the Dog in the Night-time,* 2003, whose narrator is a 15-year-old boy with Asperger's syndrome. The boy sees details in things that most people ignore, such as the pattern of the material on the seats on the underground trains, and we understand what it must be like to see the world as he does.

Who's that man?

An example of defamiliarisation in my own life is when I spent a month travelling in Thailand and Burma. I'd visited innumerable Buddhist temples with stone or gilded images of the Buddha sitting in meditation, reclining or standing. Eventually, in Mandalay, I came across a strange Christian church. On the wall were depicted the seven deadly sins, which seemed bizarre and monstrous. Then I saw a statue of a strange man with a beard and a flaming heart on his chest reaching out his hand in exactly the same gesture as the Buddha I'd just seen on Mandalay Hill. I stared at this image for a few seconds before I realised with a jolt that I was looking at an image of Christ. Immediately, the image became familiar and no longer alarming.

This taught me something that I've never forgotten: aspects of my own culture can look as foreign to people from other cultures as theirs can do to me.

Defamiliarisation is also often used in science fiction. By describing an alien race or civilisation, science-fiction writers are often describing aspects of human society, but in a different context to make people re-evaluate them.

In *Gulliver's Travels* (1726), Jonathan Swift uses the technique of defamiliarisation for comic and satirical effect. When Gulliver finds himself among the gigantic Brobdingnagians, he comes face to face with a gigantic breast, which he perceives to be covered in 'spots, pimples and freckles'. He finds the sight nauseating instead of beautiful.

Try this exercise in defamiliarisation. Remember that you are trying to convey an ordinary experience in a new way so the reader will see it afresh:

✔ Write about an object, describing it as if you or the character have never seen it before.

✔ Write about an everyday scene as if you are:

- A small child

- An animal

- A visitor from overseas

- An alien from another planet

Experimenting with the rhythm of sentences

The rhythm of sentences can create very powerful effects. Long, meandering sentences produce an impression of tranquillity and leisure. Short, abrupt sentences create a feeling of urgency and pace. The direct sound of the sentences is what creates an effect on readers, regardless of the actual words used.

Look at the difference between these two sentences:

> He walked into the room and looked around, wondering if anyone was there and whether he might be waiting here for hours.

> He walked into the room. He looked around. Was anyone there? He might be waiting for hours.

In the first sentence we have an impression of spaciousness and leisure, in the second of urgency and haste. Our emotions are directly affected by the long and short sentences.

You can keep sentences fairly flat and plain, or you can play with rhythm, having your sentences build to a crescendo and then fade away, as with a piece of music. Of course, you usually match the rhythm of the sentences to your subject matter – but you can create a shock by occasionally doing the opposite.

Always read your work aloud to see how it sounds. You can tell when your mouth and tongue trip up over awkward combinations of words, or when the prose flows smoothly.

Listening to the sounds of words

How a word sounds in poetry and fiction can be as important as its meaning. People associate certain sounds with softness and others with hardness. Words with 's', 'h' and 'sh' sound soft, while words with 'b', 'k' and 't' sound hard. Long vowel sounds also create an impression of softness, while short vowels give an impression of hardness.

You can consciously use the sounds of words to create an impression of a feeling without stating anything explicitly to the readers. Here are some of the devices you can try:

- ✔ **Alliteration:** The repeated use of words with the same consonant at the beginning, such as in the description of the sacred river in Coleridge's famous 1816 poem 'Kubla Khan': 'Five miles meandering with a mazy motion'.

- ✔ **Assonance:** The same vowel sounds are repeated in the same phrase. 'Lolita, light of my life, fire of my loins' from the beginning of Vladimir Nabokov's 1955 *Lolita* uses the 'i' sound repeatedly (with some alliteration too!).

- ✔ **Consonance:** The same consonants are repeated in words close to one another. John Updike uses consonance in his 1964 poem 'Player Piano', where he writes 'Chuckling, they knuckle the keys'.

- ✔ **Dissonance:** When word sounds clash and are awkward to say, such as 'crunched splints' or 'drop print clashes'.

- ✔ **Onomatopoeia:** The use of words that have a similar sound to the thing that produces the sound. For example, the moo of cows, the baa of sheep, the tweet of a bird, the tick-tock of a clock, the beep of a horn, the plop of a frog jumping into a pond.

- ✔ **Sibilance:** The use of hissing sounds at the beginning or within words: 'Sing a Song of Sixpence' is a good example.

'Fresh-firecoal chestnut-falls' from the Gerard Manley Hopkins poem 'Pied Beauty', written in 1877, uses alliteration, consonance, assonance and dissonance in one brief phrase! The poet used many literary devices to convey mysterious religious experiences and images.

All the devices in this section can be used to create emotions and sensations in the reader that go far beyond the meaning of the words themselves. Try this for yourself in the following exercise:

1. **Play around with the techniques in this section, writing sentences that use some or all of these devices.**

2. **See whether you can use any of these sentences in a story or scene that you're writing.**

Using the Contradictory to Communicate the Ineffable

In this section I describe two techniques that rely on their inherent impossibility to help readers approach hard-to-convey experiences.

Playing with paradox

A *paradox* is a statement that contradicts itself. Paradoxes can be useful, because they reveal flaws in the way that people think. Scientists and mathematicians use apparent paradoxes to find solutions to knotty problems and refine their thinking.

A good example of a simple paradox is this sentence: 'This sentence is false.' Think about it! If the sentence *is* false then it must be true, but it can't be true or it wouldn't be false!

Paradoxes have been used in religious language to try to force people beyond their assumptions and into a new way of thinking. Zen Buddhism uses paradoxical sentences called *koans,* such as 'Listen to the sound of one hand clapping'. Their purpose is to force people beyond their limited conceptions and to destroy the naive and inadequate flaws in their thinking. Koans are intended to 'wake us up'.

Paradoxes have been used in Christianity too. Think of a mother who's a virgin and a being who's both man and God. The Christian mystics also used paradoxical language to try to convey their experience of God. For example, the apostle Paul uses paradox when he writes, 'When I am weak, then I am strong' (*King James Bible,* 2 Corinthians 12:10). The basic claim in all religions that everything is one is, in itself, a paradox.

An *oxymoron* is a particular kind of paradox, when two opposing words are placed together, such as the 'living dead' or a 'deafening silence'. It's often used in poetry to give a powerful effect.

Examples of oxymorons occur in Shakespeare, where, in *Romeo and Juliet,* Romeo refers to parting as 'such such sweet sorrow'. Henry Vaughan's 17th-century mystical poem 'The Night' includes the line 'There is in God, some say, a deep but dazzling darkness . . . '. Wilfred Owen's poem 'The Send-Off' (1918) refers to soldiers leaving for the front line, who 'lined the train with faces grimly gay'.

These juxtapositions of opposites work because they're close to people's lived experience. Extreme joy can make you weep just as much as great sorrow, and sometimes knowing whether you're laughing or crying can be difficult. Athletes know that if you push through the pain barrier you can feel extreme elation. Paradoxes can also be profoundly truthful, as in Socrates's famous saying, 'The more you know, the less you know.'

Paradoxes reveal flaws in our conception of the universe and have often been explored in science fiction. Many of these are to do with the logistics of time travel. One paradox is known as the grandfather paradox – when you go back in time and kill your grandfather, which of course means that you'd never have been born!

Creating oxymorons and paradoxes is not easy. Have a go here to help you to develop this skill:

- ✔ Write a list of six oxymorons and see whether you can use any of them in your fiction.

- ✔ Write about a paradox. What does it mean for your characters? Does it give them a new insight?

Creating ambiguity

Generally, you try to avoid ambiguity in fiction. Often a piece of writing is ambiguous because the writer has simply failed to make clear to readers what's happening. You can all too easily refer to more than one character as 'he' when describing a scene, thus not being clear who's speaking or acting. Another form of unwanted ambiguity is a sentence that's capable of two interpretations, such as 'Jeremy enjoyed painting his models in the nude'.

Ambiguity can also creep in when you don't describe situations in enough detail. For example, in one scene written by a student of mine, two characters were talking, and someone came down the aisle and sat down near them. Because the location wasn't made clear, some of the class thought the characters were in a church waiting for a ceremony to begin, others that they were sitting in a cinema, and others still imagined them in a large concert hall. In fact, the characters were on the top deck of a bus!

Sometimes, however, intentional ambiguity in a piece of writing can be a powerful technique. When you leave something undetermined, you open up multiple possible meanings.

In Christos Tsiolkas's 2008 novel *The Slap,* various characters react to the same event in different ways. A man slaps a misbehaving child at a barbecue on a late-summer afternoon. The force with which the child is struck is deliberately left unclear. As a result, readers are able to empathise with different characters, depending on how hard they think the man hit the child.

You can also make use of ambiguity to create a strange or even other-worldly atmosphere. Many works of fiction leave unclear whether a character is hallucinating or imagining a ghost or supernatural being, or whether the figure is really present – as in Henry James's classic story *The Turn of the Screw* (1898).

You can also make your characters' motivations ambiguous – people don't always understand what they feel or why they decide to do something. In this sense, ambiguity in fiction is what makes your characters believably lifelike. In reality, people often don't know what goes on inside the head of another human being; fiction where motivation is too obvious always seems contrived.

Sometimes a work of literature or a film deliberately doesn't give readers or viewers enough information to make sense of the story. In prose, Shirley Jackson's 1949 short story 'The Daemon Lover' seems to be about a woman who's stood up on her wedding day. Then you begin to think, from other people's reactions, that the woman may have imagined her fiancé. In film, David Lynch's *Mulholland Drive* (2001) and Alain Resnais's *Last Year in Marienbad* (1961) create a spooky feeling because you aren't sure what's happening.

If you're tempted to try this approach, bear in mind that it's really hard to pull it off without alienating your audience. If you don't do it well, more often than not the reader or viewer will simply be left confused – and irritated.

You can also use ambiguity effectively at the end of a piece of fiction. In her 1853 novel *Villette,* Charlotte Brontë deliberately leaves the ending ambiguous. Although Lucy says that she wants to allow readers to imagine a happy ending, she gives a strong hint that M Paul's ship was destroyed by a storm during his return journey from the West Indies. A good recent example of an ambiguous ending is that in Mohsin Hamid's novel *The Reluctant Fundamentalist* (2007). I look more at endings in Chapter 23.

Now is the time to try out an exercise in ambiguity. Write a scene that has two possible interpretations. Make sure that both are possible – for example, a character hears a sound in the night and sees a shadow on the stairs. Make it clear that your character thinks he has seen a ghost, but also that there's a perfectly reasonable alternative, such as that there was a burglar.

You may need to show the piece to several people and ask them what they think. Ideally, you want half of them to think it's a ghost, and half a burglar!

Part IV
Developing Your Plot and Structure

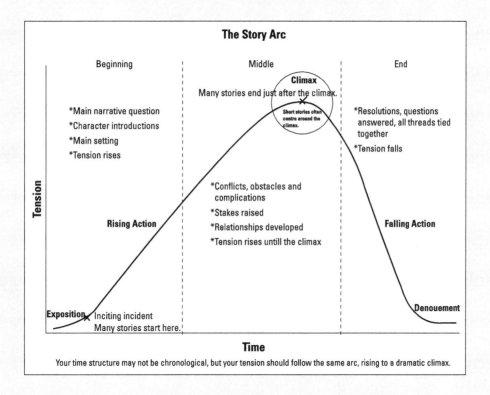

The Story Arc

Beginning | Middle | End

Climax
Many stories end just after the climax.

Short stories often centre around the climax.

*Main narrative question
*Character introductions
*Main setting
*Tension rises

*Resolutions, questions answered, all threads tied together
*Tension falls

Tension

*Conflicts, obstacles and complications
*Stakes raised
*Relationships developed
*Tension rises untill the climax

Rising Action

Falling Action

Denouement

Exposition Inciting incident
Many stories start here.

Time

Your time structure may not be chronological, but your tension should follow the same arc, rising to a dramatic climax.

Find more information on generating your plot and structure at www.dummies.com/
extras/creativewritingexercises.

In this part . . .

- ✔ Find an appropriate overall structure and timeline to whatever kind of story you're writing. Structuring and plotting your story are essential to its success.

- ✔ Strengthen your skills to identify the best way to begin, work out how to build suspense and complicate and expand the narrative, write a thrilling climax and end the story with a satisfying conclusion.

- ✔ Get taken step by step through the plotting process and look at all the different ways you can keep readers hooked – until you're ready to let them go!

Chapter 17

Writing a Gripping Opening

*O*ften people say to me, 'I've got a great idea for a story, but I don't know where to begin.' The answer is simple: just start writing. Don't worry about whether you're writing the beginning of your tale or not – just start writing about something that interests you, and feel confident that you'll find the best place to begin the story later.

When you do start producing your opening lines, you're sure to find this chapter invaluable. I lead you into the task and describe several types of opening that have kicked off some classic novels.

Don't be too intimidated by the need to produce a perfect opening that blows your readers' minds. In the end, the opening line has only one purpose: to make readers want to read the next line . . . and then the line after that . . . and so on.

Introducing the Art of the Opening

An old German proverb says that 'all beginnings are difficult'. The more you sit around musing about the beginning, the harder it becomes.

Most opening lines or paragraphs of books aren't the first lines the author produces. Many writers find that they need to write themselves into their stories before they know where the tale starts. Sometimes the opening lines are the very last words the author writes!

Starting somewhere, anywhere

You do have to write your opening at some point. So, here's a list of all the things a good opening has to do. You don't have to do them all in the first line, but maybe in the first paragraph and definitely on the first page:

- ✔ **Introduce the characters:** By name if you're writing in the third person, or by individual voice if in the first person (check out Chapter 8 for more on voices and point-of-view narration).
- ✔ **Set the scene – the time and the place:** You can do so simply with a place and date, or by describing the scene.
- ✔ **Create a mood:** You create atmosphere by description, but also by style, length of sentences and choice of vocabulary.
- ✔ **Describe an action or situation – including dialogue if needed:** The more dramatic, the more arresting your opening is likely to be.
- ✔ **Ask a question:** Don't try to give too much information – provide enough to orientate readers in the story, but leave questions to entice them to read on.

Your readers may know nothing about the tale they're about to read – except the title and a brief summary. Your duty is to help them into the world of the story. Don't hold back too much or they become confused, but don't bombard them with information that they're unable to take in. When in doubt, clarity is the best policy!

Knowing which kind of opening is going to suit your story is difficult. The best way to find out is to have a go at several different types (like the ones I describe in the later 'Discovering Openings from the Greats' section).

In this exercise, think of the situation that kicks off your story and then write four different kinds of opening for it:

- ✔ A piece of description
- ✔ An action
- ✔ A dialogue
- ✔ A philosophical statement

Write a whole page. Put it aside and then return to it later and have another go. If it helps, find one of the books I quote from in the later section 'Discovering Openings from the Greats' that you really like the sound of and imitate the way the prose works (not the subject matter). Take your own characters and your own situation and write the opening in that style.

Now select a kind of opening you don't like from the later section, and write in that style too. You may be surprised: sometimes this one works better than the one you thought you'd like, perhaps because it forces you to think extra carefully and be more creative.

Just start somewhere. I can't emphasise this enough, so I say it again: don't let your search for the perfect opening hold you up. You don't truly know where your story begins until you've finished it. You can always come back and change the beginning later. So just get writing!

Locating a great place to start

If you're not sure where to begin your story, try to think of the event that causes the main action to happen. If your character is going to fall in love, she needs to meet the person she'll fall for. Therefore, a good place to begin the story is their first meeting.

If you don't want to give too much away too early, you can scroll back a scene or two. So for the love example, instead of introducing the romantic interest straight away, you can begin with the character breaking up with her former lover. The important thing is to find a concrete, preferably dramatic event that sets out the main focus of the story.

Here are some examples of how not to delay too long before delivering some action for different genres:

- **Murder mystery:** Consider beginning with the murder – or the discovery of the body.
- **Ghost story:** Perhaps start with the ghost appearing – or arriving at a house and being told that it's haunted.
- **Coming-of-age story:** Maybe begin with a character leaving home – preferably for some dramatic reason.

The important thing is to be clear in your mind what the story is about. Don't worry if you don't know that at first. Just start writing and keep writing until you do. Then you can go back and write the opening. You may find that the object of your protagonist's desire dies and your romance develops into a ghost story!

Avoiding common mistakes

Here are some of the errors people make when writing the opening scene:

- ✔ **Nothing happens:** The story starts with characters chatting or going about their day-to-day lives, or with descriptions of scenery, but nothing significant occurs. Readers don't find your location and characters as fascinating as you do unless you inject some action and a dilemma.

- ✔ **Too much back story:** Back story is death to the opening of the novel – in fact, too much can be death to any novel. At the start, readers want to get into what's happening now, before finding out what happened earlier. Maybe they never need to know earlier events, because it's ancient history. (More on back story in Chapter 19.)

- ✔ **Point of view is unclear or inconsistent:** If readers don't know who's narrating the story or who's the main character they need to identify with, they have great difficulty getting involved with your writing. Naming the character right away is a great help, unless it's a first-person narrative, and even then readers need to find out sooner rather than later, unless you have a strong artistic reason for holding it back (such as in Robert Harris's 2007 novel *The Ghost*, where the character's name is never revealed – a play on the fact that ghostwriters' names are not acknowledged in the books they've worked on).

- ✔ **Characters are unbelievable:** If the characters don't come across as real people with flaws and foibles, readers aren't likely to want to know what happens to them. You need something interesting and unique about your characters in order to arouse your readers' curiosity.

- ✔ **Voice is neutral and uninteresting:** The voice and tone of your story have to grab readers. Defining this aspect precisely is difficult, but it's almost certainly a kind of confidence and energy and conviction in the writing that makes readers feel that the writer has something important and interesting to communicate. You feel that the writer knows what she's doing and you, the reader, are picked up and carried along by it. You know it when you read it!

When I look at this list, I realise that people make these mistakes throughout pieces of fiction, not just at the start. Clearly, the first page of a story can reveal many of the faults that occur later, and so sorting them out early really helps you with the whole project.

Discovering Openings from the Greats

The best way to discover how to write successful beginnings is to look at the famously successful openings of great novels, short stories, films and plays. Think about which ones grab you and why, and notice which ones you remember and which ones you forget.

Take down the books on your bookshelf at home and look at the opening paragraphs; or go to a bookshop or library. You can also use the 'look inside' function on Amazon – almost always this shows the first few pages. Examine books that you've read or ones you'd like to read. In particular, look at books in the kind of genre that you want to write.

In this section I look at some of my favourite opening lines and talk about why I like them and why I think they work. Many of these lines turn up regularly on lists of the best-known openings or are remembered by people who love books. I've organised them into groups to allow you to see easily the different kinds of beginnings available to you.

Don't over-egg your opening sentences by trying too hard. If you can't come up with something stunning, being simple and direct is far better than being too clever or complicated.

After you've read through all my favourites, get down to business. Write as many opening lines as you can think of. Fill a whole page. Don't worry if you don't use any of them.

Making a statement: Philosophical openings

The three openings in this section are grand philosophical statements, and yet each one is closely linked to the theme of the novel. The following opening captures the character of Bendrix the narrator, a writer who plays games with himself and with other characters and is trying to avoid the painful truth:

> A story has no beginning or end: arbitrarily one chooses that moment of experience from which to look back or from which to look ahead.
>
> —*Graham Greene (The End of the Affair, Heinemann, 1951)*

In *Pride and Prejudice* the whole theme of the story is encapsulated in the following sentence, together with Jane Austen's dry and ironic tone. Readers soon discover that Mrs Bennet is *very* keen to marry her daughters off to rich men:

> It is a truth universally acknowledged, that a single man in possession of a good fortune, must be in want of a wife.
>
> —*Jane Austen (Pride and Prejudice, Dover Publications, 1995, first published 1813)*

In *Anna Karenina* the theme is marriage – its success and failure. Immediately after this sentence readers are plunged into a crisis in Anna's family involving adultery:

> Happy families are all alike; every unhappy family is unhappy in its own way.
>
> —*Leo Tolstoy (Anna Karenina, translated by Constance Garnett, Modern Library, 2000, first published 1877)*

Speaking from the start: Dialogue openings

I've heard people say that you should never start a novel with dialogue, and so perhaps that's why all this section's opening lines have a mixture of dialogue and prose. The great thing about dialogue is that it gets straight into the characters and the action. It's immediate and compelling, as if readers are overhearing a snatch of an intriguing conversation. In this quote, the whole premise of the novel is made clear:

> 'You too will marry a boy I choose,' said Mrs Rupa Mehra firmly to her younger daughter.
>
> —*Vikram Seth (A Suitable Boy, HarperCollins, 1993)*

This next quote is fairly dramatic, because the author plunges readers into the middle of a tense conversation:

> He said, 'Save yourself if you can,' and I said firmly enough, though I was trembling and clutching at straws, 'I intend to'.
>
> —*Beryl Bainbridge (Every Man for Himself, Gerald Duckworth, 1996)*

The following quote is intriguing: who are the American and Leamas and who are they waiting for?

The American handed Leamas another cup of coffee and said, 'Why don't you go back and sleep?'

> —*John le Carré (The Spy Who Came in from the Cold, Gollancz, 1963)*

Intriguing readers with odd-narrator openings

All the quotes in this section immediately make readers curious about the narrator. This narrator features a distinctive voice:

You better not never tell nobody but God.

> —*Alice Walker (The Color Purple, Harcourt Brace Jovanovich, 1982)*

Here's an intriguing narrator suggesting an intriguing scenario:

I was born twice: first, as a baby girl, on a remarkably smogless Detroit day in January of 1960; and then again, as a teenage boy, in an emergency room near Petoskey, Michigan, in August of 1974.

> —*Jeffrey Eugenides (Middlesex, Farrar, Straus and Giroux, 2002)*

Clearly, the following narrator has something odd about him:

I may have found a solution to the Wife Problem.

> —*Graeme Simsion (The Rosie Project, Michael Joseph, 2013)*

Holding on for an exciting ride: Dramatic events

If you want to grab your readers from the word go and hold on to them, relating a dramatic event is certainly a way to do it. Consider how difficult you'd find not carrying on after these three dramatic starts. Here we want to know who the people are, and what the effect of their deaths is:

On Friday noon, July the twentieth, 1714, the finest bridge in all Peru broke and precipitated five travelers into the gulf below.

> —*Thornton Wilder (The Bridge of San Luis Rey, Longman's Green & Co, 1927)*

Here we want to know what will happen to this innocent man:

> Someone must have slandered Josef K., for one morning, without having done anything wrong, he was arrested.
>
> —*Franz Kafka (The Trial, translated by Breon Mitchell, Schocken Books, 1998, first published 1925)*

This opening has so many intriguing threads in it that you have to read on:

> It was a wrong number that started it, the telephone ringing three times in the dead of night, and the voice on the other end asking for someone he was not.
>
> —*Paul Auster (City of Glass, Faber and Faber, 1985)*

Beginning with a bang: Firing-squad openings

This section contains three attention-grabbing openings, although only the first two have firing squads – the third has an electric chair! This opening is like looking down a long telescope of time, knowing that a character is going to face a firing squad. Will he survive? Why is he facing it? Will readers have to wait for the rest of the novel to find out?

> Many years later, as he faced the firing squad, Colonel Aureliano Buendía was to remember that distant afternoon when his father took him to discover ice.
>
> —*Gabriel García Márquez (One Hundred Years of Solitude, translated by Gregory Rabassa, Harper and Row, 1967)*

The next opening is in the here and now of a cold March morning in Paris, and readers wonder who's going to be executed and, of course, why:

> It is cold at six-forty in the morning of a March day in Paris, and seems even colder when a man is about to be executed by firing squad.
>
> —*Frederick Forsyth (The Day of the Jackal, Hutchinson, 1971)*

The mention of an execution creates an uneasy feeling, and makes readers wonder whether something unpleasant or even similar is going to happen to the main character . . . which, in Plath's novel, tragically it does:

It was a queer, sultry summer, the summer they electrocuted the Rosenbergs, and I didn't know what I was doing in New York.

—*Sylvia Plath (The Bell Jar, Heinemann, 1963)*

Setting the scene with descriptive openings

Although books often used to start with a long passage of description, especially in the 19th century, that technique is unfashionable nowadays. However, a great piece of description can without doubt set the scene for a novel effectively, especially if that location is important, as is the case in these three examples.

 Getting only a great first line from a descriptive opening is difficult, because the effect is usually cumulative. I suggest you go away and read these three beginnings in full.

This quote, featuring Hemingway's famous direct prose style, draws us straight into the world of the story:

In the late summer of that year we lived in a house in a village that looked across the river and the plain to the mountains.

—*Ernest Hemingway (A Farewell to Arms, Scribner, 1929)*

This simple statement of fact tells us exactly where we are:

I had a farm in Africa, at the foot of the Ngong Hills.

—*Karen Blixen (Out of Africa, Putnam, 1937)*

I cheat with the next quote and include three sentences. Conveying the full brilliance of this opening with one sentence is impossible, especially because Dickens breaks up his sentences into fragments. The success lies in the sense of atmosphere conveyed and the mysterious hint that the description of the world outside somehow also relates to the man sitting indoors:

Michaelmas Term lately over, and the Lord Chancellor sitting in Lincoln's Inn Hall. Implacable November weather. As much mud in the streets as if the waters had but newly retired from the face of the earth . . .

—*Charles Dickens (Bleak House, Penguin, 1985, first published 1852–1853)*

Waking up your readers: Science-fiction openings

In all the openings in this section, something isn't quite right. In the first introductory sentence, readers are forced to ask themselves, 'In what world do clocks strike 13?' You know at once that you're in another time or another world:

> It was a bright cold day in April, and the clocks were striking thirteen.
>
> —*George Orwell (Nineteen Eighty-Four, Penguin, 2003, first published 1949)*

In the second opening, you wonder what place has such a strange sky:

> The sky above the port was the colour of television, tuned to a dead channel.
>
> —*William Gibson (Neuromancer, Ace Books, 1984)*

In the next witty opening, something is clearly radically wrong (the earth's sun, the source of all life on this planet, is small and disregarded?):

> Far out in the uncharted backwaters of the unfashionable end of the Western Spiral arm of the Galaxy lies a small unregarded yellow sun.
>
> —*Douglas Adams (The Hitchhiker's Guide to the Galaxy, Pan, 1979)*

Going for the obvious: Statement-of-fact openings

These great lines go to show that you don't have to be a genius to start a novel effectively. The first opening is a complete cliché – but all the same, readers want to know who's fallen for whom:

> It was love at first sight.
>
> —*Joseph Heller (Catch-22, Simon & Schuster, 1961)*

Besides, the subsequent line delivers a suitable twist: 'The first time Yossarian saw the chaplain he fell madly in love with him.'

Similarly, the opening line in Camus's masterpiece is followed by the sentence, 'Or was it yesterday?' This immediately makes readers intrigued about the state of mind of the narrator:

> Mother died today.
>
> —*Albert Camus (The Outsider, translated by Stuart Gilbert, Penguin 1961, first published 1942)*

Chapter 18

Plotting Your Way to Great Stories

In This Chapter

▷ Choosing an engrossing central question

▷ Motivating characters (and readers!)

▷ Dealing with coincidences

▷ Ensuring that your plot stays interesting

*P*lot (or narrative) is the central thread that holds together all the other elements of your fiction. It's important because people's minds process and recall information in the form of narrative. A mere series of dates and events is utterly unmemorable, but a story can stay with you forever. That's why the earliest pieces of writing in the world are all narratives (such as *Beowulf* or the *Epic of Gilgamesh* or the *One Thousand and One Nights*) – oral stories passed on through generations before they're finally written down.

You don't need your whole story plotted out before you begin writing – only the most formulaic stories work that way. Most writers find that the story unfolds as they go. So don't worry if you sometimes find yourself going down blind alleys or feel that the story is petering out – it's inevitable. Keeping the story going in the middle of the narrative is particularly difficult, even if the beginning and end are fairly clear.

In this chapter I look at some of the tricks writers use to keep the narrative flowing and gripping for readers: an intriguing central premise or dilemma; believable character motivation and conflict; the canny use of coincidence; and twists and surprises.

Intriguing Readers with a Core Question

Every story needs a central dramatic question to hook readers. Aim to ask this question near the beginning of your story and not to answer it until the end.

Here are some examples of questions in different kinds of story:

- ✔ **Romance:** Do the lovers get together and live happily, or do they separate and feel miserable?

- ✔ **Mystery story or quest:** Will the character solve the mystery or find what he seeks?

- ✔ **Adventure or war story:** Does the character survive the hostile environment he's battling against or overcome the enemy?

- ✔ **Rags to riches:** Will the character succeed or fail?

- ✔ **Redemption story:** Will the character save others, or transform himself?

- ✔ **Coming of age:** Does the character grow up, and if so, how and why?

- ✔ **Tragedy:** Does the character escape his fate or not, and if not, why?

 Ensure that you create an equal balance between the two presented possibilities. If the outcome is too obvious from the start, readers aren't going to be as gripped as if the outcome is uncertain.

 If your story is more psychological (in other words, centring on the protagonist's personal growth and development), you may need to find a symbolic device to create a clear narrative goal for your character – an object that he wants that represents his goal of happiness. (Check out Chapter 15 for more on using symbols in your writing.)

 Many plots revolve around an object that everyone wants. Try out the following exercise to find out how useful such objects can be:

1. **Think of an object that your character and everyone else in the story wants: perhaps something inherited, secret, valuable, useful and so on.**

2. **Make this object in some way symbolic of the character's interior goal, if possible.**

3. **Write three scenes in your story in which this object appears – one near the beginning, one in the middle and one towards the end.**

Propelling Your Plot with Motivation and Conflict

To be successful, the plot of a piece of fiction requires a lot of things to come together, but two essentials top the list: your characters need to desire something (this is their motivation) and they need to face obstacles and conflict in achieving their aim.

Revealing characters' motivation

In order to identify with a character's journey, readers need to know what the person wants. The character's motivation is the engine of your story. A character with no motivation has no reason to struggle forwards through the pages of your story.

Most people have fairly simple long-term goals: to be happy, to be successful, to avoid premature death. They also have short-term goals: to complete a project at work, to pass an exam, to buy something they want. In a narrative, characters commonly have short-term goals that drive them through, chapter by chapter, and one overall goal that they don't achieve until the end of the story.

1. **Write down your character's main long-term goal.**

2. **Come up with three short-term goals and write a scene involving each one.**

3. **Look at how the short-term goals take your character towards the long-term goal.**

If you're tempted to write about a character who doesn't know what he wants, try to make sure that *you* as the author know what your character wants. You can then make your readers understand what's motivating the character, even if he doesn't know himself.

Although a rough distinction, you can break down characters' motivations into two groups:

- ✔ **Unconscious:** Most motivation comes from unconscious factors related to the character's past. Many people want things that they didn't have in childhood: money, security, love, success at school, to name some of the most common ones. This is why exploring your character's childhood is so important (as I discuss in Chapter 3).

✔ **Conscious:** Even a conscious motivation (such as becoming famous, so that you're rich and successful) may have an unconscious motivation behind it of which you're unaware. The unconscious motivation behind a desire for success may be that, as a child, you were ignored by busy parents and overlooked at school.

Characters' motivations are often related to their values as well. A character who wants to be rich and famous values money and success, and so is likely to be materialistic. This is very different from a character who wants to become rich and famous so that he can use the money and fame to do something significant – either for himself (such as building the world's highest skyscraper) or for others (building a hospital in a poor country).

Creating conflict

Conflict is a major ingredient necessary for all fiction. Without conflict, your story is over in five minutes. A woman meets an attractive man, the pair fancy one another like mad, go on a date, leap into bed, decide to get married and live happily ever after. Where's the story? How is this possibly interesting for readers?

Or suppose that someone is murdered, only one person is in the house, he's found holding a bloody knife, and he confesses immediately to the crime. Or that a man is in debt and wants to raise money, and wins the lottery the next day. Without suspense arising from a conflict of some sort, the whole story is quickly done and dusted.

Without obstacles, difficulties and conflict you don't have a story!

Conflict can exist at many levels. The most obvious and least interesting kind of conflict is simply having a villain – the technical term is *antagonist* – who for no particular reason is determined to prevent your main character, the *protagonist,* from getting what he wants. You can make this more sophisticated by giving your villain a reason for wanting to get in the way of your character.

In real life, people with whom you're in conflict aren't usually out-and-out villains. They're simply people who want something different to what you want. If you build your antagonist up into a fully fledged character with good points and bad points, you usually find good reasons why that person desires a different outcome from that which your main character wants.

Sometimes conflict is expressed openly, sometimes it's hidden away. Often a hidden conflict can be more useful in narrative terms, because it simmers away under the surface and readers know that it's going to erupt dramatically at some point.

Conflict can be within the person as well as outside him. A character may desire something but have been told throughout his childhood that this is bad. He may find that his desires aren't approved of in the wider world.

Take your main character and write about:

- ✔ **An internal conflict:** A conflict with part of himself. An example may be someone who wants to climb a mountain for a challenge, but is afraid of heights.
- ✔ **A personal conflict:** A conflict with another person. An example may be someone who is at war with his spouse, his child or his boss.
- ✔ **A social conflict:** A conflict with social customs or laws. An example may be someone who wants to have a relationship with someone from a different religion, culture or a group that is ostracised by a community.

Handling Plot Coincidences – with Care

Coincidences are almost impossible to avoid in a piece of fiction, because everything has to fit together in a narrative in a way that doesn't usually happen in reality. Most often in life you lose touch with people and never find out what happens to them, events occur that don't have much effect on your life, and you forget about people or events without ever having a need to remember them.

Things like this have no part in a fictional narrative. Everything you include has to be present for a reason. Something that happens early in the novel needs to influence a character or return in some way by the end.

Many stories begin with an initial coincidence. Two people happen to bump into one another, someone happens to be in the right place at the right time – or the wrong place at the wrong time! Readers aren't usually worried by initial coincidences. They accept that the story simply wouldn't take place if these events didn't happen.

What does bother readers, however, is when coincidences multiply beyond what's reasonably believable, especially when they occur whenever your character is in a spot of difficulty. This robs your fiction of any tension, because readers suspect that your character will always be rescued by some improbable coincidence just in the nick of time.

On the positive side, coincidences can have a powerful impression on readers because they provide a feeling that something is 'meant to be'. You can make use of this tendency in your fiction to influence your character's behaviour. In a romance, for example, your character may feel that the relationship 'has to happen' because of the extraordinary coincidence that led to the couple meeting. In a crime story, a detective may become convinced that something was intended when in fact it was only a coincidence, taking the investigation in the wrong direction and making a useful red herring.

Coincidences used to be more acceptable in fiction in the past because they were seen as the working of providence or fate. Plot coincidences are a staple of much Victorian fiction and play a major part in the works of Thomas Hardy, where they fit in with his pessimistic view of life, in which his characters struggle against their destiny to no avail.

A recent novel that makes deliberate and effective use of coincidence is Ian McEwan's *Black Dogs,* which explores the tension between materialism and spirituality. When faced with what some would read as a meaningful coincidence, Bernard, the materialist and rationalist, ignores it, saying:

> 'Yes. Quite a coincidence, I suppose. Now for goodness sake Jeremy, get me home!'
>
> —Ian McEwan (Black Dogs, Jonathan Cape, 1992)

Here are some useful aspects about coincidences in fiction:

- ✔ They make a meaningful pattern.
- ✔ They link things up.
- ✔ They can resolve plot problems.

But bad things about coincidences in fiction include the following:

- ✔ They can seem contrived.
- ✔ The writer may seem lazy.
- ✔ The story loses credibility.

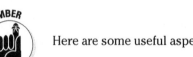

Write a scene involving a coincidence. For instance, have character A talking to character B about someone else they know. Then character B meets this person in a completely unrelated context. Consider how the characters react. Can you invent a reason for this meeting to happen that means it's not a coincidence at all?

Some people believe that coincidences contain meanings (check out the nearby sidebar 'Synchronicity' for an example). Write about a meaningful coincidence that occurs in the life of one of your characters. How does this change the character's viewpoint or feelings?

Synchronicity

Carl Jung, one of the founders of psychoanalysis, came up with the concept of *synchronicity* – or meaningful coincidence. He felt that people can connect through the inferred meanings of events that aren't related in a clear cause-and-effect manner.

Jung described the story of woman he was treating who had a dream in which she was given a golden scarab. At that moment, Jung heard a tapping at the window and saw that an insect was banging against it. He opened the window and caught the creature, which was a scarab beetle, astonishing his patient and forcing her to change her overly rationalistic way of thinking. She made a breakthrough in her analysis as a result.

Jung was convinced that life wasn't a series of random events but an expression of a deeper order, a view backed up by his own experience of psychoanalysis.

Coincidences do happen in real life, so you can always get away with an occasional one in your fiction. Your characters should, however, always recognise that it's a coincidence themselves!

Keeping Readers on Their Toes

Readers like being shocked and surprised when they're reading a story – strangely, in a way that they don't in real life! Perhaps it's the chance to experience excitement with a safety net. Therefore, in some ways the worst comment that readers can pass on your work is that the plot is predictable.

Making twists and turns

Try to make sure that your narrative doesn't stay on one level. You want to keep your readers in doubt as to whether the story will end well or badly for your protagonist, and so you need to alternate scenes where everything goes well for the character with scenes in which something goes badly.

Generally, you can think of this as a question of two steps forward, one step back. You need to keep a fairly equal balance between the two possible outcomes of the story. If things are too clearly weighted in favour of your main character, a positive outcome is too obvious. If everything seems doomed from the beginning and then goes from bad to worse, your readers probably give up long before they get to the tragic ending.

From time to time, your character is sure to hit a major setback and go back several steps, or to make a sudden leap forwards, rather like in a game of snakes and ladders (or chutes and ladders). These major twists and turns can inject new energy into your story when it seems to be going a bit stale.

Draw a 'snakes and ladders' diagram for your story. At the end, put your character's goal. Write in incidents that take your character nearer to this goal (ladders), and write in incidents that take him farther away (snakes).

Take a look at the layout of the board for a game of snakes and ladders. It contains lots of small snakes and ladders throughout the game, and a few really big ones. In particular, the board nearly always features a very long snake near the end that takes you almost right back to the beginning. You can see this like the tendency in fiction for the character to hit the biggest obstacle just before the end of the story, making readers fear that he may indeed go right back to square one.

Remember to keep the character's feelings changing throughout the narrative. At the end of one scene he can feel more optimistic; at the end of the following scene he can be convinced that everything is going to go wrong. If every scene ends on the same note, the narrative has a static feel to it, whereas a rollercoaster of emotions keeps readers hooked. The ancient Greek philosopher and writer Aristotle called these moments *reversals*. They're essential to a good story, a fact that hasn't changed for thousands of years!

Try out this exercise to put your character on an emotional roller-coaster that will grip your readers. Don't worry if you exaggerate the emotions to begin with – you can always tone them down later:

1. **Write a scene in which your character ends up feeling positive about achieving his goal.** End on an emotional high.

2. **Write a scene in which something goes wrong for him.** End on an emotional low.

Delivering shocks and surprises

You can't avoid a certain element of predictability in fiction. Readers need to have some idea of the road ahead, the kinds of obstacles in the path of the main character, and the possibilities for overcoming them. You also need to foreshadow some future events (see Chapter 14 for how to do so). But when the story is completely predictable, it can't possibly be interesting. Throwing in some shocks and surprises helps develop your narrative and revive readers' interest.

Use this exercise to spice up your story by introducing random shocks and surprises:

1. **Write down about a dozen surprises that can happen to a person.**
2. **Put each one on a separate piece of paper (if necessary, ask friends for ideas; get others from a newspaper).**
3. **Shuffle the pieces of paper.**
4. **Pick one at random and write it into your story.**
5. **Think about whether it works and whether it's worth keeping.**

Considering ways to surprise

One common surprise in fiction is to have a character that readers think is a friend turn out to be a foe, and the opposite (an enemy turns out to be on the main character's side).

Remember that you need a good motive for a betrayal, or for an opponent to change his mind. You will need to go back and sow some clues into the story earlier so that the surprise, while unexpected, does make sense – you don't want to make your characters have a sudden personality switch!

1. **Write a scene in which a friend betrays the main character.**
2. **Write a scene where an enemy decides to help him.**

In the following list I identify the kinds of surprises that occur in fictional plots. I don't name the books, because it would completely spoil the pleasure of reading them. But if you've read them, you may well recognise the descriptions:

- ✔ In a wedding scene the groom is revealed to be married already.
- ✔ The main character is suddenly run over, just when you think everything is going to turn out happily.
- ✔ The narrator of the story is revealed to have committed the murder.
- ✔ A character turns out to be the child of someone other than he thought.
- ✔ An inheritance turns out to be from someone completely unexpected and undesirable, not the person the protagonist assumed.
- ✔ The individual doesn't marry the person readers assumed the character would, but someone completely different.
- ✔ A main supporting character is killed at an unexpected moment.
- ✔ Someone readers assumed to be dead turns out to be alive.

Timing your surprise

Shocks and surprises can occur at different points in your narrative: some fairly near the beginning; others around the middle of your story – where they're often incredibly effective; and some towards the end. You can also have a final twist (I consider endings in Chapter 23).

Although you generally need to introduce all the main characters near the beginning of your story, you can create a surprise by bringing in a significant new character part-way through the story. This character can change the direction of the story, perhaps by helping the main character, getting in the way or acting as a new love interest.

Try this exercise to introduce a new and surprising character into your story. To add that extra element of unpredictability, why not get someone else to choose this character for you – after all, you can't predict the next person who will come into your life:

1. **Write about a stranger who appears during your story.** If possible, ask a friend to give you a brief description of a character, or choose this character at random by picking a name out of a newspaper or a picture out of a book of portraits (remember to open it at random and stick to your choice!).

2. **Write about what your main character thinks at two points:**

    • When the stranger first appears.

    • After the character gets to know the person.

Surprise yourself, not just your readers! Write something completely unexpected and see whether you like it and whether you can find a place for it in your story. Well-judged surprises can send your story in a new direction and introduce new aspects to your main characters.

Follow Raymond Chandler's advice: when you're in doubt, bring on a man with a gun. (It doesn't have to be a literal gun, of course – it can be anything that raises the tension level a few notches.)

Chapter 19

Making Good (Use of) Time in Your Writing

Time is an illusion. Lunchtime doubly so.

—Douglas Adams (The Hitchhiker's Guide to the Galaxy, Pan, 1979)

*A*ll stories unfold in time. Even the shortest short story takes place over a number of minutes. Some stories tell of a whole life from birth until death. Long stories can even take place over generations, obviously with gaps in between.

The way you structure a story in time changes its nature. If you start a novel with the characters meeting and end with them getting married, you have a quite different story to one where you begin with their marriage and end with their divorce!

You also have options about how you organise time in a piece of fiction. You can start at the beginning and move forwards, you can jump around between past and present, or you can leap forwards into the future; you can even tell a story backwards (something I describe in more detail in Chapter 20). In science fiction, you also have the option of exploring physical time travel and the distant future.

In this chapter I look at different ways to handle time in fiction and how the structure of a novel depends on your arrangement of the time sequence.

Working with Time in Conventional Narratives

The simplest kind of story is called a *linear narrative*. The story starts at the beginning, usually with a dramatic event, and carries on forwards in time through to the end, whether that's 24 hours or a lifetime later.

If you're telling this kind of story, it's a good idea to map the main events along a timeline. (For more on plotting, flip to Chapter 18.)

Your timeline is never set in stone. You can always go back and change it later – it's just a guideline.

With one of your stories in mind, use this exercise to create a timeline for it:

1. **Draw a horizontal line on a large piece of paper.**

2. **Add in the main events of your story, making sure that you have an initial dramatic event, major turning points, a climax and a resolution.**

If you haven't thought about the length of time over which your story will take place, reflect on this aspect now. Maybe you think that the action should take place over roughly a year; or perhaps that's too long and six months will do – or even a week is enough. Or maybe your story needs to cover a whole lifetime or several generations. Condensing the action as much as you possibly can is helpful, though, because it helps create narrative tension (as I discuss in Chapter 21).

Timelines really come into their own when you're working with dual narratives, as I discuss in the later section 'Handling flashbacks'.

Jumping over the dull bits

Most fiction consists of scenes that happen in real time and interludes in between that summarise what happens between the scenes. More and more contemporary novels jump from scene to scene, leaving a gap in between. This approach saves the need to write sentences like: 'For the next three weeks nothing much happened' or 'Three years passed without John meeting Sally'. These kinds of linking passages tend to be boring for readers, so it's best to leave them out.

Whenever you think that the writing is getting a little dull, just jump forwards to the next interesting scene!

One novel that proceeds in a series of jumps is Marina Lewycka's *A Short History of Tractors in Ukrainian* (2005). She includes many short scenes and passages, with gaps in between.

The action of *One Day* by David Nicholls (2009) takes place on just one day – 15 July, St Swithin's Day – over 20 successive years. By seeing what the characters are doing and thinking on this one day, the whole story becomes clear. The full significance of the choice of this date is revealed near the end.

Try this exercise to see how leaping through time in your story can be useful – and fun:

1. **Write a dramatic scene at the beginning of your story.**

2. **Write as separate scenes what the characters are doing at exactly the following moments (jumping the time in between): five hours, five days, five weeks, five months and five years later.**

These jumps in time are effective because they get readers' imaginations working and draw them into your story. Readers fill in the gaps for themselves.

Stretching out with sagas and lifetimes

Many books with big themes take place over the lifetime of one character, from birth to death. In this case, even though you're covering the whole lifetime of a person, readers don't need every detail of the character's life, just the most important ones (otherwise your novel takes a lifetime to read, which tests even the most determined reader!). Often, the most significant part of the story takes place in the middle of the character's life.

Many 19th-century novels use this technique, from Thackeray's 1844 novel *Barry Lyndon* to Charles Dickens's 1850 *David Copperfield*. Recent examples include William Boyd's 2002 novel *Any Human Heart*.

Other stories span several generations. Daphne du Maurier's 1943 *Hungry Hill* is a case in point, telling the tale of three generations of an Irish family. Jung Chang's 1991 *Wild Swans: Three Daughters of China* is a true life story about three generations of a Chinese family, showing how the major political changes in China affect the characters' individual lives.

Write a short piece about your character's life, her mother's and father's lives, and her grandmother's or grandfather's life. Think about how different life is for each generation.

You may not want to write a novel that spans three generations, but understanding the lives of the parents and grandparents of your character can give you a good insight into her upbringing and motivation. (I discuss the importance of the latter in Chapter 18.)

Living life in one hectic day

If you really want to condense your book, you can make the whole action take place over a mere 24 hours – or less. Most books with such a tight timeframe use flashbacks and memories in order to flesh the book out. Here are some famous examples to check out:

- ✔ James Joyce's 1922 *Ulysses* and Virginia Woolf's 1925 *Mrs Dalloway* use extensive flashbacks to give a sense of the main character's whole life.

- ✔ *The Apartment* by Greg Baxter (2012) describes a man's search for an apartment in an unnamed European city. Much of the tension comes from his reflections on his unusual past.

- ✔ *One Day in the Life of Ivan Denisovich* by Aleksandr Solzhenitsyn (1962) describes one grim day in the character's life in a Soviet gulag. The fact that the story is set on one day among many almost identical days creates a feeling of timelessness.

- ✔ *24 Hours* by Greg Iles (2000) gives the characters 24 hours to rescue their kidnapped daughter, and *Saturday* by Ian McEwan (2005) is set on the day of the anti-Iraq war demonstration in London. These writers use the 24-hour device to increase dramatic tension.

Try writing your own 'story in a day'. You can expand it by adding in other characters' stories, flashbacks and memories, and thoughts about the future:

1. **Write a story that takes place on one day.**

2. **Think of ways to expand it into a longer piece of fiction, and then write some more scenes.**

Looking Over Your Shoulder at the Past

Things often seem better when looking back – the summers were longer and warmer, everyone was friendlier and so on. Nostalgia works that way. But whether remembering the past gives you a warm glow or makes you shiver, looking back is a natural human impulse. And so your characters wanting to remember or tell tales of their pasts in your fiction is equally natural.

In this section you get to examine your characters' pasts through flashbacks or hindsight narration.

Handling flashbacks

Flashbacks into the past are the most common type of time shifting in fiction. You can find lots more on flashbacks and memories in Chapters 3 and 13.

Keeping flashbacks clear

Flashbacks always work best when you keep them short. That way they don't hold up the forward momentum of your story. If you want to write a long flashback, you can do so by weaving individual flashbacks into the present, touching base with what's happening now at regular intervals.

1. **Write a short flashback.** Remember to include the trigger for the flashback, and to come back into the present at the end.

2. **Think of something the character can be doing in the present that takes more than a few minutes.** Write three sentences about what the character is doing now, and then three sentences of the memory, and then another three sentences of what's happening now, followed by another three sentences of memory, and so on until you get to the end of what you want to say. Always end in the present.

Don't write a flashback within a flashback; it's too confusing. Instead, return to the present before you go into the second flashback. If you must have a double flashback, make sure that you keep it very short.

Duelling narratives in harmony

If you have a number of short flashbacks in your story, write them as they occur to you, and when the time seems right for readers to know the information that the flashback contains. If you find that you have a larger number of longer flashbacks, you may be better off writing a *dual narrative,* which has one story taking place in the present and one story taking place in the past – a 'now' story and a 'then' story.

If you're writing a dual narrative, try writing the 'now' story in the present tense and the 'then' story in the past tense. This enables you to switch from one to the other without readers becoming confused.

Other ways to help ensure clarity are to use alternate chapters between the present and past or to put the dates at the start of each chapter.

One problem with dual narratives is that one strand of the story can be more interesting than the other. Sometimes readers care more about what the character is doing now and sometimes more about what happened in the past. Try to keep your narratives equally gripping to stop readers skipping through one strand of the story to get back to the other!

A common approach is to have a dual narrative in which a modern-day character uncovers information from the past, often involving her family. Sometimes the information from the past is revealed at least partly through letters and diaries.

An example of a novel in which information is revealed from the past is *Asta's Book* (1993) by Barbara Vine, in which Asta's granddaughter Ann unearths secrets from nearly a hundred years earlier. *Possession* (2002) by AS Byatt tells the story of two contemporary academics who research the love affair between two famous fictional poets. The novel moves between the present day and the Victorian era. *The Map of Love* by Ahdaf Soueif (1999) moves back and forth between 1997 and the first decade of the 20th century as the American Isabel uncovers the story of her great-grandmother.

You can even stretch this multiple-narrative technique to three generations. For example, *The Historian* by Elizabeth Kostova (2005) involves three timelines: the historical period, the point of view of the father and the point of view of his daughter 30 years afterwards.

You can also use two timelines based on different parts of the same character's life. *Cat's Eye* by Margaret Atwood (1988) alternates between her present life as an artist and her childhood in Toronto.

When using the dual-narrative technique, you have to make connections between the past and present. Perhaps you can employ parallel themes; for example, in *Possession* a romance between the two academics parallels the love affair in the past. Plus, always separate out the different timelines clearly. Alternate the two timelines scenes by scene, chapter by chapter or section by section.

1. **Plan out a dual narrative with one thread about what happens to the character now and another thread about what happens to another character in the past.**

2. Draw two timelines, one for each character in the story (for how to produce a timeline, flick to the earlier section 'Working with Time in Conventional Narratives').

3. See whether you can work out parallel events for the two narratives.

I knew that would happen! Writing with hindsight

Telling a story with hindsight, when the narrator is looking back at events that happened previously, is a common technique in contemporary writing. It enables the narrator of the story to have a degree of omniscience, because she knows the whole story and what will happen at the end; as a result she's able to comment on events as they happen, to hint at what's going to happen and even to jump forwards and tell readers. I look briefly at telling a story with hindsight in Chapter 8.

Enjoying the freedom

A story narrated retrospectively gives you considerable freedom to jump around in time and tell the tale in a different order. As long as the narrator is clear and tells the story in a way that makes sense, readers go along with it.

Kazuo Ishiguro uses this technique in *Never Let Me Go* (Faber and Faber, 2005). Paragraphs and sections begin with phrases such as 'All of this . . . reminds me of something that happened about three years later' and 'I want to move on now to our last years'. The unfolding of the story is carefully controlled but sounds entirely natural, as if the narrator is telling the story to readers directly.

You can relate a story with hindsight in a number of different ways:

- ✔ The narrator tells a story to others, with a conversational tone.
- ✔ The narrator writes a journal, diary or letter, either to a specific person such as her child or for posterity.
- ✔ The narrator addresses readers, although this usually isn't stated explicitly but taken for granted.

In some stories, the narrator tells the story just after the final events took place. In others, she relates events that happened many, many years ago. These stories are a little different in that generally the narrator of a more recent story is able to recall the story with much greater accuracy. A story narrated many years after the final events may become slightly unreliable, as the narrator points out in Kazuo Ishiguro's *Never Let Me Go*. At the beginning of the second chapter he writes: 'This was all a long time ago now so I might have some of it wrong; but my memory of it is . . .'.

You can also use a frame in which the narrator introduces the story and sums up at the end, while telling the actual story in between. Sometimes you can develop your tale into a story within a story. Or you can return readers to the narrator in the present at intervals throughout, in order for her to comment on what happened. Sometimes the narrator is present throughout the whole story, constantly commenting and reflecting on events.

Avoiding the pitfalls of hindsight

You have to watch out for a few potential problems when writing a retrospective novel. For example, an elderly narrator recounting highly accurate memories of early childhood can sound contrived. Can she really remember everything that well? You may need to work quite hard to make this convincing.

Also, you need to create a gap between the experienced view of the adult narrator and their younger self. The longer the distance between the narrator experiencing the events and relating them, the bigger the gap.

Here are some classic examples that are well worth reading:

- ✔ *To Kill a Mockingbird* **by Harper Lee (1960):** The author combines the narrator's voice as a child observing the events with the voice of a grown woman reflecting back on herself as a child. The novel's ironic adult language gives away the fact that the narrator is now adult.

- ✔ *The Remains of the Day* **by Kazuo Ishiguro (1989):** The main events are told with hindsight, but in the foreground of the story the protagonist is travelling to a meeting with the woman who's the focus of his recollections.

- ✔ *Enduring Love* **by Ian McEwan (1997):** A big gap doesn't exist between the end of the story and the events the narrator is relating, which gives a feeling of great immediacy.

Another problem with a retrospective novel is that it does give away one aspect of the story: the fact that the narrator is still alive to tell the tale. If you want a high suspense story where the narrator's life is at stake, this may not be the best way to tell your story.

Write a story or a scene told with hindsight in these three ways:

✔ The narrator relates the story to a friend immediately afterwards.

✔ The narrator relates the story to an acquaintance ten years later.

✔ The narrator writes the story down at the end of her life.

Playing Around with Time

One of the greatest aspects of creative writing is the immense possibilities it offers you as an author. You aren't restricted by budgets, as with films, or the physical limitations of a stage, as in theatre. You can cover any story you like and set it in any place or time you desire.

In this section I discuss jumping forwards in time with flash forwards, messing with time (and perhaps your readers' minds) and travelling physically through time.

Leaping into the future

Sometimes you can create a breathtaking literary effect by jumping forwards in time. Giving your readers an insight into what's going to happen next allows you to rack up the tension.

The technique of jumping forwards in a narrative is known as a *flash forward* (or more technically *prolepsis*). Of course, you can hint at what's going to happen in the future through foreshadowing – using dreams, oracles and so on (as I describe in Chapter 14), or by describing characters thinking about what will happen or even imagining future scenes. But some writers simply jump forwards and tell readers what's going to happen later in the narrative.

A great example is in Muriel Spark's 1970 novel *The Driver's Seat.* The main character is in an airport about to go on holiday when the narrative suddenly flashes forwards and informs readers what's going to happen to her when she arrives at a destination. It's a shocking and completely breathtaking moment, transforming what seems to be a fairly pedestrian narrative suddenly into something compelling.

Write a scene that involves a sudden flash forward. You can just jump forwards or, if it suits the style of your narrative better, you can give your character a prophetic dream, have her fortune told or make her convinced that a future event will happen.

Beware of simply writing 'little did she know' or similar phrases – you need to be more subtle, especially if you're writing in the point of view of a character: after all, if she doesn't know, she can hardly write about it!

Flash forwards work best in a narrative where the narrator is in the future and telling a story that happened in the past. This enables the narrator to keep jumping forwards and letting readers know what's going to happen. For a discussion on the technique of writing with hindsight, check out the earlier section 'I knew that would happen! Writing with hindsight'.

Mixing up time

You can write some pretty complex narratives that jump around in time. If you're going to use this technique, however, you have to know exactly when events are taking place, and you need to find ways of letting readers know.

When you're oscillating between several different time periods, a good idea is to give readers times and dates and places at the opening of each chapter, so they don't have to work too hard to know where they are.

Novels with complex time structures include the following:

- ✔ **Audrey Niffenegger's *The Time Traveller's Wife* (2003):** Features Henry, who as a time traveller can move back and forth from the past to the future, and Clare, whose life moves chronologically. The author helps readers out by giving dates and both characters' ages at the start of every chapter.

- ✔ **Arundhati Roy's *The God of Small Things* (1997):** Weaves back and forth between the present and past, foreshadowing future events. I don't analyse the complete structure, because the author admits that she wrote the book as a linear narrative and then cut it up into pieces and rearranged them!

- ✔ **Lionel Shriver's *The Post-Birthday World* (2007):** Starts with an initial chapter and then splits into two with alternating chapters showing two different possible futures depending on the choice the character makes at the end of the first chapter.

- ✔ **Kate Atkinson's *Life After Life* (2013):** Describes many possible versions of one character's life.

- ✔ **David Mitchell's *Cloud Atlas* (2004):** Consists of six different stories nestled within one another like Russian dolls.

Plan a novel with an unusual structure. Don't worry if you never write it – it's just an exercise! On the other hand, you may get some good ideas that help you in a more conventional narrative.

This exercise is a useful way to create a non-linear narrative. You may need to try out several different arrangements of the story, and you may decide it worked better as it was. Sometimes, however, you will find changing the order sheds a new light on the characters or situation, and in any event your story will be stronger for having explored it in this way.

1. **Write a short story with a conventional linear narrative.**

2. **Chop it up, rearrange it to see what happens, and decide which version you think is better.**

Nothing's wrong with a conventional linear narrative – many great novels are still written this way. The safest approach is probably to write a straightforward narrative before you start experimenting with complicated structures.

Travelling through time

In science fiction, characters can travel physically in time, as opposed to thinking about the past or imagining the future. The theme of time travel has been incredibly popular: the BBC drama *Doctor Who* involving a time-travelling Time Lord is one of the most popular TV series ever.

Some writers avoid travelling back to the past because of the philosophical problem that any action taken in the past changes the future that the character came from (the so-called grandfather paradox: see Chapter 16). However, time travel has been used to explore historical themes, as Daphne du Maurier does in her 1969 novel *The House on the Strand,* in which a character uses a drug to take himself back to the early 14th century – though he's only able to observe what happens, not interfere with it.

Other novels explore the possibility of characters from the future travelling back into contemporary society. This enables the writer to view the current world from a different point of view and explore social themes.

One of the first novels to use this device was HG Wells's *The Time Machine* (1895). A gentleman scientist and inventor demonstrates his time machine, which takes him into AD 802,701. Here he meets the Eloi, small childlike adults who do no work and live in a futuristic environment, before discovering the Morlocks, apelike cave dwellers who live in darkness underground and work the machinery that makes the aboveground paradise possible. He escapes and travels even farther into the future, where the earth is dying. He returns to his laboratory only three hours after he originally left.

Many of the themes of this novel have appeared in science fiction ever since, especially ideas about utopias and dystopias.

Write a story involving time travel. If this doesn't work for you, write a scene in which your character imagines what it would be like to be able to travel in time – perhaps to jump forward to see whether she marries the right person or go backwards to undo a mistake she made.

Chapter 20

Structuring a Longer Work of Fiction

*A*ll products – whether they're enormous skyscrapers or small coffee tables – are built with an underlying supporting structure. Otherwise, they crumble to the ground. Your stories are no different. In order for your creative writing to be comprehensible to readers, your stories and novels need a solid, clear framework. However, you may not actually construct this until you have a working draft, so don't let the lack of structure hold you up in the early stages.

You can structure a narrative in all sorts of different ways. Sometimes you know from the beginning that you want to divide your book into two or three parts, or that you need a certain number of chapters. On other occasions you just write and arrange the structure later. Your preferred approach doesn't matter as long as you end up with a well-structured book. In this chapter I look at some of the issues involved in structuring a longer piece of fiction, including handling different plots and subplots and even experimenting a little.

Dividing Your Work into Parts, Chapters and Scenes

Most long narratives such as novels are structured and divided into parts and then chapters, to help organise the text and make the book easier to read. It is all too easy to lose your place in a book with no chapters, and picking it up again is then hard!

Chapters often contain a number of separate scenes. A *scene* is defined as a piece of writing that happens at one time, in one place, and with one set of characters. Sometimes, within in a scene, you can bring in an extra character or have one leave, or go from one place to another, but in some sense the action should be continuous.

Here, I take a look at parts and chapters, which you mark as discrete sections in your novel, and scenes, which you don't necessarily have to separate for readers with a heading.

Partitioning into parts

If you have a number of characters from whose viewpoint you want to narrate the story, you want to think about separating your novel into parts. If you have two main characters, for instance, you may want to divide your book into two parts: the first part telling one character's story and the second part the other person's.

You may also want to divide your book into parts when it involves different locations or timeframes. If you're telling a story that involves three different generations of the same family, for instance, consider dividing your book into three parts, one for each generation. For more on writing novels that span several generations, flick to Chapter 19.

Chatting about chapters

Most books are divided into chapters, which are useful because they help give readers time to pause between different scenes. They're also great for marking transitions between scenes in different viewpoints or ones set in different locations or at different times.

Although chapters are often roughly the same length, they don't need to be. You can vary their length, perhaps because one scene is complex and needs a lot of time to unravel, while other scenes can be short though no less effective.

Throwing in a really short chapter can be an effective way to grab readers' attention.

Heading off to a chapter name

You can number your chapters, give them titles, head them with the name of the character whose viewpoint is contained, or include the time and place of the action. Different systems suit different kinds of books, and the decision of how to label the chapters is purely up to you.

Titling your chapters is a useful way of increasing narrative suspense by indicating that something dramatic is about to happen. If you title a chapter 'A Firestorm' or 'Lightning Strikes', you pique readers' interest.

Think of those old-fashioned books that give a summary of what's going to happen at the start of each chapter, such as in the children's novel *Winnie-the-Pooh*:

> Chapter 2 . . . in which Pooh goes visiting and gets into a tight place

> —AA Milne (Winnie-the-Pooh, Methuen, 1926)

Another great example of a novel with chapter headings is Cormac McCarthy's *Blood Meridian, or The Evening Redness in the West* (1985). The neutral tone of the headings contrasts brilliantly with the amoral savagery of the text.

Giving each chapter a title can help you to focus on what the chapter is about and allow you to spot when a chapter is too 'bitty' and made up of too many strands.

Just for fun, give your chapters titles. These can be working titles you write as you go, or you may prefer to come up with titles for each chapter after you finish writing.

Thinking about chapter patterns

Organising your chapters into a pattern is useful. You may have a thematic reason for the book including a certain number of chapters. Although this isn't strictly necessary, a pattern can give you a template to work within. Also, readers are often unconsciously aware of symmetry within a story and respond to it positively.

Here are some examples of chapter patterns in novels:

- ✔ **Elizabeth Gilbert's *Eat, Pray, Love* (2006):** Contains 108 chapters and is divided into three sections of 36 chapters each. Gilbert chose the number 108 because the 'rosary' of beads used by Hindus is made up of that number of beads. One hundred and eight is considered an auspicious number because it divides into threes, and because the three digits 108 add up to nine, which is three times three. Gilbert also said that she was 36 years old when she wrote the book.

✔ **Charles Palliser's** *The Quincunx* **(1989):** Is divided, like the quincunx itself (a geometric pattern consisting of five points arranged in a cross with one point in the centre, like a five on a die), into five parts consisting of five books, each of which is divided into five chapters.

✔ **Henry Fielding's** *Tom Jones* **(1749):** Has 198 chapters, divided into 18 books, the first 6 of which are set in the country, the second 6 on the road, and the last 6 in London.

Look at similar kinds of books to the one you're writing to see how the authors structure them. Look at whether the chapters are numbered or titled and how many chapters the book contains. See whether you can discern a reason for this choice.

Writing complete scenes

Extended pieces of fiction work best when they proceed with a series of complete dramatised scenes. Each scene works as a little short story with a beginning, a middle and an end. In a short story, of course, the end completes the story, while in a longer piece of fiction the end of the scene has to open out into the next one and make readers want to find out what happens next.

Structuring your book to a 'T'

When I wrote the first draft of my novel *The Resurrection of the Body* (1995) for a competition to write a novel in 24 hours (which I won!), I gave each chapter a title to help me keep track of the story, because I wrote it under this extreme pressure. Doing so was really helpful when I wanted to scroll back and amend a particular scene.

When the book was rushed straight into print, the typesetter noticed that most of the chapter headings happened to begin with a 'T'. As the main character was a vicar, he wanted to use the typographical device of making each T at the start of the chapter a Christian cross. I immediately changed the remaining chapter titles so that they started with a 'T' as well. What began as a means to help me find my place in the novel became an important stylistic feature of the book.

Here's an exercise to help you to write a good scene with a beginning, middle and end:

1. **Divide your page into quarters, making four squares.**

2. **Sketch out your scene with simple pictures to show what the characters are doing (Figure 20-1 is an example to illustrate how this process can work).**

3. **Add in some extra visual details such as facial features, landscape or weather, and any objects or props that might be in the scene.**

4. **Write each part of the scene in order, starting with the first box and ending with the last.**

Adeoga is at home when the phone rings. It is her father, who wants to see her.

Her father appears with a bunch of flowers. He says he needs to talk to her.

Over tea, Adeoga's father tells her that he is not her biological father. Adeoga's mother is the only one who knows his identity.

Adeoga rushes from the room in tears, knocking over the tea things.

Figure 20-1: A sketch for a four-part scene.

You may find that drawing images for your scene makes it more dramatic. Filmmakers work with visual images and so they often storyboard the narrative in this way, but it can be very helpful when writing prose fiction too.

I can't stress enough the importance of writing your fiction in complete scenes: it's the best way to 'show' and not 'tell'. Try to avoid passages in which you tell readers what happens in between scenes or summarise events that you haven't dramatised. One common problem when writing is that you're so keen to get on with the next section that you skip ahead without giving enough weight to each scene in your story. Slow down and enjoy writing each scene, remembering that everything is in the detail.

You can write a whole novel in this way. Sketch out each scene before you write it, and end by writing the first sentence of the following scene so that you have something to pick up on the next time you sit down to write. Hemingway always said that it was his practice to finish a morning's writing at a place where he knew what was going to happen next!

Linking Different Narrative Threads

If you're writing a book that has more than one narrative line – for example, you may have a main plot and a subplot, or one story in the present and another story in the past, or three main characters whose stories interweave – you need to structure and connect the separate threads. You can think of this process as a bit like making a braid or plait.

Whatever happens in your subplot has to connect with and change what happens in the main plot. What happens in the main plot can then affect the subplot too, creating a chain of consequences that grips and holds readers. Flip to Chapter 18 for loads more on plotting.

Spinning subplots

Subplots are incredibly useful in fiction. Here's just some of what they can do:

- ✔ **Reveal a different aspect of your character's life.** If your main story involves your character's personal life, consider introducing a work subplot or one involving a friend or a hobby. This approach can help to develop the characters and introduce new themes.

- ✔ **Create obstacles.** Events that happen in your subplot can get in the way of what the character wants in the main plot, thus helping to increase tension and suspense.

- ✔ **Introduce contrast.** A subplot can introduce a change in mood or pace. For example, in a thriller you can introduce a romantic subplot or in a romantic novel you can add a darker subplot such as a local crime wave.

✔ **Mirror the theme.** Authors commonly use the subplot to mirror the main theme and offer a different potential outcome. For example, in Tolstoy's *Anna Karenina* (1877), the main story is a tragic adulterous love affair, but the subplot, which is equally important in the novel, is about a more successful marriage.

The most common way to structure subplots is simply to alternate one scene of the main plot with one scene of the subplot. In this case, the subplot is usually almost as important as the main plot. However, you can also take up most of the story with the main plot and just drop in short scenes from the subplot at regular intervals.

You can make your subplot as major or minor as you like – although at a certain point it can become too insignificant to really matter.

If you want, you can introduce a subplot and then drop it for a considerable time, only to return to it at the end of the story. This approach can work if the subplot is memorable enough for your readers to hang on to for all that time. The return of the subplot at the end, usually to perform an important function in the plot, can be very satisfying.

The Lord of the Rings by JRR Tolkien (1954) is a great example of a big story with several subplots. The main story concerns Frodo's mission to take the One Ring first to Rivendell and then to Mordor to destroy it, accompanied by the faithful Sam. The narrative contains many other important characters as well, however, and at the end of the first volume it splits in two. The first strand continues with Frodo and Sam's journey into Mordor, while the second strand follows the other members of the Fellowship – including Aragorn, Legolas and Gimli, and the two other hobbits, Merry and Pippin – as they travel to Gondor to defend it against the Dark Lord Sauron's armies.

The narrative cuts back and forth between the two threads. If you read closely, you spot that some events that occur in one part of the story are noticed by characters in the other. Finally, you realise that Frodo and Sam's journey only succeeds because Sauron had been distracted from them by the battle fought by the other characters. Both strands of the narrative are equally important to the outcome of the plot.

Developing subplots is a fun way to clarify what you want to say with your story, and create more tension and conflict. Try this exercise to see how this works:

1. **Think of three different possible subplots for your story.**

2. **Plot the subplots on a piece of paper as three lines in parallel with your main story.**

3. **Note down some key incidents in each subplot and see how they connect both with the other subplots and with the main narrative.**

4. **Write the key incidents as self-contained scenes.**

Trying different subplot structures

You can experiment with different ways of tying subplots into the main story. One common structure is to tell two separate stories that only meet near the climax or ending of the story. These subplots don't intersect beforehand, but readers usually sense that they're going to come together – otherwise the second story wouldn't exist!

Another way of using subplots is to have lots of smaller subplots that weave their way in and out of the story. Each little subplot needs to work as a story on its own as well as having an effect on the main plot line.

Create tension by leaving one strand of the plot at a moment of high tension and swapping to the other strand. Then leave that second strand at a moment of high tension before you switch back to the first.

Don't have so many subplots that you end up with a knotty tangle instead of a neat braid. Ensure that you keep the main narrative line clear.

Look up some short stories you've written and see whether you can use one of them as a small subplot in a bigger story. If not, write some new stories now!

Playing with Structure

You can structure your piece of fiction in all sorts of complicated ways. Many modern novels in particular play with structure.

You don't need to worry too much about organising your story when you begin. Concentrate on writing separate well-defined and dramatic scenes. You can mentally peg them on a washing line and then move them around later.

If you ever glance at the back of a tapestry, you'll see that it looks like a complete tangle with yarns crossed all over the place in different colours, knots that stick out and the occasional loop. Your novel may well feel similar while it's a work in progress. The lucky thing in writing is that words can be completely deleted, unlike pieces of yarn!

Write a brief summary of each scene in your story on an index card. Lay all the cards out on the floor and play with the order.

Becoming more complex

In this section I describe just two ways to experiment with your novel's structure.

Different versions of the same story

Some contemporary novels start the story in the same place but then split into two or more separate narratives, usually based on the choice a character makes.

Check out Lionel Shriver's *The Post-Birthday World* (2007) and Peter Howitt's 1998 film *Sliding Doors*. Both start with an initial event and then split into two different possibilities – as the result of a character's choice in the first, and by accidentally colliding with someone and so missing an underground train in the second.

In her 2013 novel *Life After Life*, author Kate Atkinson makes the heroine either repeatedly die or have a close brush with death. Each time she dies, the narrative starts again and works out differently. The author offers readers different possibilities of a life, without them ever giving one 'true' version.

Fragmented stories

In a novel, story or film, the scenes don't always have to occur in the right sequence. You can break up a conventional linear narrative into a different order, or even allow readers to select their own preferred order in which to read the book.

In his 1963 novel *Hopscotch,* Julio Cortázar suggests that the book can be read in one of two possible ways: consecutively, from Chapters 1 to 56 (the remaining 99 chapters are then 'expendable'), or by 'hopscotching' through all 155 chapters in an order he gives in the author's table of instructions. Cortázar also offers readers the option of choosing their own unique path through the narrative.

Jennifer Egan's 2010 novel *A Visit from the Goon Squad* pieces the story together using different characters, different points of view and non-consecutive events set in different times and places, each of which revolves around the same characters: Bennie Salazar, an ageing rock music executive, and his onetime assistant, Sasha, as well as their various friends and associates. The author plays with different voices and even includes one section as an onscreen-style presentation.

Have you ever had the experience of making a choice and then wishing you had done something else? Try this out with your characters to explore different narrative options:

1. **Think of a point in your story at which your character has a simple choice (for example, to go to a party).**

2. **Create three different choices for your character (for example, to go, to stay at home or to go somewhere else).**

3. **Write all the scenarios and see which one you like best and which one offers the most interesting possibilities for the rest of your story.**

Chapter 21

Tightening the Tension to Enthral Readers

*M*iddles are often neglected. We all know about the middle-child syndrome, middle managers often complain that they are caught between two stools, and the piggy in the middle seldom gets the ball. The same is true with writing. The beginning and the end of the story are usually dramatic scenes that are easy to identify and focus on. But when you get to the middle, things start to get tough.

The middle part of your story is always the most difficult to write. After you've introduced the characters and created an arresting opening (as I discuss in Chapter 17), you often you find yourself wondering what to do next and how to keep readers turning the pages.

To increase and maintain the required narrative tension through the main part of your story, you have to create suspense. One great way to do so is to hold back information from readers to raise the stakes for the characters and to create time pressure. Clues help keep your readers on track, and leaving tantalising gaps also helps you to build suspense. You can also create cliffhangers at the end of your chapters and sections to keep readers' palms sweaty with tension.

But that's enough tantalising hints. Read on to find out more about all these devices and how you can use them to make your story un-putdownable!

Introducing the Art of Creating Suspense

Suspense is a combination of anticipation and uncertainty. Therefore, you create it in your narrative by flagging up something that's likely to happen and then delaying its happening, so that readers remain uncertain which way the story's going to go.

Make your character's goals, hopes and fears clear, so that readers know what they're looking forward to or dreading and can engage with the story. Along the way, reveal enough information to keep readers interested, while holding back enough to make them want to keep going until they find the missing details.

Unfortunately, no foolproof, one-size-fits-all method exists to achieve this aim. Some writers do it instinctively, others learn from reading lots of fiction and working out how it's done, while still others have to rework their fiction time and again until they get there.

Read some really gripping thrillers, because these are largely plot led and designed to keep you hooked. Even if you're writing something more character based or literary, you can still discover a lot about how to keep your readers hooked from studying good thrillers.

Suspense comes from waiting. If you keep delivering non-stop action, readers don't have the space to wait and worry. The best approach is to alternate high drama and action scenes with quieter ones.

Here are two exercises that will help you to create suspense:

1. **Write a scene in which your character is told that a character she hasn't met before is about to arrive.**

2. **Delay the character's arrival.**

3. **Write a conversation between the two people who're waiting for the character – don't forget to describe their surroundings too, as they can help foreshadow events and actions to come (see Chapter 14).**

This second exercise helps you to develop tension by building up something the reader knows will happen:

1. **Write a scene in which your protagonist has to tell a person some very bad news; begin by describing her journey to see the person.**

2. **Compose a scene where the other character isn't present when the main character arrives.**

3. **Depict your protagonist waiting for the other character to arrive, again remembering to describe the surroundings.**

Familiarity breeds suspense

Suspense contains a peculiar paradox: if you read a book that you've read before, you can still enjoy a pleasurable build-up even though you know what's going to happen. Here are three suggested explanations for why I think this is the case:

✔ You may simply have forgotten many of the details, so that in some sense you're reading the story for the first time.

✔ Some aspects of suspense occur *because* you know what's going to happen – if you're watching a comedy and see somebody about to walk under a ladder where a worker's holding a pot of paint, you just know that the paint will fall all over the passer-by. But you still enjoy the anticipation and the character's reaction when the inevitable happens.

✔ All reading of fiction involves a certain willing suspension of disbelief. When you re-read a book, you're prepared to still believe on some level that the story may turn out differently this time, even though you know rationally that can't be true.

 Don't keep your character waiting too long: you have to keep the narrative interesting. If you want to spin it out, bring in another diversion or another character to avoid readers getting fed up and skipping to the next page – or even another story!

Investigating Ways to Turn the Screws

You can produce suspense in your stories in all sorts of creative ways. Here I discuss four methods: how to retain narrative movement and momentum; how to sow clues that sprout surprises; how to build vertigo-inducing cliff-hangers; and how to fill your novel with intriguing gaps!

Pushing the narrative for tension's sake

One of the essential aspects of narrative pace is to keep up momentum by introducing new questions and challenges after you've answered a previous one.

 As soon as one thread of the story starts to be resolved, open up a new one.

Suppose your protagonist wants to gain an interview with an important person. Finally, she succeeds. The tension is over. But imagine that the important person has to break off the interview halfway through, and then sets up another one later on. That way you keep the tension going.

Or suppose that a character wakes up in the night after hearing a sound downstairs. She descends the stairs nervously, expecting a burglar. She discovers that she left a large window open ('must've been the wind'). The tension drops. But then imagine that she sees something else that drives the action forwards – the neighbours fighting in the next-door house, a note pinned to the fridge or some drops of blood on the floor. . . .

Try this exercise to show how to keep spinning out the tension. Don't leave too long a gap between the goal achieved and the new challenge:

1. **Write a scene in which a character achieves a minor goal in her story.**

2. **Introduce, before the end of the scene, a new element that opens up a new question, challenge or goal.**

Inflicting change

Another aspect of maintaining narrative tension is to create constant change. Change brings up new conflicts and challenges for your characters, and often makes them uncomfortable. If the situations in your story keep changing, readers are far less likely to get bored.

Characters often react negatively to change. They may actively fight against it or passively resist it, creating more conflict. If changes occur rapidly, the character and readers have to think on their feet. The character may well make bad decisions, which create more problems (in other words, additional suspense) further down the line.

This exercise will help you to create some changes that threaten your character's security, creating both conflict and suspense:

1. **Write down three significant changes that threaten your character in your story.** For example, losing a friend or partner, losing her job, having to move to a new home.

2. **Write a scene involving each change.** How does your character react? Is she overwhelmed or does she take control? What are the knock-on effects of the changes, and how will these affect your story?

Raising the stakes

Fiction always involves what's known as *rising action,* which means that the stakes get higher and higher for your main characters as they go through the story. For example, the longer the lovers have known one another, the more deeply they're in love, and the more terrible the thought of them being separated; the closer the detective gets to uncovering the identity of the serial killer, the more determined the killer becomes to corner and murder the detective.

A common reason for stories not getting going is that the stakes aren't high enough. I'm certainly not saying that all fiction has to be about saving the world – your story can simply involve saving one character who means the world to your protagonist. But whatever your character wants or fears, it must be all-important and all-encompassing to her.

Think of ways to make your character more desperate as the story proceeds. Perhaps she wants something more and more strongly, or the pressures on her grow greater and greater. In this way you get your readers biting their nails to the quick!

Using time pressure

The most common device for increasing narrative tension is to put your character under some kind of time pressure. She has 24 hours to find and defuse a bomb. Kidnappers give a couple seven days to raise the ransom money before they kill the couple's child. A married couple have a fortnight's holiday in which to decide whether they're going to divorce. A character has a month before the wedding to convince the man she loves that he's marrying the wrong woman.

Stories feature two general kinds of deadline:

- ✔ **External:** Deadlines imposed by outside forces. Examples include work deadlines, academic deadlines (such as exams or the end of a term or academic year), a wedding date, birthdays and anniversaries, major festivals, trial dates or dates for an execution, a bomb set to go off at a certain time or a kidnapping deadline, the time a journey takes, seasons, tides, an asteroid that will shortly hit the earth and so on.

- ✔ **Internal:** Deadlines that characters set themselves, such as making a resolution to return to their home town in six months, to lose half a stone in weight by six weeks, to find the right man by the end of the year and so on.

Always set your characters some kind of internal or external deadline at the start of your story, because time pressure turns a slow, meandering story into a tight, tense narrative. As well as the main deadline, you can create a series of smaller interim deadlines to create tension within each chapter or section. You also have the possibility of extending a deadline to spin out your story for longer without losing dramatic tension.

Here are some great examples of time deadlines in novels:

- ✔ In her 2004 novel *Running Hot,* Dreda Say Mitchell's protagonist, Schoolboy, has seven days to get together the money he needs to start a new life outside London.

- ✔ In Christopher Marlowe's 1604 play *Dr Faustus,* the doctor strikes a deal with the devil that he will have 24 years on earth with the devil as his personal servant, before handing himself over to him to be damned in hell for all eternity. His speech at the eleventh hour before the devil comes to claim him at midnight is harrowing.

- ✔ In the 1988 film *D.O.A.,* directed by Annabel Jankel and Rocky Morton – a remake of a 1950s film noir – Professor Dexter Cornell is poisoned. He's told that he has 24 hours to live and during that time he has to find out who killed him and why. (DOA stands for dead on arrival.)

- ✔ *Bridget Jones's Diary* by Helen Fielding (1996) starts with a list of New Year's resolutions and continues with Bridget's daily struggle to achieve them. Each chapter begins with her weight, alcohol units consumed, cigarettes smoked and calorie intake.

Here are two exercises that help you to make use of deadlines in your fiction. In the first one you practise creating external deadlines. Try to be as inventive as you can.

1. **Note down any external deadlines you can create for your character in your story.**

2. **Write a scene in which the deadline is approaching.**

In this second exercise you get to work with internal deadlines. Think about the goals that are appropriate for your character:

1. **Write a scene in which your character makes three New Year's resolutions.**

2. **Have her set a deadline for achieving each one.**

Sowing clues into the story

Clues are an essential ingredient of fiction, not just detective fiction. They're like the paper trail in a treasure hunt. If no pieces of paper point you in the right direction, you don't know where to begin. If too many exist, no one has any fun looking for them. Clues in fiction can be of three main kinds:

- **Physical clues:** Traces a person leaves behind, such as photographs, objects belonging a character, or pieces of herself such as hair or fingerprints.
- **Verbal clues:** Things people say, such as information they give, things they let slip, things they leave unsaid.
- **Action clues:** Things that people do (or don't do) that can give information away. Past actions can also lead readers to expect the character to behave in a similar way in the future.

Clues can be so obvious that readers can't possibly miss them, or so subtle that only discerning readers notice. Probably the best clues are somewhere in between.

If you want to reveal a clue, have your character notice it and describe it to readers in detail. If you want her not to pay attention to it until later, distract readers from it by immediately delivering some other important information or by making the character react emotionally to something else. You can also conceal a physical clue by burying it in a list of other objects, so that the reader doesn't recognise which is the significant one. Remember, the first and last objects in a list are always the most memorable!

Try this exercise to conceal or reveal important clues. I'll give you a clue: remember that the more detailed the description, the more memorable the object will be. Write two lists of objects in which you

- First, conceal which is the important one.
- Second, reveal which is the important one.

You can make your clues ambiguous. A shoe that the main character thinks belongs to one person can turn out to be an identical one belonging to someone else. A clue may mean nothing on its own until another one turns up somewhere else or someone else draws attention to it.

Sketch out a scene involving a clue:

- ✔ Write about a character noticing the clue and realising what it may mean.
- ✔ Write about another character who misses the clue.
- ✔ Write about a character who spots the clue but comes to the wrong conclusion.

Sometimes the best way to check how obvious a clue is (or isn't) is to try it out on a reader – this could be a friend or a fellow writer (more on this topic in Chapter 25).

Constructing cliffhangers

A *cliffhanger* is when you end a scene, chapter or part of a narrative with a main character in a precarious or difficult dilemma, or confronted with a shocking revelation. The intention is to make readers turn the page.

Cliffhangers became extremely popular when many novels were serialised in instalments in magazines, and authors and magazine editors had to tempt readers to come back for more. Nowadays they're extensively used in TV serials and soap operas.

A literal cliffhanger occurs in Thomas Hardy's 1873 novel *A Pair of Blue Eyes*. At the end of Chapter 21 Henry Knight is left suspended over the edge of a cliff, hanging onto a tuft, while Elfride runs for help.

You don't need to end every chapter with a cliffhanger, but stopping on a moment of high tension really helps. Instead of ending with the sentence revealing or resolving something, try ending just before those words and carrying them over to open the next chapter.

Creating a gap in the narrative

Although leaving a gaping hole in the plot is certainly something no one would advise, placing a deliberate gap in the narrative line is a classic device for creating suspense. It means that readers don't know what happened at a critical point in the story.

You can achieve this goal in a number of ways depending on the point of view you're using to narrate the story. (As I describe in Chapter 8, in the first- or third-person limited narrative, readers can only know what the character knows.) These are:

- ✔ **Your character loses her memory:** A contemporary example is SJ Watson's 2011 novel *Before I Go to Sleep,* in which a character suffers from amnesia and wakes up every morning not knowing who she is and what's happened to her. She tries to overcome this problem by writing a diary.

- ✔ **Your narrative leaves a character just before an important event happens, and you switch to another point of view only to return to the first character much later.** In Joseph Conrad's 1911 novel *Under Western Eyes,* the first part of the novel ends with the main character facing a dilemma. The narrative then skips forward several months and changes to the point of view of a teacher of English in Geneva, who meets the main character in exile there. Readers only find out what choice the main character made much later.

- ✔ **You break off a journal or spoken account at a certain point, leaving your readers in the dark about what happens later in the story.** A famous example is Bram Stocker's 1897 novel *Dracula,* which is told as a series of letters, diary entries and ship's log entries, occasionally supplemented with newspaper clippings. Switching from one part of the story to another helps create narrative suspense.

- ✔ **Your unreliable narrator deliberately withholds information about an event.** Agatha Christie's 1926 novel *The Murder of Roger Ackroyd* has a narrator who hides essential truths in the text through evasion, omission and obfuscation.

This last technique is difficult to achieve without readers feeling cheated. You need to develop the voice of the character in such a way that the reader realises that she may not be entirely reliable (see Chapter 8).

Try out this technique by creating a missing piece in your own story. It could be a conversation where a significant piece of information is exchanged, a meeting that one of the characters (and therefore the reader) doesn't know about, or an event the main character isn't privy to. Remember that you need to know what happened, even if the characters don't:

1. **Think of a way to create a gap in the narrative of your own story.**

2. **Make sure that what happens in this gap is vital to your story. If the plot doesn't turn on it, this exercise won't work.**

Chapter 22

Expanding Your Ideas into Larger Narratives

*H*ave you ever had the feeling that what you're doing is not working out the way it should? For example, the cake you are baking fails to rise so you put fruit on top and turn it into a weird kind of flan, or a utility room turns into a second sitting room because you knock down the wrong wall!

You may encounter a similar issue in your writing. Perhaps you start out with an idea for a novel, but realise that it's not going to be long enough or complex enough to satisfy readers, though it's far too long to be a short story. But never fear, because, as I describe in this chapter, you have plenty of effective options for complicating and expanding the basic premise of your story into a longer and more widely satisfying narrative.

One approach is to work with your characters, adding new ones, developing others into bigger roles and complicating their lives. You can do this in the present by involving them in additional plot lines, or you can add information from the past.

Alternatively, you can expand ideas from the point of view of the plot or narrative, bringing in new themes to enrich the fiction or connecting different threads of the story to make a richer and more suspenseful whole. Sometimes you may want to connect together a number of ideas and stories, perhaps thematically or by creating an overall situation (or *bridge*) that forms a link between different parts of what becomes the whole work.

Expanding Your Work with the Characters

One of the simplest ways to broaden a story is to take one or more of the minor characters and expand their roles. Doing so creates a richer texture for the story, adding characters who have different views and goals to those of your protagonist. In fact, if you don't develop the more minor characters, they fail to seem real and the narrative can appear insufficiently lifelike.

Aim to give all significant characters their own developed narrative within the overall story. For instance, your main character may be on a quest to achieve a particular goal, but his sister who lives nearby is involved in a romance. Or your main narrative may be a rags-to-riches story, but developing a minor character allows you to add a contrasting plot line of failure or tragedy.

Even the most minor character can have a big impact on how the story develops. Leo Tolstoy's *Anna Karenina* (1877) contains a scene where Karenin goes to see a lawyer with the aim of getting a divorce. While Karenin explains the situation, the lawyer kills moths flying across his desk. The lawyer is so odious to Karenin that he abandons plans to divorce his wife, thus the outcome of the novel changes. The skilful way Tolstoy describes this interaction explains Karenin's decision perfectly.

Connecting with new characters

Bringing in a new character or developing a minor one enables you to add another strand to your story. This character can be directly connected to the main character, connected to another important character or someone who occupies a whole other plot strand that meets up with the main one later.

Ensure that the new character's story intersects with that of your main character.

In Chapter 2, I provide a have-a-go exercise that helps you produce a map of character connections. If you haven't completed that exercise, you can do it now. Examine the map and think about these questions:

✔ Have you ignored any characters or not thought of who may play a bigger role in your story? If so, write about them.

✔ What do these characters want that's different from your main character's goal? For example:

- Your main character can have a sibling with financial problems who keeps borrowing money, putting them both in difficulty.

- The woman your character fancies at work is divorced but turns out to have a disabled son to care for, creating difficulties in the relationship but also demonstrating her compassion and commitment.

- An uncle dies and leaves a character a house that has to be sold. An old friend of the family turns up and starts causing problems.

When you introduce new characters, don't let them clutter up the story without influencing the main character's story. If characters don't interact, positively or negatively, they don't belong. Each new character needs to act to help your main character get what he wants or to get in the way. Also, you can have too many characters. If you find that a character isn't really doing anything in the plot, be ruthless and take him out (sorry to sound like a villain ordering a hit!).

Involving characters in new plot lines

When you extend and complicate your story by adding new plot lines involving other characters, as I discuss in the preceding section, you need to drop in the new strand of your narrative at intervals between the sections concerned with the main plot line.

Readers have to be able to see the connections as they occur or foresee trouble brewing ahead. In the end, subplots need to intersect with the main plot, ideally with a satisfying 'ah-ha!' moment as readers understand why the subplot and its characters existed all along.

I provide loads more useful info on subplots in Chapter 20.

This is a useful exercise to help you work out who your character's friends and foes are and ensure you have a good balance in your story:

1. **Divide a page into six sections, placing your main character in the top left-hand box.**

2. **Enter the names of three other characters who can help your main character get what he wants, and two others to hinder him.**

3. **Select one helper who can swap to become a hinderer, and one hinderer who turns out to be a helper.**

4. **Write some scenes where the characters interact.**

Complicating your characters' lives

A great way to expand the interest of your story is to ensure that your protagonist faces plenty of difficulties in achieving his goal. You need to find plenty of complications and challenges for your characters to struggle against.

Here's a list of some kinds of complications that you can use in your creative fiction:

- **Financial complications:** Characters can lose money, get into debt and experience financial difficulties. They can even win money or be left a legacy that causes bad feelings or resentment when they refuse to spend it on or share it with others.

- **Career complications:** Characters can lose their jobs, get new bosses, have an impossible relationship with someone in their team, be promoted and find that they're struggling, and be posted to another city or country.

- **Family complications:** Parents may get ill or die; siblings can be difficult; wives, partners or girlfriends can get pregnant. Children can experience difficulties at school, get ill, take drugs or otherwise cause problems.

- **Complications with friends:** Friends can fall out, become demanding or have problems they need to resolve. They can betray confidences or share secrets. They can take up weird hobbies or dump their problems on your main character.

- **Health complications:** Characters can become ill or worried about their health. Even minor illnesses can have an impact on your story and affect relationships between characters. Characters can become depressed or mentally unstable.

- **Housing complications:** Your characters may need to move house, may be thrown out of their homes and need to find somewhere new to live, or their houses can be flooded or need expensive repairs.

- **Political complications:** Your characters may face a political crisis, a riot or an election. Characters can disagree violently about politics or individual policies that affect them.

- **Sexual complications:** People have affairs or fancy inappropriate people. They may have sexual secrets or commit sexual indiscretions and may change their sexual orientation.

Whenever you feel that things are getting too easy for your characters, throw in something from this list. Authors need to be ruthless and inflict on their characters events they wouldn't wish on their worst enemy in real life!

Brace yourself to make things really tough for your characters with this exercise (though try not to overdo things so much that your story becomes like an over-heated soap opera!):

1. **Think of half a dozen complications from the list in this section that you can insert into your story.**

2. **Write a scene involving each one.**

Weaving characters into new timeframes

You can introduce complexity into a story by integrating information from your characters' past. You can do so via short flashbacks, but sometimes a sufficiently interesting event from your characters' past can create a whole story within the story.

Perhaps a character in the present is exploring a mystery in the past, or you can explain his current behaviour by relating events from his childhood. For instance, uncertainty may surround one grandparent, who turns out to have been mentally ill. This may explain your main character's mood swings and help him get a diagnosis. Or maybe your protagonist moved home repeatedly in childhood, which explains why he'd rather do anything than get divorced and lose the family home.

You can also introduce a thematic connection between your character's story and that of his parents, grandparents or more distant relatives, which can add another layer to your story.

Write a story based in the past that you can weave into your present work to expand it. It doesn't have to take up a large amount of space in the novel, but should reveal something important to the character in the present.

Check out the next section for all about adding themes to your work, and Chapter 19 for handling flashbacks and past stories.

Using Narrative and Plot to Expand Your Story

In the preceding section I discuss expanding your work with a focus on characters. Here I suggest using plots, themes and subject matter to add size and complexity. Of course, plots and characters are intimately intermingled, and so these areas overlap.

Bringing in big themes

One way to make your story larger and more complex, as well as raise the stakes for the characters, is to introduce a big theme. Doing so allows you to add an extra layer to the plot and make your character's choices more significant in the wider world of the story. A *theme* is a universal idea or concept that threads through an entire story. It's related not to the content of a story – which is the *subject matter* – so much as to what that *means*. Characters have experiences as they go through the story, and through these readers come to some conclusion about the human condition and perhaps how people ought to live.

For instance, your character wanting to do well at his job so that he can make lots of money is one thing, but when his job has a significant positive effect on the outside world, that's quite another, and allows you to develop this as a theme. Your character can be involved in medical research, developing a new treatment to help a large number of people; or he may be involved in environmental concerns or politics, or in preventing some kind of disaster. If his work is really important to him, it can interfere with personal relationships and be a great source of conflict for your story, making it more interesting.

When your piece of fiction explores a theme, let your readers arrive at their conclusions instead of making your personal position clear. For example, if you want to write a book about the evils of the financial markets, it works best when you just write the story of the characters and let readers decide which characters they identify with and what they feel is right and wrong.

Making the theme of the story controversial is helpful in developing your readers' interest. Having an issue about which readers can disagree makes people want to discuss the book and even argue about it!

Themes to consider

Here are some common themes you can use to give weight to your fiction:

- ✔ Individual will versus fate or destiny

- ✔ Conflict between the individual and society

- ✔ People in conflict with technology

- ✔ Love against ambition

- ✔ Faith against doubt

- ✔ Growing up and coming of age

- ✔ Loss and fear of death

- ✔ Love and sacrifice

- ✔ Exposing corruption

- ✔ Humans against nature

You can introduce such themes into your story in several ways. For instance, perhaps one of your characters is ill and suffering from a particular condition. This can provide an interesting contrast in a romantic novel or a thriller. Or another character has a religious conversion that brings him into conflict with other friends and relatives, and challenges the views of all the characters in the story.

Large themes are played out in very different ways in different works of fiction. Much 19th-century fiction is concerned with the position of women in society: the fact that men could control a woman's wealth, the double standard that men could divorce their wives but women couldn't divorce their husbands, and that it was acceptable for men to be unfaithful while women were utterly disgraced. This theme appears in Leo Tolstoy's *Anna Karenina* (1877), Henry James's *The Portrait of a Lady* (1881) and Thomas Hardy's *Tess of the d'Urbervilles* (1891).

Charles Dickens explored themes of poverty and exploitation of workers and children in many of his novels, including *Oliver Twist* (1838), *Little Dorrit* (1857) and *Bleak House* (1853). His portrayals so upset people that they brought about real legal change and social improvements.

In the 20th century, the two brutal world wars inspired writers to explore the horror of military conflict. Erich Maria Remarque's *All Quiet on the Western Front* (1929) gives a brutally realistic account of the horrors of trench warfare in the First World War from the perspective of a German soldier, and Ernest Hemingway's *For Whom the Bell Tolls* (1941) is set during the Spanish Civil War.

Novels such as Graham Greene's *The Quiet American* (1955) explore the origins of the war in Vietnam, and John le Carré investigated the psychology of the Cold War through a series of gripping espionage books.

Science fiction was a popular genre during this period and tackled big themes connected with how future technological developments will affect human society and the dangers they may present.

In the later part of the 20th century going into the 21st, much fiction has explored the voices of members of society who had previously been marginalised: gay people, people from ethnic minorities, those with disabilities and so on.

The need for research

When you bring in a big theme, you may well need to research it to produce the important facts and details to shape how your story develops.

In such cases, do your research at the same time as you're writing – first, because you know what information you need and what's irrelevant, thus reducing the overall amount of research necessary; second, because if you do all your research before you start writing, you run the risk of never actually starting to write! (I discuss doing research in Chapter 2.)

When you're writing a scene and you need a specific piece of information, don't break the flow by stopping and rushing off to do research. Make a note of what you want to know and carry on with the scene. You may find that you need two or three additional pieces of information, and then you can do all the research together.

You can research for a story in two main ways:

- ✔ **First-hand research:** If you can, getting first-hand information is the best way to go. First-hand research includes activities such as going to the Victoria and Albert Museum to look at the costumes worn by people in a particular era, or visiting a place where your story is set or where a particular event occurred – provided it hasn't changed too much, of course, and even then it can be helpful.

    Many professional people are surprisingly helpful when you tell them you're writing a piece of fiction. If you ask around, you're bound to find someone who knows someone who has a friend who's an expert in whatever field you need information about.

Many writers make sure that they've directly participated in or observed the subject they want to include in their fiction. Crime novelist Patricia Cornwell covered police work at the *Charlotte Observer* and then took a job in the Office of the Chief Medical Examiner, which enabled her to write knowledgeably about police investigations and autopsies. Ian McEwan observed a brain surgeon at work so that he could create a realistic scene in his novel *Saturday* (2005).

✔ **Second-hand research:** If you can't observe something directly, you can always talk to somebody who has. If you're researching a historical subject, you can often find first-hand accounts written down at that time. You can also research facts through libraries and via the Internet.

Try this exercise to find out how useful doing research can be. Try to pick a limited topic and set yourself a time limit for doing the research – otherwise it might take years(!):

1. **Write a scene where you need to do some research.** Do the research.

2. **Ring someone knowledgeable to get some information.** Write a scene that includes what you find.

You never know which little detail is going to be important or give your story the right touch of authenticity, so do keep a note or file of everything you've researched. But don't just dump information in the text to show that you've done your research. Readers notice and it breaks their concentration.

Sensory details are important in convincing readers. The colour or texture of something, the smell or sound, is what you get through direct observation or talking to someone who has witnessed a similar event to the one you are describing. These details will also help you to expand your book into something more complex.

Threading together themes and subjects

If you have a theme or specific subject matter for your story, you need to tie all the other threads into it when producing a longer piece of work. Different strands within your story can all provide a different angle on the same theme. You can have fun placing little connections in your story as you go.

You can connect different stories or threads of stories to one another in loads of ways:

- **Characters living in the same place:** Sherwood Anderson's 1919 *Winesburg, Ohio* and Rohinton Mistry's *Tales from Firozsha Baag* (1987) are linked by the characters living in the same town or apartment block.

- **Characters thrown together by circumstance:** *If Nobody Speaks of Remarkable Things* (2002) by Jon McGregor portrays a day in the life of a suburban British street, following the lives of the street's various inhabitants. Readers gradually realise that something terrible happened that day that links the various stories.

- **Characters linked by an object handed from one to another:** Annie Proulx's *Accordion Crimes* (1996) tells the stories of immigrants to America through the eyes of the descendants of Mexicans, Poles, Africans, Irish-Scots, Franco-Canadians and many others, all linked by their successive ownership of a green accordion.

- **Stories within stories, which characters narrate, write down or read:** Italo Calvino's *If On a Winter's Night a Traveller* (1979) contains several incomplete narratives. The frame story is about someone trying to read a book called *If On a Winter's Night a Traveller.* Alternating between chapters of this story are the first chapters from ten different novels, of widely varying style, genre and subject matter; all are interrupted for reasons that are explained in the frame story.

- **Stories from different stages of a character's life:** *The Girls' Guide to Hunting and Fishing* (1988) by Melissa Bank contains short stories linked through being different episodes from the protagonist's life.

- **Stories linked by a theme such as love, death or money:** David Mitchell's novel *Cloud Atlas* (2004) has an ingenious structure in which six stories from different eras, written in different styles, are nested inside one another. Each story has a connection to the previous one, and part of the fun of reading each new story is to discover the link. The novel also seems to show that many of the characters may be one soul reincarnated in different bodies, pointing to the theme that we are all interconnected.

Try this exercise to find ways of connecting separate stories. If the first version doesn't work, then keep trying the various options until you find one that does:

1. **Pick one of the six structures in the preceding list and plan a novel.**

2. **Invent an additional, unusual way to combine different characters and their stories.**

Spanning events with a bridge story

If you have a number of short-story ideas, sketches based on different characters or an episodic story that doesn't seem to hang together, here's an excellent way to bring them all together: connect them with a narrative that functions like a bridge, linking all the other stories together.

For this approach to work, you need an overall situation that has its own narrative arc but also connects a number of characters. For example, suppose you've written some pieces about five different characters in contemporary London. None of the stories really leads anywhere, and you don't know what to do with them all.

But now imagine that you put all the characters in the same carriage on an underground train, and that a terrorist incident traps the train in the tunnel. You now have a story unfolding in the present that deals with how the five characters react to this situation, as well as what happens in the end, interspersed with the individual stories about the five characters and how they come to be on the train that day. Check out the nearby sidebar 'Building bridges' to read about a couple of examples.

Building bridges

The bridge narrative is used in Danny Boyle's 2008 film *Slumdog Millionaire* (based on the 2005 novel *Q&A* by Vikas Swarup). Here the overall arc concerns whether the protagonist cheated in the Indian *Who Wants to Be a Millionaire?* TV show. The film starts with the main character's arrest and is interspersed with scenes of his interrogation, during which he recounts several important episodes from his life that reveal why he knows the answer to each of the questions.

Another book with this structure is *The Bridge of San Luis Rey* (1927) by Thornton Wilder. In fact I call this structure a *bridge story* not only because the main narrative arcs over the other stories like a bridge, supporting each individual story, but also because the name pays homage to Thornton Wilder's book, in which a bridge in the Andes collapses, throwing five characters into the abyss. The priest who sees this event finds his faith in God challenged. He investigates the lives of these five people and discovers that each one of them seems to have died for a reason, and so his faith in God is ultimately restored.

The minimum number of stories you can connect with this kind of structure is three, and the most about six, because after this number the overall story tends to become too fragmented and readers may have difficulty engaging with the number of characters.

It's not always easy to find ways of linking characters, but this exercise should help you:

1. **Take three to six characters you've been working with and make notes on each one, detailing their interests, routines and work and family lives.**

2. **Now use these to help you think of a situation that can bring the characters unexpectedly together and throw them into close proximity. These could involve an accident, a holiday, a marriage, a neighbourhood or a common interest.**

Short-story collections always sell fewer copies than novels do, and so a good idea is to link short stories together if you can. You can then sell and market the book as a novel.

Chapter 23

Approaching the Grand Finale: The End's in Sight!

*A*s readers get near to finishing your story or novel, they need to be able to feel the tension mounting. (For loads more on creating tension and suspense, read Chapter 21.) At some point, the story can't get any more dramatic and everything has to come to a head. This climax to your story is the most important part of all – except for the beginning!

In the climax you bring together all the threads that you set up throughout your narrative, and the story reaches the point of no return. You then follow the climax with the resolution and a final ending. How you complete a story matters, because that's what readers take away with them. Many a potentially great book is spoilt by an inadequate end.

As with beginnings (see Chapter 17), take down some books from your shelves and study the climaxes, resolutions and endings to see which ones work for you and which ones don't.

Preparing for the End

The *ending* of your novel (that is, its final scene) is different to its climax, resolution and *end* (in the sense of the beginning, middle and end). Appreciating just how important the overall end is requires you to understand its role within the wider narrative, how to bring various story threads together and how to approach that all-important climactic scene effectively.

Climbing aboard the story arc

Your work's end takes place within your work's whole narrative structure, as I depict in Figure 23-1.

The Story Arc

Beginning   Middle   End

Climax
Many stories end just after the climax.

Short stories often centre around the climax.

*Main narrative question
*Character introductions
*Main setting
*Tension rises

*Resolutions, questions answered, all threads tied together
*Tension falls

*Conflicts, obstacles and complications
*Stakes raised
*Relationships developed
*Tension rises untill the climax

Rising Action

Falling Action

Tension

Exposition Inciting incident
Many stories start here.

Denouement

Time

Your time structure may not be chronological, but your tension should follow the same arc, rising to a dramatic climax.

Figure 23-1: The story arc from beginning to middle and end, including the position of the climax.

REMEMBER

✔ **Beginning:** The story starts by setting the scene, introducing the characters and asking the central narrative question, often dramatised through an inciting incident that kicks off the story.

✔ **Middle:** The characters encounter obstacles and conflicts, and readers experience rising action as the stakes get higher and emotions intensify. Scenes where the main characters get nearer to their goals alternate with scenes where they're knocked back, as the story twists and turns to keep readers hooked.

At the top of the curve comes the climax – the point of highest tension. (Check out the later section 'Producing Your Story's Highpoint: The Climax'.)

> ✔ **End:** Contains the resolution and ending. As you can see, the climax isn't the same as the ending (which I discuss later in 'Writing the Final Scene').

Follow this classic structure for your stories and you can't go far wrong!

Bringing all the threads together

Tying all the separate threads of your story together before the climactic scene is very important. You can do this by bringing together characters from different strands and forcing an interaction between them.

Anna Karenina by Leo Tolstoy (1877) has two main threads to its story. The first one concerns Anna's failed marriage to Karenin and her affair with Vronsky. The second one concerns Levin and his marriage to Kitty. Connections between the two stories go deeper than the fact that they're all part of the same social network. Kitty was engaged to Vronsky but broke off the engagement when Vronsky fell for Anna.

Shortly before the climax of the novel, Levin goes to visit Anna. Although Tolstoy reveals no obvious result of this meeting, the meeting is satisfying for readers because it reveals some parallels between the two stories.

In JRR Tolkien's *The Lord of the Rings* (1954), the mithril coat stolen from Frodo in one strand of the story is shown to the rest of the fellowship in front of the Gates of Mordor just before the final battle. Not only does this lead the fellowship to the wrong conclusion, but it also neatly brings the two timelines together.

If you're not sure how to bring your characters together, stage a big event – a party, a wedding, a funeral, a trial, a battle, a performance at the theatre or opera – where all the characters converge. This has the added bonus of creating time pressure in advance as well.

Building up to the climax

As the climax of your story comes closer, you need to create the impression of increasing speed. You want readers to turn the pages faster and faster. One way to do this is to create a series of short scenes in which characters prepare for the action at the climax. They may need to buy guns and transport them across town to defend themselves at the final confrontation, or get dressed and prepare for the wedding or stage performance or appearance at the trial, or slog up the final slopes of the mountain.

Write a series of short scenes building up to a climactic scene. Keep individual scenes brief and sentences within them short as well.

'Wait until you see the whites of their eyes!'

If you've plotted your story well, your main character has gone through a series of crises and disasters on her way towards the grand finale. Each crisis creates obstacles and challenges but also opportunities for your character.

Sometimes earlier scenes can act as a minor version of your climax. If your climax is going to be a big battle, try writing a small battle earlier in your story. If the climax is going to be the revelation of a mystery, write a scene in which some small aspect of this mystery is revealed sooner.

As you move towards the ending of the story, the pace increases as the tension builds and you have more action. Often, just before the climax, you need a scene when the main character discovers some sort of information or revelation that propels her towards a final confrontation.

Tension has to mount throughout your story, and at some point you just can't hold off any longer. Readers can take only so much of a character agonising, vacillating, hanging onto a cliff by her fingertips or anxiously awaiting a marriage proposal. And your character can trek across the desert for only so long before dying.

If you keep the tension going for too long, it becomes too much for your readers. You need enough tension, but not too much. Short scenes on the way to the climax work well because readers can stand only so much tension before they start skipping over the pages or give up and put the book down. A long, drawn-out scene before the climax is asking for trouble, because readers can't concentrate on it and it slows down the narrative pace.

When you reach the point of maximum tension, jump ahead to the climax. I describe writing the climax in the next section, 'Producing Your Story's Highpoint: The Climax'.

'I can't take it any more!' Reaching breaking point

When you've wound up the tension to the maximum, it has to snap like a coiled spring. Explaining exactly how much tension a narrative can take is difficult because it varies with every story – it's partly a matter of trial and error and partly a matter of learning from reading and analysing books and seeing how they work.

Pay attention to the mood and pace of your scene to discover the right moment, just as you find the beat of a piece of music and join in at the right time. That's when to cut the tension by bringing in your climax.

Producing Your Story's Highpoint: The Climax

The climactic scene of your story is the most difficult of all to write. The whole story stands or falls on how you deliver your climax. This scene needs to be dramatic, believable and carry an emotional punch, all without being melodramatic or over the top.

Understanding the climactic scene

You can easily fall into the trap of putting off writing the climactic scene; after all, it's hard to write and you need to showcase all your skills. You may be afraid that your scene will be too dramatic and you may veer away from writing about strong emotions and using 'purple prose' (overwritten language). The problem is, this can make your scene lacklustre and bland. The fear of overwriting can make you skip over the most significant parts of the story. Don't make this mistake!

A short story is essentially the climactic event on its own. Whereas a novel takes time to build up to and fall away from the climax, the short story homes in on the dramatic event that changes a character's life forever; it's like a snapshot of that scene instead of a whole movie.

Just as the scenes before the climax tend to be short and breathless (see the earlier section 'Building up to the climax'), time often slows down completely in the climactic scene, almost as if it's happening in slow motion. The climactic scene needs to show off all your skills as a writer – the description of the scene, the characters' emotions, the dialogue and the action. The climactic scene is what the whole story's been building up to, and so it has to be the best you can possibly produce.

The climax tends to be one of two types:

- ✔ **Confrontation:** Can consist of a battle involving large numbers of characters as well as your protagonist, or a dual between the protagonist and the antagonist. It doesn't necessarily have to be a physical fight – it can be a war of words or an emotional scene – but it has to involve struggle, and one or other character has to 'win'. In a comedy, however, both characters can win, and in some tragedies you can convey a sense in which both characters lose.

- ✔ **Revelation:** Comes in two kinds:

  - **External revelation:** Reveals a piece of information that explains everything that's happened before or is the answer to the main character's quest.

  - **Internal revelation:** Often also called an *epiphany,* this happens when the main character has a sudden revelation and understands something about herself or the world that changes her forever.

An epiphany almost always means that a character has to change; for example, unless she gives up alcohol her life will continue to fall apart, or unless she gives up searching for the perfect man she'll never have a satisfying relationship, or unless she gives up her greedy desire for more wealth she'll never be happy. It can also be a moment of transcendence – a realisation that life consists of something more than the material world.

This moment of transformation can be extremely satisfying in a story. Readers don't want to read through a whole novel just for the characters to turn out the same at the end as they were in the beginning. Something has to change – and if it doesn't change, that's a tragedy: readers recognise the moment when something should've happened but didn't.

Kazuo Ishiguro's *The Remains of the Day* (1989) has a moment when readers realise that Stevens still has the chance to confess his love for Miss Kenton. The moment when they do part from one another is almost unbearably painful, because Stevens never admits his true feelings even to himself.

Beware of writing cheap epiphanies. Sometimes a story says 'Suddenly she realised that . . . ' and out comes a realisation that has nothing to do with what happened previously. A true epiphany needs to occur for a reason and emerge from everything the character learned during the story.

Write a dramatic scene that can be the climax of your story. Slow down the pace and really take time over the scene. You don't need to drag out the scene or write in irrelevant details – but the climactic scene does need to feel to your readers as if it is happening in 'real time' so that they can experience it directly along with the characters.

If you're writing a story divided into books or parts, each section needs a climactic scene, though a less dramatic one than the final one. In any story, you require a number of dramatic set pieces that form major turning points in the narrative.

Changing everything in a single line

The remarkable thing about the climax of a story is that it can often be pinned down to a single sentence. It's as if all the threads of your story narrow down and down until they pass through the eye of a needle! The climax happens in one instant – when a character dies or realises the truth or discovers the secret. If your climax is strung out over many pages or even chapters, try instead to pin it down to one single moment.

I look at a few examples of famous single-line moments in the following list. Note that after these moments have happened, the story can't go back. In theory, at any other point up to the climax, the character can retreat back to her former state of knowledge or give up her struggle:

✔ ***Emma:*** The climactic line is:

> It went through her with the speed of an arrow, that Mr Knightley must marry no one but herself!
>
> —*Jane Austen (Emma, Penguin, 1968, first published 1815)*

At this moment, Emma realises how wrong she was to encourage her protégée, Harriet, to fall in love with a man above her station in life. Now Harriet has fallen for the very man Emma loves and wants to marry. Emma can never be the same person again, and regardless of what happens at the end of the story, she'll lead her life differently.

✔ ***The Wings of the Dove:*** The last line goes:

> We shall never be again as we were!
>
> —*Henry James (The Wings of the Dove, Penguin, 2008, first published, 1902)*

Kate Croy and Merton Densher aren't rich and so in the world of Henry James novels they can't marry. They plot for Merton to marry a rich American heiress who's dying of tuberculosis, and then he'll inherit her fortune and marry Kate. Unfortunately, things don't quite work out as planned: at the end Merton has the money but Kate no longer feels that they can marry one another, because what they've done has made everything look different.

✔ ***The Lord of the Rings:*** The line is:

> And with that, even as his eyes were lifted up to gloat on his prize, he stepped too far, toppled, wavered for a moment on the brink, and then with a shriek he fell.
>
> —*JRR Tolkien, The Lord of the Rings, George Allen & Unwin, 1954)*

After the Ring is destroyed by Gollum falling into the Crack of Doom, it can't be made again. The climax really is the point of no return.

Take the climax scene you create in the preceding section and see whether you can locate the single line where everything changes.

If you can't, write one in at the appropriate place.

Answering the central narrative question

The climax of the story has to answer the main narrative question that you ask at the beginning. Therefore, in a detective story the climax is the revelation of the murderer's identity. In a romance, it's the moment when the characters propose or decide to be together. In a quest, it's achieving whatever the character desires. In a tragedy, it's the moment of the protagonist's undoing.

In *Pride and Prejudice* (1813) by Jane Austen, the question is: will the Bennets succeed in marrying off their daughters, and will the daughters have to choose between love and money when they marry? In Dostoyevsky's *Crime and Punishment* (1886) the question is: will Raskolnikov be found out after the murder? In *Cold Mountain* (1997) by Charles Frazier, the question is: will Inman survive and return to Ada? In all these stories, readers have to wait almost to the end before they find out the answers.

You can write a story in which the question isn't answered, but then the whole point of the story becomes that fact. Samuel Beckett does this in his 1953 play *Waiting for Godot,* because Godot never appears. The whole point of the work is that salvation never arrives and yet humans continue to wait for it (cheery!). The play seeks to subvert the audience's narrative expectations.

Before you attempt to try this type of subversion, make sure that you've mastered traditional narrative structure. Otherwise your story may fall completely flat.

See whether you can frame the central narrative question of your story in a couple of lines. If not, why not? Try to narrow it down until you are clear. When you're ready, write the scene in which this question is answered.

Throwing in the unexpected

Most readers are aware that the climactic scene answers the central question, and because you've usually foreshadowed it and built up to it throughout your story, they often also know roughly what's going to happen. As a result, the climax works best when you throw some unexpected element into the mix. For example, perhaps the detective is right about who committed the murder but wrong about the murderer's motives, or the right man proposes but also announces beforehand that he has to move to a foreign country for his work. The character can achieve the object of her quest but discover that she doesn't want it after all.

Here are examples of a twist at the climax:

- *Pygmalion* **(1912) by George Bernard Shaw:** Henry Higgins wins his bet that he can turn a flower girl into a convincing duchess, but Eliza makes an unexpected choice as a result.

- *The Lord of the Rings* **(1954) by JRR Tolkien:** The climax comes when Frodo finally reaches Mount Doom. When I first read the book, all my attention was on him getting there – I never imagined that when he did, he'd be unable to destroy the Ring and would need Gollum's intervention to bring this about.

- *Bleak House* **(1853) by Charles Dickens:** Richard and Ada finally win their case in the Court of Chancery, but then readers discover that the money has all been spent on legal costs.

Write a climactic scene with a twist. If you can't think of one, do the exercise on shocks and surprises in Chapter 18 and bring one of these surprises into your climactic scene.

Writing the Final Scene

After the climax (see the preceding section), readers need some time to see what will happen as a result of the climactic scene's events. They need to see the dust settle and understand the consequences.

The climactic scene is seldom the end of the story. You usually want to include some quieter scenes to wind down after all the drama. Everything needs to be slowing down, bringing readers gently to rest at the end of their journey.

Often the ending also looks backwards, reviewing the action of the story. In some novels, however, after the action of the main story finishes, the character steps forward into a new world – one that readers can never know about but may be able to imagine.

A story takes in the critical events of a character's life, and because the choices made and the actions taken have changed her forever, readers can often imagine how the rest of the character's life will be.

Tying up loose ends

Make sure that you don't leave any major unanswered questions in readers' minds. This doesn't mean that you have to cross every single 't' and dot every single 'i', but you do have to satisfy readers' curiosity about the most important issues in your story.

Everything in your story needs to play some part, and readers should be able to recognise the role of everything at the end of the story. You don't want readers to wonder what happened to a character you introduced early on and who hasn't been heard of since, or to wonder why the dialogue in the middle of the book hinted at something that's never happened or been revealed.

Choosing your type of ending

Basically, you can opt for five kinds of ending:

- **Happy ending:** You can have your main character getting what she desires: marrying the right person, coming home safely, achieving the object of her quest, defeating the monster and so on.

Pros:

- Promotes a feel-good factor, because readers come away feeling happy and that life's basically good

- Creates a feeling of satisfaction that the story is complete

- Can make the main character earn the outcome, rewarding good behaviour

Cons:

- Can seem sentimental and contrived

- Often feels too easy or glib

- Can be too predictable

✔ **Sad or tragic ending:** You can defeat your character (perhaps she brings down other people with her), usually as the result of a fatal flaw in her character.

Pros:

- Can be cathartic, because readers come away feeling that their own lives aren't so bad in comparison

- Warns readers of the danger of bad behaviour, because the character gets her comeuppance, which can be satisfying

- Can feel profound and more true to life than a happy ending, because in the end everyone dies!

Cons:

- Can be depressing

- No possibility of a sequel if your main character is dead

- Readers can feel cheated if the main character doesn't deserve her dreadful fate

✔ **Open ending:** You can leave the story's ending open for readers to decide what finally happens. If you opt for an open ending, make sure that you have a great climax, otherwise the story feel unresolved.

Pros:

- Often resonates with readers for longer, because they imagine all the possible outcomes

- Can seem more realistic than a cut-and-dried ending

- Leaves things open for a sequel

Cons:

- Can feel unsatisfactory or unfinished

- Can seem deliberately clever or playing with readers

- Has to be handled carefully to work well

✔ **Twist ending:** The story ends with a twist that makes readers re-examine everything that came before. A good twist makes readers think, 'Of course, why didn't I realise that before?' while a bad twist pulls the rug out from under readers and makes them feel cheated. After all, a writer can easily not tell readers something that they need to know in order to understand the story. You have to be clever about the way you handle a twist, and you need to have a good reason for it that fits into the theme of your book.

Pros:

- Can make readers want to read the story again in the light of their new knowledge, if it's a clever twist, giving them two books for the price of one

- Can be more thought-provoking than a conventional ending

- Can give readers a pleasurable shock

Cons:

- Can undermine readers' trust in the writer

- Can leave readers feeling cheated

- Can seem too clever by half!

✔ **Bittersweet ending:** Here the character essentially gets what she wants but also loses something significant along the way. For example, a sad ending can contain an element of redemption as well as seeds of hope for the future. Sometimes where you have more than one plot strand in a story, one strand can end happily while the other one doesn't.

Pros:

- Can make a happy ending more realistic or soften a tragic one

- Can create a more lifelike feel to the story

- Can have more subtlety than the two extremes

Cons:

- Can be disappointing, seen to be neither one thing nor the other

- Can feel confusing or anti-climactic

- Can be difficult to get right

Here are some of the kinds of endings to avoid:

- **Utterly predictable endings:** Here readers realise on page 3, say, that Alex will marry Pat or kill Tony. If readers can be bothered to read the story at all, they'll probably hurl the book across the room when they get to the ending.

- **Fizzle-out endings:** End your story with a bang not a whimper. Don't skip the climax (check out the earlier section 'Producing Your Story's Highpoint: The Climax') and don't let your story trail away into a series of bland and uninteresting scenes.

- **Outstayed-welcome endings:** Don't go on and on and on long past the natural end point of the story. This often happens because you can't bear to let go of your lovely characters or because you can't face the hard work of revising the book or the agony of showing it to your friends, but in the end you have to let it go.

- ***Deus ex machina* endings:** In ancient Greek drama, the gods used to arrive in a chariot at the end and dispense justice to the hapless mortals. It worked then, but nowadays it jars. Beware of rolling a character on at the end of your story who sorts everything out. If you do want this kind of ending, you need to foreshadow it carefully from much earlier in the story.

- **'Asteroid' endings:** My term for when a random event happens out of the blue and scatters or kills everyone. It can work in a certain genre of fiction, particularly surrealist humour, but is best avoided in most fiction.

- **It-was-all-a-dream endings:** Don't completely undermine the whole premise of your story at the end. Your readers have engaged with your characters over many pages and chapters; they don't want to be told it was all in vain. William Golding got away with it in *Pincher Martin* (1956), but he's a genius and the ending is ambiguous enough that you can read it as genuine if you want to.

Perfecting Your Last Line

You'll probably discover that you work as hard on the last line of your story as you do on your first.

A last line not only reflects the beginning and gives that sense of a completed journey, but also needs to have a 'music' of its own. It often has a certain cadence to it, like the 'dying fall' in the music referred to in Shakespeare's *Twelfth Night*.

Looking at types of great last line

Here I look at some last lines from novels. Most of these are cited regularly as great examples.

Eternal recurrence

These three endings show that although times change, human nature stays essentially the same. The following chilling ending shows a suicide bomber walking out of the pages of Conrad's novel into the future in a moment of incredible foresight on the part of the author:

> He passed on unsuspected and deadly, like a pest in the street full of men.
>
> —*Joseph Conrad (The Secret Agent, Oxford World Classics, 2004,*
> *first published 1907)*

Orwell's prescient novel *Animal Farm* and its last line reveal the truth that while everything changes, everything remains the same:

> The creatures outside looked from pig to man, and from man to pig, and from pig to man again: but already it was impossible to say which was which.
>
> —*George Orwell (Animal Farm, Secker & Warburg, 1945)*

The ending of AA Milne's classic tale manages to be incredibly simple but incredibly profound at the same time, in that after a story is written it exists forever and can be enjoyed again and again by each new generation, as the Pooh stories have:

> But wherever they go, and whatever happens to them on the way, in that enchanted place on the top of the Forest, a little boy and his Bear will always be playing.
>
> —*AA Milne (The House at Pooh Corner, Methuen, 1928)*

Philosophical statement

Sometimes a book ends with a statement that seems to reach beyond the individual story itself and makes a point about a culture or the whole of life. Achebe's extraordinary story of political corruption in Nigeria ends with this statement that someone may exist who'd do something for principle and not for money:

> In such a regime, I say you died a good death if your life had inspired someone to come forward and shoot your murderer in the chest – without asking to be paid.
>
> —*Chinua Achebe (A Man of the People, Heinemann, 1966)*

This famous ending of Fitzgerald's masterpiece shows that although people are caught up in the flow of time, the roots of their behaviour lie always in their pasts:

> So we beat on, boats against the current, borne back ceaselessly into the past.
>
> —*F Scott Fitzgerald (The Great Gatsby, Penguin, 1974, first published 1925)*

In the concluding passage of *A Tale of Two Cities,* Dickens's character, about to be guillotined, still envisages a brighter future for the city and its people, and hope – even in death:

> It is a far, far better thing that I do than I have ever done; it is a far, far better rest that I go to than I have ever known.
>
> —*Charles Dickens (A Tale of Two Cities, Penguin Classics, 2003, first published 1859)*

Death

These three novels from different periods all show that, to use a biblical quote from the Song of Songs, 'Love is strong as death.' Eliot's well-known last line gives a slight upturn to the tragic end of brother and sister when they drown in a flood. The fact that it's a quote from the Book of Samuel in the Bible, about the love between Saul and Jonathan, gives a hint of immortality in the love between members of a family:

> In their death they were not divided.
>
> —*George Eliot (The Mill on the Floss, Wordsworth Classics, 1999, first published 1860)*

The following quiet ending to the story of Stoner's life marks the moment of his death, but the preceding paragraphs are incredibly beautiful and give a depth of meaning and significance to his whole life:

> The fingers loosened, and the book they had held moved slowly and then swiftly across the still body and fell into the silence of the room.
>
> —*John Williams (Stoner, Viking, 1965)*

In the last line of Wharton's novel, readers assume that the unspoken word is 'love':

> He knelt by the bed and bent over her, draining their last moment to its lees; and in the silence there passed between them the word which made all clear.
>
> —*Edith Wharton (The House of Mirth, Everyman's Library, 1991,*
> *first published 1905)*

Dialogue

Many books end with a line of dialogue – as if a character is summing up what has gone before. One advantage of using dialogue is that it can be ironic, as the reader may understand what the character does not:

The last words of Hemingway's novel are from a conversation in a taxi, showing that the characters' relationship is slipping away forever, and ends with a lovely irony:

> 'Yes,' I said. 'Isn't it pretty to think so?'
>
> —*Ernest Hemingway (The Sun Also Rises, Scribner's, 1926)*

I love this last line of *Candide:* that if you can't deal with the big things, just deal with the smaller things of life – and enjoy them!

> 'All that is very well,' answered Candide, 'but let us cultivate our garden.'
>
> —*Voltaire (Candide, translated by Robert M Adams, Norton, 1991,*
> *first published 1759)*

The end of Woolf's novel is splendid too. The whole book is about Clarissa Dalloway, and so ending this way is perfect. Like any other great character in fiction, there she is – to be encountered again and again whenever you pick up the book:

> It is Clarissa, he said. For there she was.
>
> —*Mrs Dalloway (Virginia Woolf, Hogarth Press, 1925)*

Action

A novel can end with an action – something appropriate to the tale that's been told. An action can also point towards the future.

The contemptuous action at the end of Lowry's novel shows how cheaply life is valued in the Mexico where the character lives, and adds a final note of despair:

> Somebody threw a dead dog after him down the ravine.
>
> —*Malcolm Lowry (Under the Volcano, Jonathan Cape, 1947)*

Catch-22 is a novel about war and therefore death. Yossarian manages not to despair and to survive, and this theme keeps going to the very last line:

> The knife came down, missing him by inches, and he took off.
>
> —*Joseph Heller (Catch-22, Simon & Schuster, 1961)*

The end of a novel is also a new beginning, and Plath's character fittingly steps out into a new world that readers can only imagine:

> The eyes and the faces all turned themselves toward me, and guiding myself by them, as by a magical thread, I stepped into the room.
>
> —*Sylvia Plath (The Bell Jar, Heinemann, 1963)*

Description

A piece of description can round off a novel and work at a symbolic level. Here, the title of Conrad's novel is contained in the last line. The novel begins with a description of the Thames, and so ending there is fitting:

> The offing was barred by a black bank of clouds, and the tranquil water-way leading to the utmost ends of the earth flowed sombre under an overcast sky – seemed to lead into the heart of an immense darkness.
>
> —*Joseph Conrad (Heart of Darkness, Penguin, 2007, first published 1899)*

Wuthering Heights has a remarkably beautiful ending for such a dark and passionate novel; the storms of life are over, and the characters can rest at last:

> I lingered round them, under that benign sky; watched the moths fluttering among the heath, and hare-bells; listened to the soft wind breathing through the grass; and wondered how anyone could ever imagine unquiet slumbers for the sleepers in that quiet earth.
>
> —*Emily Brontë (Wuthering Heights, Penguin, 2003, first published 1847)*

The lovely use of the repeated 'w' sounds (I discuss alliteration in Chapter 16) in this description from the last line at the end of Capote's account of a brutal murder creates a beautiful image:

> Then, starting home, he walked towards the trees, and under them, leaving behind the big sky, the whisper of wind voices in the wind-bent wheat.
>
> —*Truman Capote (In Cold Blood, Random House, 1965)*

Interesting narrator

Just as the voice of a character can intrigue us at the start of a story, so it can lead us out at the end. Molly's wonderful monologue at the end of Joyce's masterwork is beautifully poetic and life-affirming:

> then he asked me would I yes to say yes my mountain flower and first I put my arms around him yes and drew him down to me so he could feel my breasts all perfume yes and his heart was going like mad and yes I said yes I will Yes.
>
> —*James Joyce (Ulysses, Bodley Head, 1955, first published 1922)*

In Greene's novel the irony of the narrator, Bendrix, talking to a being he doesn't believe in is a fitting ending to this passionate tale of faith, love and hate:

> I wrote at the start that this was a record of hate, and walking there beside Henry towards the evening glass of beer, I found the one prayer that seemed to serve the winter mood: oh God, you've done enough, you're robbed me of enough, I'm too tired and old to learn to love, leave me alone forever.
>
> —*Graham Greene (The End of the Affair, Heinemann, 1951)*

The narrative voice throughout Salinger's novel grabs readers' attention, and the last line is no different:

> Don't ever tell anybody anything. If you do, you start missing everybody.
>
> —*JD Salinger (The Catcher in the Rye, Little Brown, 1951)*

Ambiguity

An ambiguous ending can intrigue readers and keep them thinking about the novel – for hours, days or weeks after they've finished. At the end of Hamid's short and hard-hitting novel, is the narrator about to be killed? Is the American from the CIA? Readers never know:

> But why are you reaching into your jacket, sir? I detect a glint of metal. Given that you and I are now bound by a certain shared intimacy, I trust it is from the holder of your business cards.
>
> —*Mohsin Hamid (The Reluctant Fundamentalist, Hamish Hamilton, 2007)*

In Henry James's novel, will Isabel go back to her husband or in the end choose Warburton? He may wait a while to find out, but readers have to wait forever:

> She walked him away with her, however, as if she had given him now the key to patience.
>
> —*Henry James (The Portrait of a Lady, Penguin, 1974, first published 1881)*

The ending of *Great Expectations* is doubly ambiguous and is one of two that Dickens wrote. In the other version, which Dickens wrote first, Pip meets Estella briefly by chance at the end of the novel. The current ending remains ambiguous: will Pip marry Estella or is he mistaken?

> I took her hand in mine, and we went out of the ruined place; and, as the morning mists had risen long ago when I first left the forge, so, the evening mists were rising now, and in all the broad expanse of tranquil light they showed to me, I saw no shadow of another parting from her.
>
> —*Charles Dickens (Great Expectations, Penguin, 1996, first published 1861)*

Homecoming

Can characters ever truly return home, because surely either they've changed or their homes are different? The character in Anita Brookner's novel discovers that nothing will ever be just as it was:

> But, after a moment, she thought that this was not entirely accurate and, crossing out the words 'Coming home', wrote simply 'Returning'.
>
> —*Anita Brookner (Hotel du Lac, 1984, Jonathan Cape)*

Waugh's social comedy is a classic 'voyage and return' story in which the character comes back with a new identity but resumes his uneventful life, revealed in this most ordinary of endings:

> Then he turned out the light and went into his bedroom to sleep.
>
> —*Evelyn Waugh (Decline and Fall, Chapman & Hall, 1928)*

After all the adventures and drama of Tolkien's great epic, Sam arrives home to sit in front of the fire with his daughter on his lap:

> 'Well, I'm back,' he said.
>
> —*JRR Tolkien (The Lord of the Rings, Allen & Unwin, 1955)*

Fill a page with possible end lines for your novel. The beginning and ending of a novel are closely linked, and so take a look at any opening lines you created in Chapter 17. Pair up a beginning line with an end line until you run out of pairs.

Coming full circle

The first line and the last line are often related to one another: in some cases the same line begins and ends a novel, as in Lewis DeSoto's novel, *A Blade of Grass (Maia,* 2004). The first line is 'First she must wash the seeds', and the last line is 'But first she must plant the seeds.' This choice gives readers a lovely sense of completeness, and they read this sentence differently after experiencing the character's emotional journey in the novel.

Even though the last line may not be the same as or similar to the first, very often something near the beginning of your novel is picked up in the end.

If you aren't sure how to end a novel, look at the opening paragraphs and see whether you can pick up a phrase or image that you can echo at the end. And if you have your ending but aren't satisfied with your beginning, try the same in reverse.

Part V
Polishing Your Product: Revising and Editing

Top five ways to rewrite, edit and polish your book:

✔ Read your work aloud so you can hear what it sounds like and come to it afresh. You can even ask a friend to read it to you if it helps.

✔ Leave as much time between the writing and the editing as you can to help you get distance from your work and come to it as a reader would.

✔ Don't be afraid to throw away large sections if they don't fit in – you can always file these away for future stories. In particular, cut any redundant scenes and repetitions.

✔ Weed out any glaring clichés and sentences that don't make sense. Look out for continuity errors and fix them. Spell-check your work and punctuate properly!

✔ Format your manuscript according to usual publishing conventions – double-spaced, with wide margins and paragraphs indented.

Check out www.dummies.com/extras/creativewritingexercises for an extra article on rewriting and editing your work.

In this part . . .

✔ Discover all the stages of rewriting your book – from a complete restructuring down to a final polish. Most pieces of creative writing need a lot of restructuring, rewriting and editing before you can send them out into the big, bad world to make their way.

✔ Get familiar with the skills you need to check the spelling and grammar, and format your book properly before handing it over to a professional agent or publisher.

✔ Find out what you need to do to produce the best piece of work you possibly can.

Chapter 24

Reviewing and Rewriting Your Work

In This Chapter
▷ Reading your work again
▷ Taking drastic measures
▷ Tackling a second draft

*M*ost writing is rewriting. Think of your *first draft* or your initial efforts as the raw material you need in order to start putting your story together. You have to produce this material, otherwise you have nothing to work with, but you may well end up discarding much – perhaps most – of it.

After you've completed a rough A–Z of your story, the real work begins. During the first draft you're getting to know your characters, capturing their voices, finding out where the plot's going and working on some of the key scenes. Often you make a number of false starts, such as beginning to write in the first-person voice when a third-person narrative would be more effective, or in a more distant third-person style when a first-person voice would convey the character more directly.

When you get to the end of your story, you often go back to the beginning and find that your style or way of writing has developed and changed, and so you need to rewrite the start in the same style. The characters, too, may have changed. One good reason for not endlessly rewriting the first chapter while producing the first draft is that it almost always needs rewriting when you finally get to the end of your draft!

Rewriting requires a different mindset to drafting. When you draft, you let your imagination go, stop judging yourself and permit yourself to write in the white heat of creativity. When you rewrite, you have to put on your editor's hat and be more critical. At the drafting stage, though, don't be too hard on yourself – you can't expect the first draft to be perfect.

Reacquainting Yourself with Your First Draft

After finishing your first draft, you're so intimately involved with the story that you're unlikely to gain anything by starting to reread or rewrite straight away. Instead, take some time out to refresh your energy, and then print out a copy and read it all again and again, to yourself and out loud.

Leaving your first draft alone for a while

When you've completed a first draft, the single most useful thing you can do is to put it aside for as long as you can: a weekend, a week, a month or more – the longer the better.

If possible, finish the first draft just before you go on holiday, and don't take any of your writing with you: give yourself a complete break and try to forget your work.

When you put aside your work for some time before you read it again, the more distance you have and the more you're able to judge it objectively, as your future readers will.

If you don't have time to put your work away, go and do something completely different before coming back to it. Here are a few ideas for clearing your mind:

- Go for a walk.
- Cook a meal.
- Do some gardening, decorating or house cleaning.
- Sleep on it.

These activities help your conscious mind to go 'idle'. You may find that your subconscious mind works on your story while you're physically occupied with something else.

When you do something else that uses your mind actively, you don't have the spare capacity to 'think' subconsciously about your book.

Reading your work in one go

Although you can, of course, read your draft on the computer and use the Track Changes function to edit it, I find that doing so is too difficult at an early stage: far too much needs changing and you end up looking at an unwieldy sea of red!

I think that reading through a printout of your work is important. Leave wide margins so that you can write notes in them, and set the type to double spaced so that you have plenty of room to edit. I prefer to print on one side of the paper only, so that I can use the reverse side to write notes or even sketch out new scenes. Usually, you read more accurately with hard copy, and if you've so far worked on your computer, a printout looks different; plus, the experience of reading continuously on paper much more closely resembles your readers' experience.

When you're ready and have waited as long as you can, read the whole story through in one sitting, if possible, or two or three long ones, jotting notes to yourself as you go. Write in red ink so that you can see the marks.

Don't bother with small things (I discuss the next editing stage in Chapter 25) – although if you see spelling and grammatical mistakes, correcting them as you go along certainly helps to keep you on your toes.

Here's what you're looking out for at this point:

- ✔ Where the text doesn't hold your attention
- ✔ Where your mind wanders off
- ✔ Where you're muddled or unclear
- ✔ Where you spot inconsistencies or obvious errors
- ✔ Where you see a loose end or unnecessary scene
- ✔ Where scenes go on for too long
- ✔ Where something's missing or you need to expand on something.
- ✔ Where the story is too simplistic and you may need to add more layers

Don't try to deal with specific problems right now; just mark them and read on.

Don't burn your typescript or give up writing just because your first draft hasn't come out the way you wanted. Of course it hasn't! It's bound to be all over the place. Just take a deep breath and start to work out what you need to do with it.

When you write, you don't always write chronologically. You write the scenes you like best and then start trying to stitch them together. Sometimes the result is that you can't remember where anything is and the story jumps around confusingly. If this happens, it's a good idea to start at the beginning and work out a complete timeline, slotting in scenes in the right order.

Speaking up: Reading your work aloud (but perhaps not in public)

One of the best pieces of advice I give any writer is to read your work aloud to yourself. Read it slowly – don't rush through – because the purpose is to hear what the prose sounds like.

Reading aloud distances you from your work and helps you to view it as an outside reader. You immediately spot any words that clash or jar, you hear the rhythm of the sentences and when they flow well and when you stumble, and you spot any mistakes much more easily. Words that sound good when read aloud are much easier for people to read than those that sound awkward.

Reading aloud also reveals where your writing holds your interest and where things go flat. It's the best possible tool to show you what's working in your prose and what isn't.

Record yourself reading your work aloud and then listen to it later. Even better, ask a friend to read it aloud; this can be especially important if you aren't a confident reader.

Obviously, you can't get a friend to read a whole novel – but reading short extracts will help you get a feel for how your prose is flowing, and help you with scenes you don't think are working.

Making Major Changes to Your Initial Draft

Tearing up your first draft and starting again is the most drastic form of rewriting. I don't usually recommend it, but on occasions the draft can be so all over the place that putting it to one side can help, and then you can start to write your story all over again.

The first draft isn't wasted. You've found your characters and have a much better idea of the plot when you sit down to write again. Never *literally* tear up the first draft – you may need to refer to it. You may want to retrieve a lovely sentence or image or check something you wrote earlier.

Here I describe some big changes that you may need to make to a first draft.

Taking a different viewpoint

One of the largest forms of rewriting is to change the point of view. The voice and point of view are so important to a story that, inevitably, changing these aspects radically changes your story.

Here are a few common situations that you may face:

✔ Suppose you start off with a third-person limited narrative, but find that you're using long chunks of interior monologue and free indirect speech (flip to Chapter 7 for a description of these). You need to ask yourself whether the story would be more natural told in the first-person narrative. (Chapter 8 has all you need to know on third- and first-person styles.)

✔ Suppose your first-person narrative feels claustrophobic and you want to open the story up into more viewpoints. Would you be better making it third-person limited?

✔ Suppose you picked an omniscient narrator but find that the story now feels far too distant and old-fashioned. Can you personify the narrator? Can you write the story from the point of view of an observer who's also a character? Sometimes an observer narrator is the best option – someone who views the characters from the outside. Or perhaps you can recast your narrative using multiple narrators. Again, check out Chapter 8 for all about using different viewpoints.

Changing character and location names

You may be surprised that I include this type of change here. Surely, changing the character's name is fairly minor – simply a matter of searching and replacing (perhaps on the computer).

I've experienced many writers deciding to change the names of their main characters late on in the novel, and in every single case doing so changed the character so radically that the whole novel started to transform itself or fall apart. A name is so much a part of a person that when you alter it, many aspects of the character change too.

Names carry a great deal of information about characters – their age, background, parents' aspirations for them – and also often have a meaning that influences your readers. The sound of names also has an impact: a name that sounds soft creates a different impression to a name that has a lot of hard sounds in it. Ordinary names go with 'everyman' characters, while unusual names draw attention to an exceptional character.

If you're going to change a character's name, I suggest you do so straight away, before any major reworkings, and not at the last moment. If an agent or publisher asks you to change it at a late stage, as I've known happen, I recommend you do a search and replace right at the last minute before you submit your novel, or you may find you have to change everything about your character!

If you do an electronic search and replace, always check each instance. If the name forms part of many words, you find that replacing 'Ray' with 'Ralph' results in words such as 'portralphed' and phrases such as 'the first ralphs of the sun'. An apocryphal story relates that just before submitting a typescript, a writer decided to change his character's name from David to Geoff. He was horrified to later realise that this meant that in one scene his characters had been admiring Michelangelo's famous statue of Geoff!

Changing the location can also have far-reaching impacts. Each city or country has its own geography, culture and mores. A writer I know decided to change her location from London to Brighton, and had to change almost every scene.

Altering the story's structure

Unsurprisingly, deciding to alter your work's structure requires some radical change. Perhaps you told the story chronologically but now realise the story would work better if you started nearer the end and told the early part through flashback (see Chapters 3, 13 and 19). Doing so allows you to start at a high point in the story and so can be a good way to increase narrative tension.

Sometimes deciding which way to go can be hard. In his 1934 novel *Tender Is the Night,* F Scott Fitzgerald told the story with flashbacks. After Scott Fitzgerald's death, a new version was published (in 1948), based on the author's notes, that relates things chronologically. People still argue about which version works best.

You almost certainly find a much better flow to your prose and structure when you write it continuously.

Lost manuscripts

Several authors have lost entire drafts of their work, but this didn't stop them rewriting from scratch. Fortunately, this nightmare is less common in the age of computers!

✔ Ernest Hemingway's first wife, Hadley, lost a suitcase containing his early stories in 1922 when she was catching a train in Paris. After the distraught Hadley arrived in Lausanne and told him about the loss of his work, Hemingway immediately returned to Paris to see if he could recover the suitcase. He seems to have never forgiven her for the loss, although some claim that it did him a favour, because his later stories are probably much better.

✔ Malcolm's Lowry's novel *Ultramarine* (1933) was lost by his publisher, stolen from an open-top car in London. Lowry claims to have rewritten the entire novel from memory in three weeks.

✔ TE Lawrence left the manuscript of *Seven Pillars of Wisdom* (1922) in the café at Reading station. It was never found, and the famous version is an earlier draft.

✔ Jilly Cooper took her only copy of the manuscript of her novel *Riders* (1985) with her when she went out to lunch, and left it behind on a London bus. She didn't finish rewriting it for 14 years.

✔ Robert Louis Stevenson wrote the first draft of *Dr Jekyll and Mr Hyde* (1886) in three weeks. His wife dismissed the book as nonsense and he burnt it. He swiftly rewrote it, and it went on to be a major success.

Considering other large reworkings

When you've written the first loose draft and looked through it, you may spot all sorts of major problems that require large revisions. In such situations, here are some questions to ask yourself:

✔ Is the overall goal for my main character clear?

✔ Do I have enough conflict?

✔ Does the story need more suspense?

✔ Should I divide the story into parts or sections (for guidance, check out the later section 'Working on the overall structure')?

To address these issues, you can introduce time pressure, increase obstacles and create more complications for the characters.

After you answer these questions and think of solutions (by consulting Chapter 21), you're ready to start on your second draft.

Restructuring Your Story: Second Draft

In the *second draft* you start shaping the structure of your story, tying plot lines together, considering your timeline and addressing any serious problems.

Working on the overall structure

At this stage you review all the material you have and think about whether it needs to be divided into parts, sections and chapters.

Thinking about the following issues can help you create a satisfying sense of symmetry:

✔ Does a major change of location occur part-way through the book? If so, think about dividing the book into a separate part for each location.

✔ Does a change in point of view exist? Again, look at how many points of view you have and in what order, and see whether you can divide the typescript into a pattern of alternating points of view.

✔ Do you make a major leap or several leaps in time? Again, dividing the book into parts may work.

✔ Do you have a number of linked stories? If so, see whether you can link them via an overall 'bridge' story (as I describe in Chapter 22).

After you've decided on your structure, you can work on the material you have to make it fit.

Inevitably, at this stage you find yourself

✔ Cutting whole scenes

✔ Writing in new scenes you realise you need

✔ Shortening scenes that go on for too long

✔ Extending scenes that are too short or undeveloped

✔ Moving whole scenes and chunks of the story around

These tips can help you through this process:

✔ Keep track of the scenes by making a grid or using index cards you can shuffle, with each scene or chapter written on them.

✔ If you have a number of plot lines, you may like to isolate each plot thread and look at each one on its own. This often shows that some threads are weaker than others and need strengthening.

✔ Create a separate computer file for each thread in the story, and then you can make each one work on its own before slotting it back in again – preferably in a regular pattern.

✔ Create columns for each plot line and write the events in the correct column in the order they occur. This is an excellent way of revealing when one column has much more material than another, or when you have long gaps in one column. As a result, you can see the overall structure.

Weaving in those loose threads

When you're writing the second draft, look out for any threads that don't really fit. You have a choice here:

✔ Cut them out entirely.

✔ Make them relevant to your main story.

Often at the beginning of a story you write in scenes or characters because you're not sure what to write and feel you have to write something. Or you feel that you want to cover a number of issues, and you put them in regardless of whether they're part of this story.

A common mistake when writing your first big project is to feel the need to put into this one work everything you want to write about. Then the story gets overcrowded and muddled. Most likely you have many books or stories in you, not just one, and so leave some things over for the next project!

No matter how much you love a particular character, scene or subplot, if it doesn't work or fit in this story, take it out! If you have threads you want to keep, try giving the characters a bigger role in the story. Create scenes where these characters interact with the main characters.

Checking the timeline

When you write your first draft, you're not usually too bothered about the timeline. You tend to jump ahead with phrases such as 'the next day', 'two weeks later' and so on just to keep your story moving ahead.

When you get to the second draft, you have the chance to check the timeline of your story. If you've set the story in a particular year, get the calendar for that year and choose the start date for your story. Plot each scene into the

You're how old?!

I edited one book that seemed fine on first reading. But when I looked at it more closely, the characters' ages seemed a bit off. I worked out that one of them was 20 years younger than he should have been based on early events in his life, which happened in wartime! On checking with the author, I discovered that she'd begun by setting the novel in the 1970s but then decided to make it contemporary – but she forgot to change the flashbacks to the character's childhood!

Sometimes the unexpected success of a book or character requires the author to rethink. John le Carré's hero George Smiley first appeared in *Call for the Dead* (1961), with hints that he was born in about 1906. But he was so popular that nearly 30 years later (in *The Secret Pilgrim* in 1990) he was lecturing newly trained agents, and so le Carré had to rethink Smiley's birthdate, bringing it forward to 1915! Losing nine years at the stroke of a pen; now that's the power of literature!

calendar and see how long the story takes to unfold. Sometimes this exercise causes some unpleasant surprises. For example, your characters are sunning themselves in the back garden admiring the roses in one scene, but when you plot it on your timeline you find that you're now in late November! I discuss timelines in more detail in Chapters 3 and 19.

Putting your novel into a calendar is an extremely useful exercise. You can not only check that everything fits together, but also weed out any potential problems with the timeline.

Sometimes you can make use of seasons or festivals to tighten and focus your narrative. Everything in your story may need to unfold by the summer holiday, Christmas or the end of the year. If your novel takes place over a very long period, ask yourself whether this is necessary. Can you shorten the time-span of the story, perhaps reducing it by months or years?

Also, do check for characters' birthdates and see whether significant birthdays fall during your novel. If your story takes place over an extended period of time, you also need to make sure that your characters don't end up older or younger than they should be.

Fixing fundamental flaws

At this second-draft stage you can be as ruthless as you like in fixing any flaws in your narrative. Take bold steps now and you can save yourself a lot of rewriting later, when it is much more difficult to make changes.

In particular, now's the time to root out any *plot holes* (gaps or inconsistencies in your story). Events that couldn't happen, or that contradict scenes you've previously written, can be fatal to your story.

Is it too long or too short?

Knowing when your story's the right length is tricky. I say make your story the length it wants to be and then look at it. Here are some rough guidelines:

- ✔ A short story can be as short as 1,000 words or as long as about 20,000. Most short-story competitions or anthologies ask for stories of up to 3,000 or 5,000 words.

- ✔ After 20,000 words a story starts to get into novella territory. *Novellas* are short novels, which usually have a tighter focus than longer novels. They often have less room for subplots or large numbers of characters.

  People often fear that novellas aren't popular. You can worry about this later, when you get an agent or publisher interested in your work. Otherwise let your book be the length you want it to be.

- ✔ After about 40,000 words the novella label tends to get dropped and a book becomes a short novel. Exactly when this happens is the cause of some controversy: both *On Chesil Beach* (2007) by Ian McEwan (about 38,000 words) and *The Testament of Mary* (2012) by Colm Tóibín (only about 30,000 words) were shortlisted for the Man Booker Prize, even though the rules specify that the story must be a 'full-length work'.

- ✔ A full-length novel is usually somewhere between 70,000 and 100,000 words. After 100,000 words, a novel starts to feel quite long, and you need a very good reason for a novel to be more than 120,000 words. Agents and publishers may well want a long book shortened, because otherwise the length may reduce the readership – and publishers can be wary because long books are more expensive to print.

When you see how long your first draft is, you can start to focus on how long you want the final version to be. You may want to adapt your novel to fit the expectations of the genre (see the next section). Many novels start out much shorter than you want them, and grow as you rewrite them; others start out long and are cut back dramatically. Some writers sketch scenes out and need to go back and fill them in later; others write densely and need to go back and prune.

John le Carré said about writing *The Spy Who Came in from the Cold* (1963) that the first draft was much, much longer than the final version, and he cut away at the material until the story became the final tense, spare narrative. Mohsin Hamid said the same thing about his 2007 novel, *The Reluctant Fundamentalist.*

At the opposite extreme, when JRR Tolkien started to write *The Lord of the Rings* (1954), he had in mind another book for young readers, about the length of the much shorter *The Hobbit* (1937).

Is it in the right genre?

At this stage you can also consider whether your book fits into a particular genre, and look at whether it fulfils the expectations of that genre.

Genre is important because that's how books are sold and marketed these days. Each genre has a code that shows where books are shelved in book-shops or located in online bookstores. It helps the publishers and booksellers to market your book to the right audience.

1. **Go to your nearest bookshop and look around. Find the section where you think your book may fit – crime, mystery, adventure, romance, historical, horror, fantasy or sci-fi, women's – and look at the other titles.**

2. **Pick one book, examine its cover and read the blurb on the back. Think about whether you want your book packaged this way.**

3. **Look at the length of the book, the way it's divided into chapters or sections, and whether these tend to be titled.**

4. **Select a few books that you like the look of in your chosen section and read them.** Ensuring that your book falls within what's generally expected in the relevant genre doesn't hurt.

Radical innovations in structure and style are truly appreciated only in literary fiction! Otherwise, follow the rules of your chosen genre.

Chapter 25

Whipping Your Work into Shape

*W*hen you've finished wrestling with the second, third or even fourth draft of your work (as I discuss in Chapter 24), you'll have a reasonably coherent narrative to work with. Now you need to settle down and look at the finer aspects of your writing in more detail.

At this stage, you're looking for ways to improve and streamline the story without making huge changes to the structure. You need to cut out anything that doesn't contribute to your story; after all, less is often more. Perhaps even characters or scenes that you love but that clutter up your story and distract readers from what's important have to go. And you may need to add extra information that readers need. You also want to search for ways to increase narrative tension and smooth out jarring changes of scene or transitions.

Looking with a Fresh Pair of Eyes

When you arrive at this editing stage, which is after you've got a coherent manuscript or typescript ready (see Chapter 24), you need to get yourself into a different mindset to the one that carried you through the writing. You need to take a step back from your work and become an *editor,* which involves a shift in emphasis so that you can read through your work critically and make it as good as it possibly can be.

In this section I cover taking a fresh look at aspects of your story (to see whether they work), at the roles of all your characters and at the order of scenes.

Everybody makes mistakes, and you can't be creative without them. Sometimes mistakes can even lead to original and exciting ideas, but sometimes you simply need to correct them. Developing your editorial skills helps you to spot which type of error is which.

Searching for the obvious and the obscure

One of the most awkward areas to spot in your own work is when something in your story is too blatant or too understated: you don't want to slap your readers around the face, but equally you don't want to risk them missing crucial details. Getting the balance right is tricky, because you wrote the work and you know what's going to happen; putting yourself in the situation of someone who doesn't can be difficult.

The main way you prepare readers for what's going to happen next is through foreshadowing (which I describe in Chapter 14). Ensure that your foreshadowing is subtle enough so that it doesn't scream at readers and isn't overly obvious. Sometimes you need to remind readers of an event that happened earlier or of what your character wants and what's at stake to maintain the narrative tension.

Ultimately, the best approach is to find a reader for your work. Ideally, you choose another writer – someone who understands the writing process and knows what to look for. Otherwise, ask someone who reads a lot and is good at talking about books. This person has never seen your story before and so can point out anything you've missed because you're so familiar with it.

The purpose of someone else reading your work at this stage isn't to say how 'good' or 'bad' it is. Instead, ask your reader to be analytical – to point out what doesn't work or anything she can't follow or doesn't understand. Also request that she be as calm and straightforward as possible.

Dealing with redundant characters

When you're writing, you often need many minor characters who take supporting roles. Often, however, readers have difficulty caring about these small parts or even remembering who they are. In addition, these minor characters are often quite one-dimensional, because they exist only to perform one role.

One solution to this problem is to merge as many characters as you can. Suppose that early in the novel you have a friend who introduces your main character to the man who'll become her nemesis. Later, you have a separate friend in whom your protagonist confides. Why not make these two characters the same person? This offers you the possibility of making your minor character more interesting. Maybe she feels guilty because she made the introduction and can now see that things are going wrong. Maybe she decides she must try to sort the situation out because she's responsible for it, instead of passively listening. As a result she becomes a more complex and rounded person, which adds an edge to all her conversations and introduces a new complication into the story, adding narrative tension.

Try out this exercise in merging characters:

1. **Pick two or three characters from your story who play small roles.**

2. **Now merge them into one.** Pick characteristics from the different characters and invent new ones. Now that the single character will play a bigger role, try out some of the exercises in Chapters 3 (exploring childhood and memory), 5 (embodying your characters) and 9 (complicating the characters) to build up the different aspects of your new character.

Sometimes characters seriously get in the way of what you want to achieve. You need to cut them out of your story entirely. If you watch films made of stories from books, you find that minor characters are very often merged or taken out altogether to create a smaller cast and keep the narrative line clear.

Occasionally, you find that you've made a minor character do too much in the story – she keeps popping up all over the place in an unbelievable way. In this case, split the character into two or more people.

Considering the order of scenes

When you're writing, you often include information because you can't remember whether you said something earlier, or you find that the information is in the wrong place for readers. This problem is comparatively easy to address as you read through the latest draft; you often spot scenes or parts of scenes that don't add anything to the story or repeat information that readers heard earlier. Or indeed you need to add information (see the later section 'Adding Necessary Details').

Although you don't want to have to make major changes to your work at this stage, you may need to move individual scenes around, or parts of scenes, so that the story makes more sense and reads better.

You need to handle the moving around of whole scenes carefully. The tips in Chapter 24 concerning the second draft also apply here. If you move a scene forwards, you may need to add in more details because the reader doesn't know about those yet. If you move a scene backwards, you may find you have referred to something that hasn't happened in your story yet, so you'll need to read through very thoroughly to make sure you spot any such glitches. Moving scenes always involves a degree of rewriting elsewhere – you can't just move them and be done with it!

Cutting Redundant Material

Most writers produce too many words. And that's fine, because when you're in the zone you don't want to stop and prune as you go. You leave that task to while you're reading your latest draft. Here I identify some common areas that tend to need cutting down.

Stopping overly long dialogue

Overly long dialogue is one of the most common mistakes writers make when writing, and one of the easiest to fix. Often when drafting you write out every word of a conversation – but when you edit, you need to cut back to just the important ones. (Check out Chapters 4 and 6 for lots more on dialogue.)

For example, if you have two characters in a restaurant, don't go through the whole conversation where food is discussed and ordered. A brief phrase – 'They studied the menu in silence and then ordered – fish soup for her and a steak for him' – is quite enough, and you can then jump to the important question: 'Have you seen Li Wei recently?'

Trimming interior monologue

Long passages of interior monologue (see Chapter 6) can be tiring to read. Your readers can feel trapped in the character's head and be desperate for a sight or sound of the world outside.

Interior monologue is a great tool for revealing a character's thoughts and feelings, but in general keep such passages short and intersperse them with observations and actions.

Keeping your back story to yourself

As you read through your work, you probably find passages of *back story*, which is everything that happened to your characters before your story begins (read Chapter 3 for more). If you're sufficiently distanced from your story so that you're reading objectively, you probably notice that your attention drops as soon as you get to such a passage.

If your attention drops, so will that of your readers. The problem with back story is that it makes readers look backwards, instead of looking ahead to what's coming up. As a result, it almost always reduces narrative tension.

A particular problem is when you start with a great scene in the first chapter, and then at the start of the second chapter you feel the need to go back and tell readers everything that you think they need to know about the character's early life. Resist this temptation! You may know everything about your character's childhood in order to work her out, but your readers don't need to know this info.

Think about Hamlet. Here's one of the most real and complex characters in fiction, but does Shakespeare tell the audience about Hamlet's birth, his days in nursery school, a row he had with his father on his 12th birthday, his first date, his time at university? Not at all. You just encounter Hamlet in the story's present – his thoughts, his feelings, his actions. That's all the audience needs.

If you think that readers do need to know something about the character's past, reveal it through a short flashback. (Flip to Chapters 3, 13 and 19 for more on flashbacks.) A flashback happens to the character in the 'now' of your story, as she remembers it, instead of dragging readers back into the depths of the past.

Whenever possible, *eliminate back story*. Just put a line through it. And if in any doubt, cut it out!

Getting to the point: Avoiding summary

Long passages of summary put readers off. Summary is dull to read, because it simply presents information instead of letting your readers experience a fully realised scene as if it were happening to them. It involves the great no-no of storytelling: 'telling' rather than 'showing'. You can get away with short passages of summary, but only as long as you intersperse them with fully dramatic, lively scenes.

When you write a summary you often use fewer words than when you write a fully fleshed-out, concrete scene – which can cause you to make the mistake of thinking that doing so is more economical, quickly taking readers through less important or complicated scenes. In fact, summaries often slow the pace of the book, because readers feel less engaged by a historical account than by a dramatic scene. Although summaries are sometimes necessary, generally try to avoid summarising for too long.

1. **Search through your latest draft for a piece of summary, and think about how you can replace it with a dramatic scene.**

2. **Identify the key piece of information that you want to convey, and work on doing so through the character receiving a letter, seeing a significant object or observing a clue.**

You can also bring a passage of summary to life by including some vivid images or snatches of dialogue – brief elements of 'showing' that enable readers to see or hear what happened rather than just being told.

Giving out too much information

Remember that your writing is a story: don't give readers long slabs of detailed information about characters, locations or the history of a family. They don't want to take in too much information in one go, especially if they can't see why it's relevant to the story; they'll resent having information dumped on them in this way.

Take a scene you have written that includes a lot of information to see whether you can reveal a little of this material in a more interesting way – in conversation, through direct observation or woven into action. Remember that the only information you need to include is what the reader needs to know in order to understand the story. Cut everything else out.

It's particularly important not to bombard readers with too much information when you've done a lot of research and may feel tempted to show off your knowledge. (See Chapters 2 and 22 for more on conducting research.)

Adding Necessary Details

Sometimes, when reading your draft, you discover a place where you neglected to include some important information. You may have forgotten to explain where characters are, when a scene takes place or some background information that readers need in order to understand the story.

This problem is usually easy to fix: just add the information in the subtlest way you can, so that readers don't notice any change in the flow of the story. You can weave information into description, dialogue or characters' thoughts.

Beware of shoe-horning in factual information that readers need to know in a way that's untrue to a character's thought processes. Try not to be obvious that you're presenting the information solely for the benefit of readers.

Another problem I frequently come across is when writers deliberately hold back a vital piece of information from readers, usually because they think this makes the story more interesting. Instead, it often leaves the reader bemused.

When information is vital for readers to understand the story or the character, *put it in.* Otherwise readers know something's wrong, but not why, which seriously interferes with their enjoyment of reading.

Imagine that something terrible happened to a character: perhaps she was assaulted at the age of 14. This event is frequently hinted at throughout the story, but even though the character narrates the novel, readers aren't told what happened until the end. But the character knows what happened, and so, unless you're using an unreliable narrator, readers should know too!

Sympathising with a character or understanding what she wants is difficult unless readers know what drives her; holding back something major just doesn't work.

Making Your Writing Sparkle

During the editing process, you need to take advantage of any opportunities you spot to improve the quality of your writing, such as replacing worn-out words and phrases and removing any slack.

Weeding out clichés

A major aspect of editing is taking a fresh look at your work (as I discuss in the earlier section 'Looking with a Fresh Pair of Eyes') and indeed to freshen up your prose. Of course the opposite of fresh is 'stale' – the very definition of a cliché – so as you read through your story, have your pen ready to mark any obvious and glaring clichés. See whether you can come up with a better or more original phrase; if not, just move on and return to it later.

Sometimes, in an attempt to avoid clichés and be original, writers come up with some quite bizarre metaphors or similes! If these jump out at you when you read, take them out and just use simpler expressions. Good style doesn't draw attention to itself in this way.

You can come across a whole situation that's clichéd, by which I mean that it's not sufficiently developed. I'm sure that you can think of stock situations that turn up again and again in films and novels, and play out in obvious ways (the tart with the heart of gold, the hero action who never gets shot no matter how many people shoot at him, the villains who take the time to explain their evil plan to their victim, all spring to mind.) When you encounter a scene like this, find a way of making it original – this almost always means going deeper into the characters so that they make an individual and perhaps unexpected response.

Tightening up your sentences

The word 'tight' is often used negatively ('My shoes are too tight!', 'He's really tight and never buys a drink'), but in writing, tight is good. Your read-through gives you the chance to remove all the excess flab from your prose.

You need to aim for clarity above all else, and to remove anything that clutters up your writing or makes it harder to understand:

- ✔ Delete any redundant sentences at the beginning or end of a scene. Start and end on a strong note – 'That's it, I'm leaving!' rather than 'She had a cup of tea and went to bed'.

- ✔ At the start of a paragraph remove words such as 'then', 'and', 'so', 'next they', 'suddenly' and 'after this'. You almost always find that your prose then reads more forcefully.

- ✔ Search for phrases such as 'there is', 'there was', 'it is' and 'it was', and where possible delete them. Replace them with a stronger verb: for example, instead of 'There was a man by the door' write 'A man stood by the door'.

- ✔ Take out *qualifiers* – words that precede an adjective or adverb, such as 'very', 'quite', 'somewhat' and 'extremely' – and replace them with a stronger or more accurate verb. Funnily enough, writing 'He was angry' is more powerful than 'He was very angry'. 'He was enraged' may be even better.

- ✔ Rephrase to avoid words cluttering up your sentences, such as 'situated'. So instead of 'The hotel was situated in the town centre' write 'The hotel was in the town centre'. Or, better still, make the sentence more active: 'He found the hotel in the town centre.' Redo phrases such as 'in colour', 'in size' and 'in number'; for example, instead of 'Her eyes were blue in colour' just write 'Her eyes were blue'.

- ✔ Condense long-winded phrases. Therefore 'in the vicinity of' becomes 'near', 'so that he may be in a position to go' becomes 'so he may go' and 'in order to eat' can be just 'to eat'.

- ✔ Beware of starting too many sentences with a *participle phrase* – a phrase beginning with a present or past participle – because it can sound weak. Instead of 'Sitting at the table, they ate their meal' write 'They ate their meal sitting at the table', which is clearer and easier to read.

Chapter 26

Polishing Your Work for Publication

In This Chapter

▸ Reading your story one last time

▸ Presenting your typescript for maximum impact

So you've completed the final draft of your novel. Hurrah! Take a moment to congratulate yourself, because finishing a project of that length is quite an achievement, and many people start but never see the writing through.

When you feel that your book is ready to show to a professional reader, agent or publisher, you need to do a *final read-through,* looking out for any small errors that may have slipped in. I can't overstress the importance of submitting a typescript that looks as if you've taken every possible care. You create a poor impression if you send in a story peppered with mistakes.

You also have to format your typescript as professionals expect to receive it. When I ran a publishing house, I was amazed by how many people sent in typescripts with unnumbered pages, strange fonts and single line spacing, and littered with spelling mistakes. You need to ensure that your work stands out from such shoddy submissions in the large pile of unsolicited typescripts on someone's desk.

Carrying Out Your Final Read-Through

A professional-looking typescript that demands to be taken seriously doesn't contain any continuity mistakes, grammatical errors or slips in spelling and punctuation. The final read-through is your opportunity to get rid of these slip-ups.

Correcting continuity errors

A few *continuity errors* have probably crept through into your final draft, and now's your chance to spot and correct them. (These are errors such as saying a character is an only child and later mentioning his sister, making a character younger than he should be for the birth date you've given, or saying a minor character is dead and then making him appear later!)

If you haven't already done so, make sure that you complete a proper timeline for your story (Chapter 19 shows you how). Jot down dates and times as you go through the novel. Check for consistency with character's ages and any dates.

Also check for any descriptions of people and places, and ensure that you haven't inadvertently made a mistake, although you can sometimes get away with this – Flaubert is famously supposed to have described Emma Bovary's eyes as brown, black and blue in different scenes in *Madame Bovary* (1856).

If you find that checking for continuity errors is laborious, just remember that at least as a writer you have a chance to correct any mistakes (until the novel's in print, at least). In film, continuity errors can be hard to fix, because of the huge expense of re-shooting scenes after the main filming is done.

Spelling and punctuating correctly

You need to submit a typescript without errors. I've heard people say that they think the publisher's job is to correct spelling and punctuation. No, it isn't! Doing so takes someone's time, and time means money. So make the effort to review your work and get it right – not to do so is sheer laziness. In fact, no typescript should have spelling mistakes now that everyone has word processors that spell-check.

Computer spell-checkers aren't infallible and don't replace careful reading. For example, they don't pick up correctly spelled but wrongly used words, such as misusing 'bear' and 'bare', or 'red' and 'read', or 'two' and 'too'. Also, make sure that the spell-check is set correctly to UK or US English, whichever is appropriate.

If you're in doubt about how to spell a word, use a dictionary, in book form or online.

Punctuating properly is important for two reasons: sense and style. Punctuating incorrectly can make a sentence mean something completely different to what you intend; think of the difference in meaning between 'Let's eat, Grandma!' and 'Let's eat Grandma!'.

The key punctuation marks, with a basic guide to their most common uses, are:

- ✔ **Comma:** Separates elements in a list of three or more items, before the conjunctions 'and', 'but', 'for', 'nor', 'yet', 'or' and 'so', or divides a separate clause in a sentence, as I'm doing now.

- ✔ **Colon:** Introduces a list, an idea or a quote, or divides two complete and linked sentences.

- ✔ **Semi-colon:** Divides subgroups within a list or two linked sentences. I love the semi-colon; it's elegant and subtle. You can also use it to make a pause somewhere in length between that of a full stop and a comma.

- ✔ **Hyphen:** Links two words that go together, especially when used as an adjective: hence 'We have an air-conditioned car but air conditioning in the villa' or a 'half-baked cake that's half baked'. If in doubt, look the word up.

- ✔ **Dash:** Increasingly used instead of a semi-colon to create a pause. Also used to show interrupted speech – or instead of commas to separate out a separate clause within a sentence – like this.

- ✔ **Full stop:** Comes at the end of a sentence. You can use a question mark instead for a question, or an exclamation mark to give emphasis (but not too often!).

- ✔ **Apostrophe:** Shows that part of a word is missing, as in 'it's' for 'it is' or 'don't' for 'do not'. It also shows possession as in 'John's' or 'Renuka's'. Remember that for plurals, the apostrophe comes after the 's': so you write 'I took away one boy's toy' but 'I took away all the boys' toys'.

Punctuation is also important for style. The pauses in speech as you read aloud can make all the difference to the sound of the prose.

Look at the beginning of this opening sentence:

> She waited, Kate Croy, for her father to come in . . .
>
> —*Henry James (The Wings of the Dove, Penguin Classics, 2008, first published 1909)*

James could so easily have written 'Kate Croy waited for her father to come in . . . ', but he didn't. Those commas create a little pause, a suspension, which somehow helps to keep the rest of the long opening sentence hanging lightly in the air. And it sounds beautiful.

Spotting grammatical errors

As you go through your typescript, look out for any grammatical errors and correct them.

Here are a few of the most common grammatical errors:

- Confusing 'their' (belonging to them), 'there' (a place) and 'they're' (they are).
- Confusing 'it's' ('it is') and 'its' (belonging to it).
- Confusing 'whose' (belonging to 'who') and 'who's' ('who is').
- Splitting infinitives. The opening of *Star Trek* contains a famous example: 'to boldly go' instead of 'to go boldly' or 'boldly to go'. It works. You can break this rule now and again for emphasis, as with *Star Trek*, if it sounds better, but not all the time.
- Using dangling participles; for example: 'Rushing to catch the train, Susan's purse fell out of her handbag.' This phrase means, grammatically, that Susan's purse was rushing to catch the train! The sentence should read: 'As Susan rushed to catch the train, her purse fell out of her handbag.'
- Changing tense inappropriately. Tenses should be changed for a reason – perhaps because you are writing a flashback or your character is imagining the future – and not at random.
- Subject and verb not agreeing. If you have a singular subject, you need a singular verb. Beware of phrases like: 'A list of books was lying on the table' – 'a list' is singular even though books are plural, so it's incorrect to write 'A list of books were lying on the table'.
- Getting a subjunctive wrong. Nowadays the *subjunctive* – a verb form to express the fact that something is hypothetical – is used mainly in stock phrases such as: 'If I were you' or 'I wish I knew'. It can sound old-fashioned, as in the grammatically correct 'Be they large or small'. The most common mistake is to use a subjunctive when you don't need to, especially in speech.

    ✔ Confusing 'who' and 'whom'. 'Who' is the subject (you can replace with 'I') and 'whom' is the object (you can replace with 'me'). But in speech and many informal contexts, nobody bothers with 'whom' any more, and it can make your character sound pretentious. Let your ear guide you as to whether it sounds right for a particular character's speech.

Making the Presentation Professional

One of the first things an agent or publisher notices on receiving your typescript is whether you've taken the time and effort to present your work according to accepted publishing conventions. Believe me, when you format your work correctly, you already stand out from the huge pile of typescripts that agents and publishers receive every day. Presenting dialogue is particularly problematic, and so I give it its own section.

Complying with publishing conventions

Typescripts for full-length novels should have a separate title page. Place your name and address, telephone number and email address in the upper left corner of this title page, using single line spacing. Put the title of the story in capitals halfway down. Type the author's name under the title as you want it to appear when published. You can use your real name or pseudonym, and it can of course include initials.

Ensure that all text is double line spaced, with a *ragged* right margin – don't make all the lines the same length. Indent all paragraphs except at the beginning of each chapter, and always begin with the same size indent. Don't separate paragraphs with an additional blank line, but do set generous margins of about 2.5 centimetres /1 inch.

Each page, except the title page, should include a *header* in the top margin consisting of the author's surname or pseudonym, the title of the work and the page number.

Always number your pages so that if (or when!) agents or publishers drop the typescript, they can put it back in the right order. They can also then refer to certain pages more easily if giving you useful feedback that you don't want to miss out on!

Using ellipses correctly

A brief note on the *ellipsis,* the technical term for three dots (. . .). You use it to indicate an intentional omission of a word or phrase when quoting original text. An ellipsis can also indicate a pause in speech, an unfinished thought or, at the end of a sentence, a trailing off into silence (the latter is called an *aposiopesis,* fact fans).

An ellipsis is *always* three dots, not four (though if you are using it to indicate a missing word in a quotation, it may look like four if there is a full stop before or after it – this is rare, however, in a work of fiction) and never five or even six . . . and always leave one space after the last dot, before the next word.

For your font, stick to size 12 in a standard typeface such as Times New Roman or Arial (this book's main text uses the former) – and never use anything bizarre. Also, stick to the same font in black ink throughout.

Always check that your paper size is set to the appropriate UK or US format. Europe and most of the world use A4, but the US still has its own paper sizes.

Here are a few other presentation points to note:

- ✔ Indicate your scene breaks with three asterisks (***) centred on the line. Don't simply add an extra line space, because this can all too easily be missed.

- ✔ Begin each new chapter on a new page, with the chapter number about a third of the way down the page.

- ✔ Place foreign words or short phrases that aren't used as direct quotations in italics. *Pourquoi?* That's just how it is. However, foreign words or phrases that have passed into regular English usage don't usually appear in italics. For instance, if in the denouement of your clichéd avant-garde novel, your dilettante par excellence returns to the leitmotif of a Hungarian *czárdás,* only *czárdás* is italicised.

- ✔ Use single quote marks when quoting. If you have a second quotation within the quotation, place this one in double quote marks. For example: 'Sarita told me, but without convincing evidence: "Jack burgled the house last night."'

- ✔ Include quotations of up to about 50 words in the text in the normal way, usually following a colon, but print longer quotations in a separate indented paragraph. You don't need to use quote marks for quotations printed as a separate indented paragraph.

Displaying dialogue

Laying out dialogue can be a tricky business, and if you don't get it right you can cause a great deal of confusion for your readers. Follow this dialogue and see how it works (with many thanks to Natalie Butlin for drafting the original version):

'How do I lay out my dialogue?' Gilbert asked.

'Preferably using single quote marks, because this is the British convention (Americans always use double quotes). However, my uncle Broccoli said, "Use double quotes when you have speech within speech," so that's what I always do,' Prunella said.

'But what about my punctuation?' Gilbert said.

'All punctuation – commas, full stops, question marks and so on – that belongs to the speech comes inside the quote marks. Do you see?'

'I guess so – but I always get confused at the end of a line of speech, when you say who said it.'

'Speech followed by an attribution such as "he said" or "she said" ends with a comma inside the quote marks, and the attribution always begins in lower case,' she sighed. 'Even if it follows a question mark or an exclamation mark!' she added.

'But what if –'

'Of course you don't start the attribution in lower case if it starts with a proper name. Gilbert, I could strangle you!' Prunella shrieked.

Gilbert looked into his lap. 'What about,' he began, mouse-quiet, 'when the character continues to speak after you've said who's speaking?'

'Gilbert, you are a bore,' Prunella said. 'If speech continues after the attribution then you may resume with either a capital or lower-case letter, depending on whether the speech continues as a new sentence or not. If it's a new sentence then the attribution should end with a full stop.'

Gilbert looked up and asked, 'But what about when the attribution comes before what the character says?'

Prunella answered, 'If the attribution comes before the speech act, the attribution should end with a comma and the utterance begins with a capital.' She eyed the gin in the drinks cabinet and added: 'Though alternatively the attribution could end with a colon.'

'But sometimes you don't even have to say who said it.'

'That's right. You can just end the speech with a full stop, and start a new line for the next speaker or begin the next descriptive sentence with a capital letter.' She stood, taking her glass from the table, and walked over to the cabinet. 'If the same character continues to talk after the description, you don't need to start a new line.'

'What if speech is interrupted by a moment of description?'

'In that case' – she strained at the cabinet door – 'use dashes outside the quote marks.'

'And you always begin a new paragraph, with an indent, when the speaker changes?'

'My God, you're a genius, aren't you, Gilbert? Where's the key to this cabinet?'

'I've locked that for a reason,' said Gilbert. 'And I haven't finished. So, what if your characters are doing things as well as talking – does action just run on from the speech, and you only start a new line when the next person speaks?'

Prunella glared at the blue bottle behind the glass and rattled the door again. 'If it's the other person who's acting, you should start a new paragraph. Try to keep a character's actions on the same line as their speech.' She smashed through the glass and seized the gin bottle.

Gilbert levered himself out of his chair and stood, quivering, as Prunella unscrewed the lid. 'Prunella, if I may interrupt –'

'And if a character is going –'

'Prunella, you mustn't –'

'To go on, and on and on about something, as I feel you are about to –'

'Prunella –'

'Then the end of each paragraph of their long speech doesn't close with a quote mark, but the beginning of each paragraph opens with a quote mark.

'Well, I think you've got the hang of it now, Gilbert. However, I definitely think I deserve a drink.' Prunella pressed the empty bottle to her lips and tilted it one last time, flicking her tongue into its cool neck.

You can render a character's thoughts in different ways. For example, you can put thoughts inside speech marks and follow the usual speech rules:

'Gilbert is the most terrible bore,' thought Prunella, staring out of the window. 'I really must divorce him one of these days.' She could see the cat meandering across the lawn.

Or you can use italics:

> Prunella stared out of the window. *Gilbert is the most terrible bore. I really must divorce him one of these days.* She could see the cat meandering across the lawn.

Or you can simply leave the thoughts in standard font:

> Gilbert is the most terrible bore, thought Prunella, staring out of the window. I really must divorce him one of these days. She could see the cat meandering across the lawn.

In this case, however, many writers find the following more natural:

> Gilbert was the most terrible bore, thought Prunella, staring out of the window. She really must divorce him one of these days. She could see the cat meandering across the lawn.

Which option you prefer is entirely up to you, as long as you choose one and stick to it throughout the typescript – unless you have a strong artistic reason to do otherwise.

Part VI

The Part of Tens

Find an additional Part of Tens chapter on dispelling ten myths about creative writing at www.dummies.com/extras/creativewritingexercises.

In this part . . .

- Get practical aids to make your writing easier.
- Review ways to ensure that you stay motivated and finish your written masterpiece.

Chapter 27

Ten Top Aids for Writers

In This Chapter

▷ Considering helpful equipment

▷ Discovering the best time and place to write

▷ Surrounding yourself with inspiring books

*I*f you're going to be a writer, equip yourself like one. Unlike for many forms of art and craft, you don't need much in the way of specialist tools to be a writer. That said, you can really help yourself to take your writing seriously when you put careful thought into choosing practical tools that support you on your creative writing journey.

Getting a Notebook – and Using It!

How many times have you seen or read something and thought it would make a brilliant idea for a story, only to forget the details before you got home? A notebook enables you to jot down thoughts, feelings, images, metaphors, descriptions and outlines – anything that acts as a store of ideas and helps you with what you're writing. Every writer needs a notebook.

You can, of course, use an electronic device such as a mobile phone or tablet to make notes, but I think that nothing beats a paper notebook that's small and light enough to carry around with you wherever you go. Whether it's expensive or cheap, plain or lined, with white or coloured paper, a notebook enables you to catch and record those fleeting thoughts that come to you unexpectedly during your day. You can also sketch out plans and maps, and paste or pin in photos, postcards, tickets and diagrams that you want to keep for your story.

Make sure that your notebook is small enough to fit comfortably into a pocket or bag, and not too heavy that you mind always carrying it with you. When you find the kind of notebook you like, buy a batch of them. Carry one with you and keep the rest in your room or office. If you're paranoid about losing it, photocopy it as a back-up from time to time. Put your name and contact details in the front, and write that you offer a reward for returning it.

Keep your notebook by your bed for those falling-asleep brainwaves that you're sure you'll remember in the morning – but never do. You can also record your dreams – you never know when an image, idea or sensation you experience in your sleep is going to be useful for your writing.

Write in your notebook every day. If you write even a few lines, they soon accumulate. You'll be surprised to see how much you write in a week, a month, a year. Most great writers have used notebooks – so take a cue from them and remember to keep one with you at all times.

Keeping a Decent Pen on You

Of course a notebook is no good if you don't keep a pen with it. I've found that what I write with matters a lot to me, and so I recommend that you find a pen you like and buy several. Don't buy an expensive one, however, because you may lose it if you carry it all the time – best not to use anything irreplaceable.

Keep a collection of pens on your desk, for writing and for editing, and keep one by the bed as well! Red or coloured pens (or highlighters) are really useful for editing, because the marks show up more clearly. Check out Chapter 25 for loads more tips on editing your work.

Having a Good Dictionary and Thesaurus

Although online versions are useful, I prefer to use a good printed dictionary and thesaurus. You can browse them in bed or when you're stuck for inspiration and ideas, and use them to expand your vocabulary.

Whenever you're in doubt about the meaning of a word, look it up. This includes all the words you think you know the meaning of, but when somebody asks you, you're not sure. As you read in your daily life, jot down in your notebook any words you're not that familiar with or never use, and look them up later. Work on consciously adding new words to your vocabulary every day.

If you find yourself overusing certain words in your writing, check out a thesaurus to find alternatives.

Buying the Best Computer and Printer You Can Afford

The computer is the most expensive item you use, and so before you buy, do your research carefully. Getting something you love to use is important. I once bought a cheap laptop to save money, and I hated using it so much that I became much less productive. In the end I gave it away and invested in a laptop I love. I now positively enjoy opening it up and getting to work.

I also struggled for two years with a clapped-out printer, which regularly jammed, ran out of ink and ground out the pages at a painfully slow rate. My life was revolutionised the moment I bought a reliable and quick printer–scanner – and it didn't even cost that much more than the old one!

Don't put up with inefficient equipment – it slows you down and acts as a drag. Invest in yourself as a writer and buy the best!

Make sure that you have a good keyboard and mouse that are comfortable to use. If you're getting strain from too much typing, consider using voice-recognition software. I relied on this when I was suffering from a frozen shoulder and was amazed at how quick and accurate it was. I still use it when transferring work from my paper notebook to my computer, because it's much faster than typing.

Blocking Out Your Writing Time in a Diary

I use a desk diary to mark out writing days and slots so that I don't book other appointments into them. I can also jot down my writing targets. If you do have to make another appointment during your writing times, cross out the slot and make sure that you reschedule it immediately. Try to block out regular times that suit you.

Many people now have electronic diaries, and these can help you by sending an alert that it's your writing time. If you don't have an electronic diary, try setting an alarm on your clock or mobile phone.

Investing in a Desk and Chair

Ensure that your desk and chair are at a comfortable height so you don't suffer back, neck and shoulder strain when you spend time at the computer. Invest in the best chair and work station you can. If possible, make the space welcoming and attractive, so that you want to go to it; if your desk looks like it's been hit by a bomb and is covered with dust and debris and half-drunk mugs of coffee (believe me, my desk has looked like this on occasion!), you may find yourself unconsciously avoiding it.

You can get special ergonomic chairs that help with your seating posture and prevent strain on your back, neck and shoulders. Don't use that ancient rickety chair with the wonky leg and the bar that digs into your back – find something better.

No matter how good your chair and work station are, get up regularly and stretch or run up and down the stairs to keep your muscles from seizing up. If you experience pain and discomfort every time you sit down to write, you're going to avoid doing so.

Some writers don't like to have an office. They work better in a garden shed, a café or at the kitchen table. Just find out what works for you.

Putting Up a 'Do Not Disturb' Sign

Make sure that your family, friends and flatmates don't bother you when you're writing. One writer I know puts on noise-reduction headphones, and everyone knows not to ask him anything when he's wearing them.

Put a 'do not disturb' sign on the door, turn off your phone or put it on silent, don't answer the doorbell, and tell people you know not to contact you at certain times because you'll be working.

Ask people to support you in your writing by giving you time and space. You can also try writing when no one's around: early in the morning before anyone else is awake, or late in the evening if you're a night owl.

If you can't write at home, go out to a café or library. Or find friends who're out at work all day or away on holiday and who don't mind you being in their place. You can be useful for keeping a cat or dog company, taking in deliveries or just making the home look occupied. But keep yourself focused – don't get sidetracked!

Surrounding Yourself with Great Books

My office is full of books, and I refer to them frequently when I'm writing. If I'm stuck with a dialogue scene and feel it's wooden and lifeless, I think of writers who write great dialogue – Evelyn Waugh or Anne Tyler, for example – and look up some conversations to see why they work and what's wrong with mine. If I feel a description is dull, I look at writers who use great description – Michael Ondaatje and Thomas Hardy come to mind. If I feel my writing's lacking enough tension, I look at a gripping passage in a thriller – perhaps by Michael Crichton or Ruth Rendell. You can learn more from reading than from anything else, and so don't be afraid to look at great writing in order to inspire you and show you great techniques.

Make sure that you have classic, contemporary and genre books. Buy ones about writing too. Buy as many books as you can. Remember that in buying books you're supporting other writers, and that one day you may want others to buy your books!

You can also buy books in electronic format for your ebook reader or tablet. Many of these are cheaper than print versions, and you can sometimes get classics free of charge. You have no excuse for failing to read those great books that have influenced generations of writers right down to the present day.

If you can't afford lots of books or haven't got space for them, make use of a library and look up passages from books and browse for free.

I've always been a bit of a bookworm – reading in bed under the covers with a torch when I was a child, sitting under a towel on the beach on holiday with my nose stuck into some magnum opus. Reading is my greatest pleasure – simply nothing beats becoming hooked by a great piece of writing, being taken into another world and learning something new about human nature on the way. Read as widely as you can, because you honestly discover more about writing from reading good books than any other way.

Backing Up Your Work Regularly

The worst event for writers is to lose their work. Many a writing project is abandoned when a writer becomes totally dispirited after losing a notebook or her work on a computer. Fortunately, all the available options nowadays mean that you have much less excuse for losing your work.

Back up your work regularly. Set your computer to automatically save at regular intervals. Email your work to yourself. Use a memory stick to back it up – and keep it somewhere safe. You can also use a CD or an external hard drive – but remember to keep these safely somewhere away from your computer. A writer I know was burgled, and the burglars took the hard drive as well as her laptop.

You can also use cloud storage services. These can be a more expensive option, although Google Drive and Dropbox are free.

I advise having several different kinds of back-up, because your work is precious; if you lose it, recovering the lost ground is difficult. I also print out complete drafts so that I have a paper copy. Yes, I know this may be bad for the environment, but it lets me sleep better at night!

Drinking Coffee – But Not Too Much!

Coffee or a hot drink helps me to maintain my concentration when I'm working. To stop me running up and down to the kitchen all day to reheat cups and make more tea and coffee, I have a thermos on my desk so I can top my mug up whenever I want.

Allow yourself the first coffee of the day only when you're actually sitting at your desk ready to write. That's the quickest way I know to get me to my desk in the morning. If you don't like drinking coffee but want the kick it gives you, remember that caffeine is also present in tea and chocolate.

Scientific studies show that caffeine genuinely aids concentration, but if you overindulge it stops working and even has the opposite effect. Caffeine stays in the bloodstream for some time – the amount of caffeine in the blood halves between three and four hours after drinking it – and so don't drink it shortly before bed, unless you want to be awake for hours. Bad sleep seriously affects your productivity the next day.

Caffeine can cause a 'crash' some time after you drink it, making you feel fatigued. So you can get hooked on needing another 'fix' to give you a lift again. You can even suffer withdrawal symptoms when you stop.

Chapter 28

Ten Great Ways to Stay the Course

*W*riting is difficult – no two ways about it. To complete a full-length book, you need all the help you can get. So set yourself some targets and give yourself regular rewards to help you see your project through to the end.

Bribing Yourself with a Major Reward to Finish

If you really want – and can afford – something like a special holiday, a particular piece of clothing or an item for the house, try putting off buying it until you finish your first draft. Then put off the next thing you really want until you complete the second draft. Be firm: promise yourself that you won't give in to temptation, and stick to it!

I know one writer who even made herself give up chocolate until she finished her draft. This (drastic!) method isn't for everyone, but it makes a good point: you need willpower to finish a large writing project. Maybe if you can't give up something you love for a few weeks or months, you're not going to have the strength of will to finish a book either.

Promising Yourself Minor Rewards for Meeting Targets

One of the best things you can do as a writer is to set yourself targets. They need to be SMART: Specific, Measurable, Achievable, Relevant and Time-bound.

Here are some good ideas for targets:

- ✔ A specific number of days or hours in the week to write
- ✔ A daily word count
- ✔ A certain number of pages per week
- ✔ A specific task and frequency, such as a chapter a fortnight

Make sure that these targets are something you can achieve – don't aim too high. If you're working and busy, aim to do something like three half-hour slots a week. Try to specify when, as well: for example, two lunch hours and a Tuesday evening, 500 words a week or a page a day.

If you write only one page every day, after 365 days you have a long novel.

Promise yourself a minor reward when you achieve a specific target, such as finishing a chapter: a trip out somewhere, a special meal, anything that's a particular treat.

Banishing the Inner Critic

Your first attempts at writing will be a mess. Experienced and accomplished writers know that the first draft is all over the place. Don't expect things to come out perfect first time – they don't.

Accept that your work will be far from perfect and that you'll take a long time to get it right. Banish that voice that says your writing is no good: don't listen to it – ignore it or tell it to go away. Just think that your writing is getting better and better all the time, and keep on writing.

Finding a Supportive Reader

A friend or colleague who knows about books and can support you in your writing is invaluable – someone who knows something about writing, or who's also writing, or who's studied literature, or who's simply an avid, intelligent, thoughtful reader is ideal.

Knowing that someone is waiting to read your work and prompting you for the next episode helps you no end. The person can give you targets and help you stick to them, be there on the end of the phone to listen to you talking through your problems, or just spur you on when you're flagging. If you find another writer, you can support one another.

Accepting the Bad Days Along with the Good

When you're working on any task, you're going to have good and bad days. Some days you sit down and the words come easily and you make or exceed your writing target. Other days you stare at the blank page and write a few meandering paragraphs before running out of ideas.

This book is full of exercises and ideas to get you writing. If you keep writing, your imagination will almost always come to the rescue with a good idea or a new way to write a scene. And if a day's writing really doesn't go well, don't beat yourself up about it – just have confidence that tomorrow will be better, and it usually is.

Writing Every Day

If you write something every day, no matter how little, your story stays in the front of your mind. That means you're working on it in your head even if you're not sitting down at your desk. How little you do doesn't matter – everyone can find time in their day to write a couple of sentences.

Try to write something in the morning when you get up, maybe over breakfast. Or write a few lines on the tube or bus to work or on the way home. Maybe you have one or more lunch hours in the week when you can take 10 or 20 minutes to write, or you can jot down a few lines before you go to bed. When you write something and keep thinking of your project, you make progress, however slowly.

Taking a Writing Course

Whether you're a beginner or have been writing for a long time, the perfect writing course exists for you. Universities and adult education centres run courses, as do libraries and bookshops. Some publishers and literary agents hold workshops and courses, and a number of good private courses are available. You can also find residential courses in the UK and abroad.

Always check who the tutors on the course are, their experience and whether they're writing in the same or a similar genre as you.

The great thing about a writing course is that you get an audience for your writing. You're able to read out what you've written and see which aspects are communicating well to other people, and which areas you need to work on. Trying out different exercises and approaches is a good way of developing your skills and expanding your range of techniques.

If you take a more advanced writing course, you need to be able to accept feedback from other writers and the tutor. A good tutor sets the ground rules and encourages people to look for the positives as well as what isn't working so well and will avoid over-negative or destructive feedback.

When receiving feedback, don't argue back with 'But I was trying to . . . ' or 'I did it this way in order to . . . ' or 'I wanted it to be confusing because . . . '. Just listen to what people say with all your attention and make notes. Ask for clarification if you're not quite sure what people are saying. Thank them for their comments. If you disagree with what they say when you get home and have thought about it, just ignore their remarks. Sometimes comments contradict one another – you can never please all the people all the time.

Nobody's forcing you to make changes to your work if you don't want to. Just take onboard the feedback that's helpful to you.

If several people are saying the same thing about your work, you do need to pay attention. The likelihood is that an agent or publisher's reader would feel the same. Take the time to go over your work with the comments in mind and see whether you can make changes that help you to communicate what you want to say more clearly and interestingly.

You can learn a lot about writing from listening to other writers. People often make similar 'mistakes' when writing; if you see these in others' work, picking out the same problems in your own writing is easier. If you're giving feedback, remember to 'sandwich' negative remarks between two pieces of encouragement: say something positive first; point out anything you think isn't working well; and then end with another positive comment.

Never stay on a course or in a group that undermines your confidence in your writing – find one with a more positive approach.

I founded The Complete Creative Writing Course at The Groucho Club in 1998 to provide a professional and imaginative approach to teaching creative writing. I now run a number of courses, from beginner levels to advanced workshops, and the courses are designed to be enjoyable as well as practical and informative. If you want to know more, visit the website (www. writingcourses.org.uk).

Joining a Writers' Circle

Apart from writing courses, keep a look out for groups or circles of writers who meet regularly and share their work. Often you can find out about these through local libraries, bookshops or adult education centres. If you can't find a group in your area, try starting one by putting up a sign on notice boards in local libraries, bookshops and cafés.

If you take a writing course, you'll meet other like-minded writers and may want to set up your own writers' circle at the end of the course. You can also look for online writers' groups, where people upload their work and give feedback on one another's stories.

Many writers have belonged to groups and met with other writers:

- ✔ **The Inklings:** An informal group of writers in Oxford who met at the Eagle and Child pub and included CS Lewis and JRR Tolkien.

- ✔ **The Bloomsbury Group:** An influential group of writers, intellectuals, philosophers and artists, including Virginia Woolf, EM Forster and Lytton Strachey.

- ✔ **The ex-pats who gathered in Paris in the 1920s:** These include Ernest Hemingway, John Dos Passos, F Scott Fitzgerald, James Joyce, Ezra Pound and Gertrude Stein, who all knew one another.

- ✔ **The Beat Generation of writers in late 1940s–1950s America:** Jack Kerouac, Allen Ginsberg, William Burroughs, Gregory Corso and others read one another's work and indeed often collaborated.

Searching for a Mentor

If you're looking for one-to-one support and feedback, you can try to find a writing mentor. This is a professional writer and/or editor who reads and gives feedback on your work in progress and supports you along the way. You usually have regular deadlines and meetings, which can help keep you on track, such as writing and reviewing a chapter or two a month.

This service usually doesn't come cheap. In order to get the most out of mentoring, I suggest that a mentor is most appropriate later on when you have a whole draft and want to work in a focused way on a future draft or drafts with someone who has professional knowledge.

Although a mentor can give encouragement and support and help you to develop your writing, the hardest part of the task is always yours. No one else can write your book for you (but then no one else gets his name on the cover!).

Believing in Yourself

First and foremost, believe in yourself. Keep writing, no matter how difficult it seems.

Believing in yourself doesn't mean that you have unrealistic expectations, that you boast about how brilliant your writing is or that you send it off to agents and publishers as soon as you've hacked your way through the first draft. On the contrary, you need to be as truthful as you can about your writing. Perhaps a lot of what you write isn't good enough to keep – but that applies to any writer and is nothing to be ashamed of. Like any writer, you need to work and work on your writing. But as long as you're writing, you're making progress.

If you don't have the courage to believe in yourself, how can you expect others to believe in you? Quiet confidence impresses people as well as helping you to keep working at your writing. Here are some simple tricks you can adopt to help keep up your confidence:

- ✔ Say 'when' not 'if': 'when I finish my book', not 'if I finish my book'.
- ✔ When going to your desk, say to yourself and others 'I want to write now', not 'I have to write now'.
- ✔ Say 'I can do it', not 'I can't do it'.
- ✔ Tell people you're a writer, and believe it.

Index

• C •

Notes

About the Author

Maggie Hamand is the author of two novels, *The Resurrection of the Body* and *The Rocket Man,* and has published a number of short stories, some of which have been nominated for prizes. She's the author of 18 non-fiction books, and her articles have appeared in magazines and newspapers including the *Guardian, The Sunday Times* and the *Observer.* She taught creative writing in Holloway Prison and Morley College, and also founded The Complete Creative Writing Course at the Groucho Club in 1998. She was co-founder of the award-winning small independent publisher The Maia Press and a director from 2003–2012.

Author's Acknowledgements

I'd like to thank all the people who supported and encouraged me while writing this book – especially my husband, Jeremy.

Special thanks also go to the other tutors on The Complete Creative Writing Course, past and present, from whom I've learned so much. I especially thank Rachel Knightley for helping me with research and contributing to the typescript in places, and to Natalie Butlin for the original draft of the dialogue in Chapter 26.

Publisher's Acknowledgements

Project Manager: Michelle Hacker

Project Editor: Steve Edwards

Acquisitions Editor: Mike Baker

Development Editor: Andy Finch

Copy Editor: Mary White

Technical Editor: Howard Cunnell

Project Coordinator: Sheree Montgomery

Cover Image: © istock.com/mrPliskin

Take Dummies with you everywhere you go!

Whether you're excited about e-books, want more from the web, must have your mobile apps, or swept up in social media, Dummies makes everything easier.

FOR DUMMIES®

A Wiley Brand

BUSINESS

978-1-118-73077-5

978-1-118-44349-1

978-1-119-97527-4

MUSIC

978-1-119-94276-4

978-0-470-97799-6

978-0-470-49644-2

DIGITAL PHOTOGRAPHY

978-1-118-09203-3

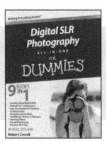

978-0-470-76878-5

978-1-118-00472-2

Algebra I For Dummies
978-0-470-55964-2

Anatomy & Physiology For Dummies, 2nd Edition
978-0-470-92326-9

Asperger's Syndrome For Dummies
978-0-470-66087-4

Basic Maths For Dummies
978-1-119-97452-9

Body Language For Dummies, 2nd Edition
978-1-119-95351-7

Bookkeeping For Dummies, 3rd Edition
978-1-118-34689-1

British Sign Language For Dummies
978-0-470-69477-0

Cricket for Dummies, 2nd Edition
978-1-118-48032-8

Currency Trading For Dummies, 2nd Edition
978-1-118-01851-4

Cycling For Dummies
978-1-118-36435-2

Diabetes For Dummies, 3rd Edition
978-0-470-97711-8

eBay For Dummies, 3rd Edition
978-1-119-94122-4

Electronics For Dummies All-in-One For Dummies
978-1-118-58973-1

English Grammar For Dummies
978-0-470-05752-0

French For Dummies, 2nd Edition
978-1-118-00464-7

Guitar For Dummies, 3rd Edition
978-1-118-11554-1

IBS For Dummies
978-0-470-51737-6

Keeping Chickens For Dummies
978-1-119-99417-6

Knitting For Dummies, 3rd Edition
978-1-118-66151-2

FOR
DUMMIES
A Wiley Brand

SELF-HELP

978-0-470-66541-1

978-1-119-99264-6

978-0-470-66086-7

LANGUAGES

978-0-470-68815-1

978-1-119-97959-3

978-0-470-69477-0

HISTORY

978-0-470-68792-5

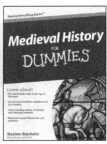
978-0-470-74783-4

978-0-470-97819-1

Laptops For Dummies 5th Edition
978-1-118-11533-6

**Management For Dummies,
2nd Edition**
978-0-470-97769-9

Nutrition For Dummies, 2nd Edition
978-0-470-97276-2

Office 2013 For Dummies
978-1-118-49715-9

Organic Gardening For Dummies
978-1-119-97706-3

Origami Kit For Dummies
978-0-470-75857-1

Overcoming Depression For Dummies
978-0-470-69430-5

Physics I For Dummies
978-0-470-90324-7

Project Management For Dummies
978-0-470-71119-4

Psychology Statistics For Dummies
978-1-119-95287-9

**Renting Out Your Property For Dummies,
3rd Edition**
978-1-119-97640-0

Rugby Union For Dummies, 3rd Edition
978-1-119-99092-5

Stargazing For Dummies
978-1-118-41156-8

**Teaching English as a Foreign Language
For Dummies**
978-0-470-74576-2

Time Management For Dummies
978-0-470-77765-7

Training Your Brain For Dummies
978-0-470-97449-0

Voice and Speaking Skills For Dummies
978-1-119-94512-3

Wedding Planning For Dummies
978-1-118-69951-5

WordPress For Dummies, 5th Edition
978-1-118-38318-6

Think you can't learn it in a day? Think again!

The *In a Day* e-book series from *For Dummies* gives you quick and easy access to learn a new skill, brush up on a hobby, or enhance your personal or professional life — all in a day. Easy!

Available as PDF, eMobi and Kindle